DISCARD

$\mathcal{M}$ine
was not a war of bugle calls and roaring engines
and magnificent defiance in the clamour of battle;

Mine
was a war of patience and endurance and stability;
of cunning and craft and stealth;
of attention to details
and giving my best to learn
all there was to learn about the job to be done.

Jesse Coffey

THE JOB
TO BE DONE

A Son's Journey Into The Story Of A
WW2 Bomber Command Aircrew

CLINT L. COFFEY

 FriesenPress

One Printers Way
Altona, MB R0G 0B0
Canada

www.friesenpress.com

ISBN
978-1-03-914654-9 (Hardcover)
978-1-03-914653-2 (Paperback)
978-1-03-914655-6 (eBook)

1. *History, Military, Aviation*

Distributed to the trade by The Ingram Book Company

"…and if they ask you what you did in the war, tell them you won it!"

- SIR ARTHUR "BOMBER" HARRIS,

SPEAKING TO DEPARTING CANADIAN AIRCREW AT THE END OF THE WAR.

Press on regardless

- UNOFFICIAL MOTTO OF BOMBER COMMAND

For Dad

TABLE OF CONTENTS

AUTHOR'S NOTE

I am not a scholar or professional researcher, and this book is not meant to be a work of history. I have heard that writing history is really just storytelling - I like the definition, and it is, in essence, what I have tried to do. But I am also keenly aware of my lack of academic credentials. So, I must state that although I have tried to include some historical facts and background in the story, (I truly felt it was essential to understanding the Coffey crew's experience), this book is a tribute, not a "history book," per se. You will find an extensive list of resources that I consulted at the back of the book, including books by *real* writers and historians!

As someone wishing to pay tribute to the valour and sacrifice of the young men of Bomber Command (in particular, of course, the Coffey crew), I make no claims of being dispassionate or impartial. Some readers may even accuse me of indulging in a bit of hero-worship at times—guilty as charged.

The opinions I have formed during my six years of research I have expressed openly and stand behind one hundred percent, but if I have gotten any facts wrong in the course of telling the story of the Coffey crew, I humbly apologize and will endeavour to correct them in any future editions. Whenever possible, I sought out the facts from the original wartime sources, like squadron Operational Record Books and interviews with those who were there, or their families. Secondary sources were books written by those who were there, and then those by post-war scholars.

There are so many people to thank—this project grew in scope faster than I felt I could keep up with at times, and it would have felt overwhelming without a lot of support.

I could not have kept up my enthusiasm if it hadn't been for the unflagging support and encouragement of the Dingwall, Hart, McWhirter, Rutherglen, Willoughby, and Bayne families. The memories, pictures, stories, maps, and logbooks the families of my Dads crewmates so generously shared with me made this project possible.

The passionate researchers on the forum at www.RAFCommands.com were lifesavers on many occasions. Someone on the forum was always able to answer my arcane questions or point me in the right direction to find it elsewhere. Thanks, in particular, to Pete Tresadern and Richard Koval - scholars and gentlemen! Very special thanks to Dave Champion, who was always encouraging and who also kindly reviewed my manuscript and pointed out some factual errors that had crept in.

Mark Evans from the Midland Aircraft Recovery Group was also very kind, helping me to understand "our" crew's training at the No. 22 Operational Training Unit.

A very special thank you to the amazing Polish CGI artist Piotr Forkasiewicz. His incredible depictions of Bomber Command in combat are breathtaking. After purchasing three prints, I contacted him to ask whether he would consider a commission—he immediately agreed, and would accept no payment. His depiction of the Coffey crew fighting for their lives over Wizernes forms the cover art for this book and I will always be grateful for his generosity. You can see his incredible work at **www.peterfor.com**.

Finally, the biggest "thank you" to my amazing wife, Tasnim—her consistent support, enthusiasm, and encouragement never failed to buoy me when the going got tough.

INTRODUCTION

I think I was more surprised than anyone when my eldest brother Gary read Dad's will out to the rest of us assembled in Mom's kitchen.

My father passed away suddenly of a heart attack in May of 1990, leaving behind four grown sons and my Mom—I am the youngest of the four boys and was only twenty-eight at the time. The reading of the will seemed a formality, as I assumed that everything would go to my Mom. However, it turned out that at some point, Dad had added a handwritten codicil at the bottom of the will, specifying that I was to have all his WW II air force memorabilia. For me, this was a completely unexpected gift, and I recall feeling more embarrassed than honoured at the time, as none of my older siblings had been bequeathed anything specific.

I had always been interested in my Dad's wartime experiences, asking him questions and reading the occasional book from the public library about the history of the Royal Canadian Air Force in World War II. When I was about ten years old, I found out that Dad had been awarded a medal for bravery. Typical of the modesty of his generation, I had to specifically ask to find out, to my surprise, that he had won, not one, but two medals for gallantry. After that, I would sometimes ask to polish the Distinguished Flying Cross and bar, which Dad kept in its original black leather presentation case at the back of his sock drawer.

I learned that the only way to get a "war story" out of Dad was to ask, as he only rarely spoke of that time in his life (I'm sure this is a common experience with many children of combat veterans). So, although I may have shown a bit more interest than my brothers in his WW II experiences, I still felt uncomfortable being singled out to receive these precious mementos. I was a grown man at the time, but I remember feeling small and uncomfortable at that moment, like a dumb kid brother who had spoken out of turn. This gathering, under sad circumstances, was the first time we had all been together in a very long time. This tension and discomfort, combined with the shock of losing my Dad and my sense of helplessness in trying to comfort my grieving mother made the whole experience overwhelming and more than a bit surreal for me.

After the funeral was over and my brothers and I had made sure Mom was comforted and settled as best we could, I loaded my Dad's memorabilia into a large box and drove the five hours back to my home in Richmond, a suburb of Vancouver.

It wasn't until several days later that I sat down to take stock of the precious items I had inherited.

The first thing I removed from the large cardboard box was Dad's uniform. Only the tunic and cap were present, and I guessed the pants had been too threadbare to save and had been thrown out years before. The blue-grey tunic was well-worn, but in good shape after spending some fifty years in the back of a closet. I was intrigued by the presence of no less than three sets of wings on the left breast. The first set was the familiar pair of sewn-on pilot's wings, but the second set was a small brass eagle, with wings spread, on the pocket flap. The third set of wings was an odd winged "O" pinned on the pocket itself, with an even odder horizontal bar hanging below it from a pair of minuscule chains.

The battered peaked cap was the epitome of the "fifty mission cap" that I had read about in history books (and that had been immortalized in song by Canadian music icons The Tragically Hip), its crushed shape and sweat-stained lining bearing clear witness to the fact that the owner was a seasoned veteran. The next item I pulled out was a sizable folded wartime map of Europe, carefully annotated with lines marking the routes and locations of dozens of targets in Germany and France. Some of the routes had the distance from their home base to the target noted, which was clear enough, but I puzzled over other notations like "Z-2023"—a coded designation for the target, perhaps? The map was well over a meter square, and I carefully folded it up exactly as I had found it. It had been folded that way for so long it was like an umbrella, just naturally returning to its original shape, almost with relief.

The next items were photos, tiny black and white pictures that felt brittle with age. There were two of a Lancaster bomber and one close-up of the bomber's nose, on which was painted a gremlin riding a bomb, with the name "Maisye" in bold letters. Another photo was a bit larger, showing Dad posing self-consciously (wearing the very same uniform that I now had spread across my sofa) in the back garden of a very English-looking home.

The last photo looked professionally taken, as it was a crystal clear eight by ten print showing Dad with two other men in uniform, posing one behind another, hands on each other's shoulders. Dad looks exhausted, with bags under his eyes and a weary smile. There were no notations on the back of the print to give any clues about the identity of the two airmen posing with Dad, nor the date or location. Next out of the box came an old wristwatch case, in which I found a small enamelled pin reading "General Service" and two shrapnel fragments, one of which had a small hole drilled in it. This item I recognized—Dad had shown it to me when I was a teenager. His "dog tags" were also in the cardboard box—a set of two hardened leather tags, embossed with his name and identity number, hanging from what I assumed was parachute cord. His Distinguished Flying Cross was here, as well as his campaign medals. Aside from one more item, this was the bulk of the collection—the rest was some miscellaneous paperwork, like his pay book and official letters and documentation from the Royal Canadian Air Force (RCAF).

The last item that I inspected was the most interesting: Dad's pilot logbook. With its slightly frayed cover and pages that were a bit brittle and brown with age, it exuded an almost tangible aura of history. As I leafed through the book, I was mystified by many of the abbreviations ("S.B.A." and "O/S") and unfathomable entries ("P-Plane factory" and "Wanganui").

Most of the many questions that came up in my mind as I examined the collection of mementos I was eventually able to answer through careful research, and I will come back to them a little later, but for now, we will leave them. Suffice to say that although I kept the collection safely stored, for the next twenty years, I spent little time with it.

Fast forward to 2013 when life, as it sometimes will, veered off the stable path I had been travelling on and into new, uncharted territory. I found myself starting over, single again after thirteen years of marriage; the choice had been my own to end a disastrous relationship, but the pain didn't feel any less because I had chosen it with eyes open. However, clichés are clichés because they are often true: the worst thing to happen to me in my life turned out to be the best thing to happen to me in my life. Later the same year, I had lunch with a lovely woman named Tasnim, and within eighteen months, she was my fiancée, and we had purchased a new home together. I had shown Tasnim my Dad's collection, and she had been particularly impressed with the map. After we moved into our new home, she suggested having it framed—she said it would look amazing on the wall of our new den. We took the folded map to a professional framer, who recommended using special backing and UV-resistant glass to protect it. The finished piece is dramatic, well over four feet square, and we were told it had been drawing a crowd as it sat on display in the shop awaiting pick up.

Once the map was up on the wall of my den, it was a constant reminder of my Dad's service, and it spurred me to look through his logbook again. I started looking things up on the internet and found quick answers to some of the mysteries. "P-Plane" for example, turned out to be another name for Hitler's V-1 flying bombs, which terrorized England in the summer of 1944. The kernel of an idea began to grow, and I started again at the beginning of the logbook, reading it line by line and making notes.

I soon realized that I was placing the seventy-year-old logbook under some stress by leafing through it and took it to a professional document preservation firm to have it scanned and reprinted. Now I had a copy I could use and make notes in while keeping the precious original safe.

Selected pages of Dad's logbook are reproduced in this book, in chronological order.

One aspect of the logbook quickly leapt out at me: Dad noted the names of the airmen who flew with him on each operation, and they were always the same. Their ranks changed as time went on, but the crew of seven stuck together (with one exception that we will come to in due course) through training and some sixty combat operations.

More and more, I began to wonder about these six other young men who relied on my Dad to bring them home safely night after night, and on whom my Dad depended to guide and defend the aircraft. Who were they, and where did they come from (and for that matter, what became of them)? And what of their families? Did they have maps and photos and stories to share? Could we exchange copies of these items and thereby get a more comprehensive picture of the incredible job our fathers had done?

In the fall of 2014, I decided to attempt to track down at least some of Dad's crewmate's families, but I didn't harbour much hope as I had nothing to go on but their ranks and last names. How in the world would I find the descendants of a "Sgt. Hart" seventy years after the fact? My goal at the time was to get lucky and track down two or three.

With this modest goal I began a three-year process of internet sleuthing and cold calls to strangers across Canada as well as in places as far away as Jamaica, Australia, and the U.K.

My efforts paid dividends, slowly but surely, and I learned not only research skills but the value of dogged persistence in the face of rejection and dead ends. I was fortunate that all of the members of the Coffey crew (aircrews, I learned, were usually referred to by their pilot's name. The pilot was in charge in the air, regardless of rank, and was invariably known as "Skipper") had been decorated (awarded medals for bravery), and this meant I could almost always find at least a brief official biographical note on them somewhere online.

The names I had to start with were:

- Sgt. Hart
- Flying Officer Bayne
- Sgt. Dingwall
- Sgt. Willoughby
- Warrant Officer Rutherglen
- Sgt. McWhirter

I decided that I might as well begin my search close to home. I had found a brief biography of my first "target," which led me to believe his family might still be in Nelson, British Columbia, some six hundred kilometres from where I live in Maple Ridge.

Warrant Officer Raymond "Ted" Rutherglen was the crew's wireless operator/air gunner - a quick internet phone directory search showed that more than one Rutherglen presently lived in Nelson, and another clue led me to a small town in Alberta. Cold calling people out of the blue is certainly outside my comfort zone, but I steeled my nerve and made the calls. I'm glad I got so lucky on my first attempt, as the memory of my quick success gave me hope and encouragement later when I hit seemingly endless roadblocks and dead-ends. That very day, I spoke not only with Ted Rutherglen's daughter, but also with his son, both of whom were excited and enthusiastic about my project and more than willing to share any memorabilia they had.

I have had many exciting moments of discovery during my research for this project. Still, nothing comes close to opening an email from Ted Rutherglen's son and finding half a dozen photos of my Dad that I never knew existed. Photos of Dad in the air, at the controls of a Halifax bomber, two photographs of him in a Sergeant's uniform reading a card from home (was that my oldest brother Gary's baby hand print faintly visible on the card…!?), and an artistic snapshot of him coolly glancing out the cockpit window into the camera, looking every inch a skipper.

It became apparent that Ted Rutherglen had been a talented amateur photographer and these unique photos took my breath away. Ted's son (also named Ted) went above and beyond generosity by insisting on sending me the original photos so I could take them to a professional to have them digitally restored, touched up, and reproduced as glorious five by seven prints. They are precious family heirlooms now, and I am forever grateful. Later, he also sent me his father's logbook, which I took to a professional to scan and reprint. Ted's daughter, Christine, enthusiastically contributed as well, sending me copies of her father's personal navigation maps, air force documentation, and photos, and writing down her memories of her Dad's life and stories.

Sgt. Digby Willoughby was the crew's flight engineer and the only one of the crew who was a member of the RAF—all the others were RCAF. I learned online that he was not Canadian and that he hailed from

Jamaica. Tracking down Sgt. Willoughby's family proved to be far more challenging than my previous quick successes! There are plenty of Willoughbys in the Kingston, Jamaica telephone directory, and I didn't even know where to start. I decided to take a different tack and contacted the National Library of Jamaica's historical research department. A very kind researcher named Genevieve dug into the matter for me and came up with several newspaper clippings from the war, which gave me some interesting information about him and his family, but she was unable to find any clues as to current family members.

Now that I had a few Willoughby family biographical nuggets of information, I decided to try Ancestry. com, and this website proved to be a great resource. I eventually connected with Francoise, who turned out to be the daughter of Digby's sister, who had come to Canada during the war. She gave me a brief rundown on the Willoughby family and their time in Jamaica, as well as solving the mystery as to why I had been unable to find any relatives there. It turned out that after the war, Digby had immigrated to Australia.

Through family connections she was able to find an email address for Digby's son, and soon Keith (and his brother Craig) Willoughby and I were corresponding. Keith was delighted to hear from me and sent me a copy of his father's logbook and stories of his father's post-war life. I was saddened to learn that Digby (known to his friends and crewmates as "Jimmy" for some reason) had died long ago, in 1965, when Keith was only nineteen. Keith's two brothers were even younger, one just a baby when they lost their father.

Sgt. Ken Hart was the crew's mid-upper gunner, and I knew he came from Ontario, but such a common last name would likely make tracking him down difficult. After many false starts and dead ends, a connection clicked when I learned Hart had been employed by a large Canadian insurance firm called London Life for many years. Via a helpful employee at London Life, who found an old company newsletter about Hart's retirement, I got the names of Hart's children, including married names, which proved to be the final hurdle in finding his family. I was soon talking to Ken Hart's daughter, Suzanne. She was enthusiastic about my project and provided me with some of her Dad's wartime documents and photos, as well as putting me in touch with her father's brother Don. He kindly sent me many stories about his older brother and insights into Hart's family and childhood. My connection with the Hart family was soon to take a more profound and troubling turn when I uncovered some disturbing information about Ken's RCAF service that I felt duty-bound to share with them.

Flight Sergeant Malcolm Dingwall was the crew's bomb aimer, and all I could find on him was that he was from Saskatchewan. Cold calling people with the same last name turned out to be a dead-end. He seemed to have no online presence, aside from one passing mention in a very old obituary, which noted that the person had worked for a baker named Malcolm Dingwall after the war in a small town in Saskatchewan. From there, the trail went dead. I enlisted the help of the Saskatchewan Genealogical Society, and they managed to track down a newspaper obituary for Dingwall, which allowed me to leave Saskatchewan and pick up the trail in my own province of British Columbia. After a few false starts, I was delighted to reach Dingwall's daughter in Prince George and shortly after, his grandson Glenn, who visited me several months later.

Connecting with navigator **Flying Officer Robert Bayne**'s family proved to be one of my more difficult tasks, but not because I couldn't find them. I found a family member relatively easily, but this person was uninterested in my project. After an initial email, he simply stopped replying to my repeated attempts to engage with him. In frustration, I dropped the search for Bayne's family for a year while I focused on other research. When I started looking again, I had better luck and connected with Bayne's grandson in Toronto, who I interviewed briefly in the spring of 2018. My conversation with him cleared up many mysteries and led me to even greater respect for the Coffey crew's navigator.

The search for the family of **Sergeant Robert McWhirter**, the crew's rear gunner (or "tail-end charlie" as they were nicknamed), turned out to be uniquely rewarding. I knew I had met McWhirter once, some twenty-five years previously, at a 405 Squadron reunion. At the time of Dad's death, he had been registered to attend and since the reunion was being held near where I lived, I had decided to go in his stead. I don't recall a lot of that evening, other than feeling a bit uncomfortable being at least forty years younger than anyone else in the room, but I remember meeting Bob and his wife, who were very kind and welcoming to me. My passionate interest in my Dad's wartime service had not germinated yet, and I am sorry to say I missed a unique opportunity to interview some of my Dad's comrades.

McWhirter came from Saskatchewan, so I started my search for him there, and after a series of connections, found myself talking on the phone to his stepson Curt. I asked Curt about his Dad's RCAF memorabilia, hoping for an introduction to the family member who might have his logbook and photos, and was astounded when Curt replied, "Oh, Dad still has his stuff in his apartment." The present tense almost left me speechless.

"Your Dad is still alive?" I asked rather stupidly.

"Oh yes, he goes curling twice a week and is sharp as a tack!"

Well, this was incredible news, and Curt soon put me in touch with his brother Tim, who lived in Kelowna, British Columbia, near his Dad. After a conversation with Tim, who assured me his Dad would be delighted to hear from me, I spoke with Bob McWhirter on the phone, and in the spring of 2015, my wife Tasnim and I drove to Kelowna to visit him in person.

Bob was the last surviving member of the Coffey crew, and I feel so grateful I had the opportunity to meet him and his son Tim. They were both unfailingly helpful, encouraging, and generous in assisting me in my research.

So now I had many more pieces of the puzzle than I had started with, and it was time to try and put them together into some sort of narrative. At first, my idea was to annotate Dad's logbook somehow, labelling various entries in it with paragraphs of explanation. This idea morphed into perhaps writing some kind of chapbook, getting it printed at Staples and sharing it with all the families I had connected with.

Finally, the idea of actually writing an actual book reared its ugly head in my mind. I rejected the idea immediately: writers write books, and I am not a writer. Some years later, the book that should have been written by a writer is in your hands.

In some ways, this book is a personal narrative, a son's journey to get to know his Dad better—but mostly, it is a tribute, an attempt to honour the awe-inspiring courage of seven seemingly ordinary young men who did something quite extraordinary.

I believe with all my heart that this story deserved to be told, and it seems it was stuck with me to try and tell it—I sincerely hope my passion for the subject can make up for my lack of talent as a writer. This book is an attempt to tell the story of these seven young men who came together from different places and disparate backgrounds and formed a team. They lived, trained, flew, and faced death together, and then went home when they had completed their part in "the job to be done."

CHAPTER ONE:
"NOT IMPRESSIVE AS AIRCREW"

FEBRUARY 1942 TO NOVEMBER 1942

Bomber Command pilots were probably the most extensively trained warriors up to that point in history: my Dad enlisted in February of 1942 and flew his first combat operation in February of 1944, almost two years of increasingly intense and sophisticated training. The chances of a new aircrew recruit surviving over two years of risk-filled training and then two tours of combat operations was shockingly low—about one in three—it's a good thing they were all unaware of their odds of making it or most of them might have chosen to join the Army instead. Nothing in Dad's background provides a clue about why he succeeded in coming home safely, where tens of thousands of other young men perished.

Jesse Ray Coffey was born into poverty in the village of Czar, Alberta, on April 16, 1921. My grandfather had brought the family to southern Alberta about twenty years previously from the American state of Arkansas, where the Coffey family had settled after emigrating from Ireland in the early-to-mid 19th century. Harry Coffey, my grandfather, worked many different jobs to support the family, but they never rose above a hardscrabble existence. I remember Dad telling me that, as a child, he could hear the bugs dropping from the ceiling at night and hitting the floor. Occasionally he and his brothers would run a burning roll of newspaper along the cracks in the ceiling to try and keep the insect population in check. I never knew my grandfather, but he was, by all accounts, a hard and ignorant man. His daughters (my aunts) wasted no time in leaving home and getting away from him as soon as they were old enough. My Dad never spoke of him, other than to tell me once that my grandfather chewed tobacco and wouldn't bother with a spittoon, preferring to spit on the floor of his own home—enough said. How my Dad grew up to be such a kind, wise, and classy gentleman coming from such a background is a bit of a mystery.

Despite these uninspiring origins, my Dad was no doubt an intelligent young man with ambitions. He managed to complete High School with above average grades, and soon landed a job as a clerk with that legendary Canadian institution, the Hudson's Bay Company. The HBC's all-pervasive presence across Canada ranged from upscale department stores in urban centres to tiny one-room trading posts in remote Indigenous communities. I don't know whether Dad had any say in his placement, but it's hard to believe that where he ended up was one of his top choices. The tiny hamlet of Port Simpson (today known as Lax Kw'alaams), on British Columbia's rugged northern coastline, was in essence an Indigenous village with a Hudson's Bay Company general store to service the community, buying furs and selling all manner of retail goods. The store had begun as a tiny trading post in 1834, but by the time Dad arrived in 1941 it was a substantial two story wooden building, with room on the second floor for employee accommodation. The natural beauty of the area must have been a real eye-opener for Dad, and his arrival in Port Simpson was the first time in his life he had seen the ocean.

I know little of Dad's life there, simply that he listed his occupation as "Senior Assistant," and to me that implies a wide variety of responsibilities. I know he became quite knowledgeable in the grading of furs during his time with the HBC, and it's almost certain his education began in Port Simpson.

However, like millions of other young men worldwide, his career plans were interrupted by the war, which was now well into its second full year. Sometime towards the end of 1941, he returned to his hometown of Czar and shortly thereafter travelled to the nearest large city to "join up."

When I first started making a timeline of my Dad's life for this time using snippets from various sources, one question began nagging at me: why had Dad travelled all the way back to Alberta to enlist? The village of Port Simpson was near the town of Prince Rupert, which likely had a recruiting office, or he could have easily taken a ferry or train south to Vancouver, one of Canada's major cities. Why make the long, convoluted journey back to Czar?

One can speculate and come up with all kinds of plausible explanations, but I choose to believe (and I admit that my mind may be clouded by sentimentality) that he made the long journey home because he was in love.

In the months before leaving Czar for British Columbia, he had worked at a variety of odd jobs, one of which was as a hired hand on a large and relatively prosperous family farm belonging to Gustav Anderson, a Swedish immigrant who had homesteaded in the area. Gustav had an eighteen-year-old daughter named Ruby, who was to become my mother.

Before leaving for his new job in Port Simpson, had Jesse promised her that he would come back as soon as he could arrange a transfer somewhere closer to Czar? I think it is a possibility. Had the two exchanged letters while Dad was far away on the wild coast of British Columbia? Again, I believe it very likely.

At any rate, Dad returned to his hometown in early 1942, and there is no doubt he spent time courting Ruby, as will soon become apparent.

In February of 1942, he travelled to Edmonton, Alberta and enlisted in the Royal Canadian Air Force. I never asked my Dad why he chose the Air Force, but it is not hard to guess at his reasoning: the Army probably held connotations of drudgery and trenches, and as a boy born and bred on the Prairies, the Navy wouldn't likely have even been in the running as a choice. On the other hand, Dad had no doubt looked up and seen many aircraft flying across the clear Albertan skies during his youth, and had read about the adventures of legendary Canadian bush pilots like Wop May and Punch Dickens.

As a young adult, he no doubt had read newspaper accounts about the heroic deeds of "the Few" in the Battle of Britain, and so he probably, like tens of thousands of other young Canadian men, had dreams of being a fighter pilot. However, his dreams would matter little to the vast bureaucracy he had just joined.

After passing all the tests and exams at the recruiting office, Dad returned to Czar for two months, waiting for a spot to open up in a new class of recruits at Manning Depot in Edmonton, which happened in May of 1942. Saying goodbye to friends, family, and sweetheart Ruby, he made his way back to Edmonton to begin his new adventure.

Every air force in the world faced the same challenge when the war started: how to find the right men for the job. They required men who not only had an aptitude for flying, but also the mental and physical stamina needed to endure the rigours of training and the unique challenges of air combat. Able-bodied men were the most valuable resource a country had as it faced war. It made no sense to waste effort and money attempting to train someone with no head for mathematics to be a navigator, for example, if he would be better suited as an air gunner or engine mechanic, which were equally vital trades. Not to take anything away from the skills it required to be a good soldier or seaman, but a Bomber Command pilot or navigator was in a different league—navigators especially had to master complex calculations, techniques, and equipment that were cutting edge (and often top secret) in the 1940s.

Being tested, retested, and tested again was going to be part of Dad's life now, as the vast machine known as the British Commonwealth Air Training Plan (BCATP) decided what role he would play in the RCAF.

A mugshot of my Dad, taken upon enlistment in the RCAF.
Photo courtesy of Library and Archives Canada.

The BCATP was one of the real success stories of the Second World War, and one in which Canada played a large role. The Canadian government saw Allied airpower as an area to which the Dominion of Canada could make a major contribution, and Canada devoted tremendous resources to its success, far out of proportion to its relatively small size. Well, "small" in terms of population and economic power perhaps, but not lacking at all in terms of geographic size, and that's where the Canadian Prime Minister saw an opportunity for Canada to make a unique contribution to the Allied cause. Lester B. Pearson called on Canada to become (in President Roosevelt's catchy phrase) the "aerodrome of democracy," and envisioned hundreds of airfields across Canada, all churning out fully trained aircrew, ready to ship to Europe to join the fray. In Canada's vast expanses of flat, well-mapped prairie, fledgling aircrew would be safe from depredation by the German Luftwaffe, and the well-lit towns (there was no need for blackout rules here as there was in England) would help rookie navigators find their way at night.

There is no doubt Pearson had an ambitious vision, but even he didn't foresee how huge the Plan would become. It eventually spread across the globe, with airfields as far away as Africa and Australia. Once the Plan was agreed on by all involved (a miracle in itself, with politicians and bureaucrats from many countries mired in wrangling over who would pay for what), it snowballed quickly, but it took a lot of time and effort to get that ball rolling. The idea had been around for years, but political wheels often turn slowly and war had already started in Europe by the time the first British students arrived in Canada. Remarkably, by the end of the war, the BCATP had trained forty-four percent of all Allied aircrew, more than 200,000 men, with Canada hosting over 130,000 of this impressive number.

So it was into this vast establishment that Dad entered in early 1942, and it was no doubt a jarring and disorienting experience. He was paid the grand sum of $1.10 a day, which was about one-third the average daily wage in Canada at the time, but his room and board (such as it was...) was, of course, provided by his new employer.

His first stop was in the city where he had joined up two months previously, at the No. 3 Manning Depot, located in the heart of Edmonton, Alberta, at the Clarke football stadium. The RCAF's Manning Depots were basically air force "boot camps," and after being issued a rough woollen uniform and stiff leather boots, Dad and his fellow Aircraftman 2s (an AC2 was the lowest form of life in the RCAF) would be shorn like sheep by a military barber and begin the process of learning what the RCAF referred to, without irony or humour, apparently, as "airmanship." The days were filled with route marches, drilling, polishing buttons and boots, a seemingly endless series of inoculations and learning to clean and fire a .303 Lee Enfield rifle—some recruits must have wondered if they had joined the Army by mistake! There were lectures and calisthenics and assigned cleaning duties to keep the days filled. The conditions were typical rustic military style, with dorms filled with bunk beds and communal washing and eating facilities that made no allowances for privacy.

Then came the testing. The BCATP management was determined to be scientific in its selection process, and got a lot of input from civilian experts, including psychologists and medical doctors. Many ingenious (though often useless) tests were devised to determine who was suitable for aircrew, and in what capacity. Although every young man joining the air force likely dreamed of being a Spitfire pilot, precious few actually achieved their goal. When I interviewed Bob McWhirter (the crew's rear gunner) in 2016, I asked him if he as well had hoped to be a pilot when he joined up. The boyish grin and the twinkle in his eye as he answered, "Oh yeah!" seemed to erase several decades from his ninety-three-year-old face. However, like so many others, his hopes were dashed due to his limited education, cut short so he could work on the family farm.

Tests administered included blowing into a glass tube and, by maintaining air pressure, keeping a column of mercury suspended at a certain level—this was supposed to test lung power. Word got around about the test and soon some cagey students learned to surreptitiously cover the opening of the tube with their tongues, which held the mercury at the correct level without having to blow!

Other tests were psychological, such as being asked odd hypothetical questions so experts could assess the answers. There were endless interviews with doctors and military officers who poked, prodded, questioned, and tested the recruits. I am fortunate to have copies of many of my Dad's medical forms and assessments courtesy of the Canadian government, which will provide military records to relatives if requested. The forms I received document the lengthy process involved to convince the RCAF that Dad was fit to fly. The questions asked and answered covered a broad range of mental and physical health subjects such as: "consumption" (negative), "nervous trouble" (none), "habits-smoking" (Dad admitted to twelve a day), and "Discomfort on Swings, Roundabouts and Switchbacks" (None). Several of the doctors made a brief, positive comment about Dad, including "good lad" and "better than average aircrew," but he certainly made a poor impression on a certain Dr. T, who wrote this dismissive assessment:

> Tall slim fair with some fine hair on body. Stuffy eyed – shy & timid – nervous tics as playing with shoe lace or coat belt. Unaggressive – satisfied with unexciting life?? store clerk. Lacks confidence. Not impressive as aircrew material for any position.

Was the good doctor just having a bad day, or did who-knows-how-many aspiring aircrew have their hopes dashed by a similar disdainful assessment? In my opinion, Dr. T had made the classic mistake of equating aggressiveness with courage and character—my father may not have been brimming over with the former, but he had the latter in spades.

In trying to be fair-minded, I must note that the attitude he expresses is reflective of the official thinking of the day, that good military men were the result of "good breeding," and that no amount of training could make up for the lack of it. Early RCAF recruiting posters depicted young men playing polo and driving sporty cars as the ideal of who they were looking for. Since such activities were well beyond the means of ninety percent of Depression era youth, one gets a sense of the snobbishness in some of the official attitudes of the day. Fortunately, Dr. T's old-fashioned prejudices did not prevent Dad from progressing towards the goal he aspired to, and he was assessed as being a suitable candidate for aircrew training, although in what capacity was still to be determined.

Dad had another run-in with another sort of doctor around the same time, this one a dentist. Dad told me he had never been to a dentist in his life before joining the RCAF, but that having a dental exam was part of the process of being deemed fit for aircrew training. The dentist performed the routine exam and informed Dad that he had two bad cavities that required filling immediately. He assured my nervous father that it was completely routine and pulled out a needle to inject some freezing into the problem area. When Dad saw the size of the needle he panicked, and insisted he didn't need it, and that the dentist should proceed without it. After much arguing, the exasperated dentist said, "sure kid, have it your way." Dad told me that the noise of the drill and the smoke coming out of his mouth was terrifying enough, but when the drill finally touched a nerve, things got infinitely worse, and he was lifted out of the chair with the pain. He now acquiesced to the anaesthetic needle, and the procedure was completed without further drama.

At this point, Dad's story follows the same path of almost all of the Manning depot graduates: he was assigned to a nearby airfield for six weeks of "tarmac duty."

Dad and a few of his fellow AC2s were transported to the No. 2 Air Observer School at Blatchford Air Field, only a few kilometres from the Manning Depot in Edmonton. There they would spend the next six to eight weeks tidying hangers, manning the entrance gates, cleaning Avro Ansons inside and out and patrolling the perimeter of the airfield. Whether the patrolling was to prevent unauthorized trips into town by the airmen, or to detect intrusion by Nazi saboteurs, I am not sure.

The Air Observer School was the first step in the training of future navigators and this particular one was headed by none other than Wop May, the WW I Sopwith Camel pilot who had pioneered the bush pilot trade in post-war Canada. On one occasion, May had helped the RCMP track down the murderous Rat River Trapper when he was on the run in the wilds of the North West Territories. It was one of the first times in history an aircraft had assisted police in such a task.

Towards the end of July 1942, Dad received a piece of information that was to change his life. I don't know the method used to convey the bombshell to Dad, but a telegram seems the likeliest: Ruby Anderson was pregnant. Sometime in April, while Dad was awaiting orders from the RCAF to report to Manning Depot, the young couple had consummated their relationship. To his credit, Dad lost no time in "doing the right thing"—somehow arranging for a pass and transportation, he met my Mom at the halfway point between them, in the small town of Lougheed, Alberta. There, on July 23, 1942 they were married by a Donald MacKie, likely the minister from the local United Church. No civilian records remain of the marriage ceremony, and as far as I know, there are no surviving photos. Not the most romantic of starts to a marriage perhaps, but their bond remained solid for over fifty years, with only death separating them in the end. I sometimes wondered growing up why not much was made of their yearly anniversary—it seemed to be downplayed a bit. It wasn't until I was an adult that my oldest brother Gary pointed out to me the time between their anniversary date and his birthday was about six months, and the penny dropped for me.

At the end of August 1942, Dad completed his stint on tarmac duty at Air Observer School. Before leaving Edmonton for his next post, he likely attended the graduation ceremony of the current class, where he and the graduating students were told to "keep their bodies clean and their minds clear and active" by their Commanding Officer.[1]

Dad's next step on the BCATP ladder was the No. 7 Initial Training School in Saskatoon, Saskatchewan. The school was located in a re-purposed teacher's college, the Saskatchewan Normal School, whose former occupants were relocated to make room for the Air Force trainees. It is a beautiful brick and stone building, still in use today as a film studio, and is a designated heritage site.

Initial Training School's purpose was to give the Air Force the information they needed to finally separate the pilots from the navigators. Other trades, like wireless operators and air gunners, had already been identified at Manning Depot, and been sent on their way to their respective schools, but making final decisions about the pilots and navigators would require still more training and testing. The School curriculum was tough, and was meant to be: everything from algebra and trigonometry to sitting in a decompression chamber (to test tolerance to oxygen deprivation) was involved. An especially long medical exam was an integral part of the course: it was known as the M2, and ranged from psychological tests to balance tests, and even included an EEG over the course of some four gruelling hours. Dad would also make the acquaintance of a piece of equipment that he would become very familiar with over the next two years, the Link trainer.

The Link trainer was the brainchild of Ed Link, an American entrepreneur, who had seen the need for some kind of tool to train would-be pilots while keeping them safely on the ground. In a way, the trainer

---

1   Still good advice even today!

was a precursor to modern flight simulators. Link struggled through the Depression, but when war came he was flooded with orders, especially as the BCATP got up to speed. Although the Link became more sophisticated as time went on, it was essentially a plywood box with stubby wings and an instrument panel and control stick. It was rigged up with pulleys and cables (later models used a system of bellows), and moved in a somewhat realistic manner based on how the student sitting in it moved the control stick and rudder pedals. The wooden hood could be closed to simulate night flying, the student using just the instrument panel to follow the instructor's directions over his headset.

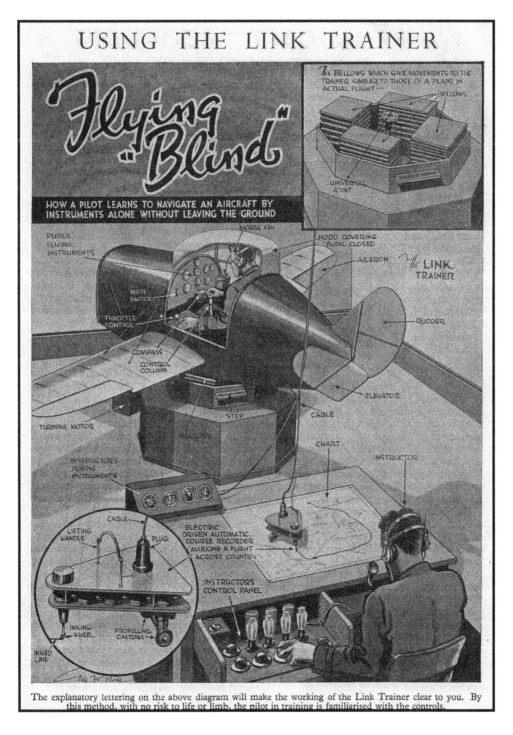

A Link Trainer depicted in a WW2 magazine article from Australia. Author's collection.

For the most part, aircrew trainees loathed the machine and many a would-be pilot saw his career hopes come to a (simulated!) crashing end inside the claustrophobic confines of a Link Trainer. There is little doubt, however, that the Link saved thousands of lives, and I think it is one of the unsung heroes of World War II. It was certainly an improvement over the method used in the First World War, where pilots flew a couple of flights as a passenger and then were simply sent off solo to see how they did, leading to many unnecessary and wasteful deaths. The training provided in the first war had also promoted aerial stunting as a way of building skills and demonstrating "keenness," with equally tragic results. In contrast, the BCATP taught professionalism—it was a different kind of war.

At the end of eight weeks of this intense program of testing and training, each of the students would spend a few crucial (and no doubt extremely stressful) minutes being interviewed by a panel of three or four senior officers, the Aircrew Selection Board. The results and postings were announced shortly afterwards, and there would be groans of disappointment and hoots of joy as the young men learned what the powers that be had decided about their futures. Dad was selected for pilot training, and along with all the other graduates, received a promotion to Leading Aircraftman and a propeller patch to sew on his left sleeve. He and his fellow LACs also were given a white flash to place in their caps, which signified they were aircrew in training. In what one must admit was a brilliant propaganda coup, soldiers across Canada soon spread the rumour to local girls that the white flashes meant the airman in question had an STD.

In the collection of my Dad's memorabilia, I found a group photo of Dad with his fellow students and their officers, taken on the front steps of the Saskatoon Normal School. On the back is scribbled the names (and nicknames) of twenty-eight of the sixty or so young men who graduated, and I was able to find out a bit about some of them.

Hugh Campbell gleefully wrote "L.A.C.!" after his name, obviously proud of his new status. Campbell went on to flying school but was unsuccessful, having "washed out" (to use the somewhat heartless phrase common at the time), and redirected to Bombing and Gunnery School. Campbell ended up a very successful and respected bomb aimer with 427 Squadron, rising to the rank of Flying Officer and being awarded the DFC. He never gave up on his dream of being a pilot, and after the war he finally earned his wings, becoming a Sikorsky helicopter pilot with the RCAF's Search and Rescue Squadron.

Jack "Hotcake" Burch completed his flying training and went on to be a pilot with 433 Squadron and another DFC winner. He, too, returned home safely and became an instructor, teaching student pilots to fly the famous Chipmunk, an aircraft almost as beloved as the Tiger Moth, which it had replaced as the RCAF's primary training aircraft.

Charles "Russian" Clegg was a classmate of Dad's at both Elementary Flying Training School and Service Flying Training School. He went on to be the skipper of a Handley-Page Halifax with the RAF's 51 Squadron, returning home safely to Alberta after completing two combat tours.

Others were not so lucky.

John "Angus" Black died when his Lancaster was shot down while attacking a V-1 flying bomb site in June of 1944. "Jock" Ramsay lost his life in January of 1944, shot down over Berlin. Ramsay had been a theatre usher in Nanaimo, British Columbia prior to joining up. He was an impossibly fresh-faced and boyish-looking young man, with tousled blond hair and an innocent smile—he looks like he belongs in a Boy Scout uniform rather than an Air Force uniform. In fact, he was twenty years old at Initial Training School (ITS), only a few months younger than Dad. For whatever reason, Ramsay was sent on to Bombing and Gunnery School after ITS rather than flying school—perhaps his grades were not quite there, or he may have failed to suitably impress the Aircrew Selection Board. He eventually became a bomb aimer with 429 Squadron, and on the night of January 20, 1944, he died over Berlin, along with all but one of his crew, when their Halifax was shot down, likely the victim of flak. Their pitiful, mangled remains were impossible to separate in the wreckage, and the Germans buried them together in a group grave. They had trained, bunked, flown, and then died together, and in the end were buried together, as a crew. Something tells me they would not have minded the arrangement in the least.

Adding even more poignancy to the story of "Jock" Ramsay is a letter sent by RCAF headquarters in July of 1945 to a young Nursing Sister at the No. 24 Canadian General Hospital in Surrey, England. The letter, which began, "Dear Miss Sparks," advised that Ramsay's death had been confirmed and expressed deepest sympathy "in the loss of your friend." It is hard not to jump to the conclusion that the two were more than "friends," and not difficult to imagine the grief and sorrow this young nurse must have felt to have her deepest fear come true. She may have lived for eighteen months hoping against hope that her lover was safe in a German prison camp and they would be reunited after the war was over.

Although the fates of Dad's classmates who were awarded decorations were relatively simple to find, the majority proved untraceable, at least with the admittedly rudimentary skills I brought to the task.

What, I wondered, had happened to Bill "Coat'n Hat" Cotton, A. L. "Signalgram" Seligman or "Machine Gun Louis" Bean? It is sobering to look at the photo of Initial Training School Class 61 and realize that, statistically speaking, more than half of these eager, smiling young men never made it home, dying over Germany or France, or in training accidents in England.

Upon graduating, Dad was given twelve days of leave, and he no doubt went home to Provost, Alberta, to spend time with his wife Ruby. When it was time to part, it was not far by train to Prince Albert, Saskatchewan, some 150 kilometres north of Saskatoon. His destination was the No. 6 Elementary Flying Training School. It was the next stopping point on the BCATP conveyor belt: he would be taught to fly, and it is here that his logbook begins.

CHAPTER TWO:
FROM NOSE TO TAIL

NOVEMBER 1942 TO MAY 1943

In 1940, when the British Commonwealth Aircrew Training Plan was getting up to speed, there had been a frenzy of construction across Canada. Some of the training facilities had been created by expanding existing airfields, but many were carved from scratch out of the Canadian prairie, a massive engineering feat. Scouts flew around Canada, searching for suitable locations from the air and marking them on maps, which were then passed on to engineers on the ground. These ground surveyors would then visit the site and assess it. Many factors had to be considered: everything from water drainage to the proximity of a town to supply services had to be scrutinized and weighed against competing locations. The logistics of finding a site, assessing it, and then constructing what amounted to a small town from nothing were mind-boggling. Somehow it all came together—it seems there was an almost tangible "can-do" spirit at the time, and nothing seemed too big an obstacle to overcome in the fight against Hitler.

No. 6 Elementary Flying Training School was one of the facilities built from the ground up on the banks of the South Saskatchewan River, just across the water from the town of Prince Albert. Today the site is still in use, home of the Prince Albert Airport, although only one building remains from the World War II era. Like the Air Observer School, the EFTS was run by civilians under RCAF auspices—there is a stamp in Dad's logbook that says, "Northern Saskatchewan Flying Training School Ltd." I also noted the "Mr." rather than military rank preceding the names of some of his instructors.

Leading Aircraftman Jesse Coffey arrived in Prince Albert on November 9th, 1942 on what was likely a bitterly cold winter's day. The first two weeks of his time at EFTS would have been spent in the classroom and the aircraft hangar, learning the theory of flight and the parts and workings of the aircraft he would be flying. He also would have been issued two vital components of his new career as a pilot, the first being his flying kit, consisting of a pair of heavy, lined canvas overalls with a fur collar, heavy gauntlet gloves, and a pair of sheepskin-lined boots.

The second piece of "equipment" was a brand new Royal Canadian Air Force Pilot's Flying Log Book, which would be his constant companion for the next two years. Every minute of training and combat flying had to be recorded in detail, and losing one's logbook was a court-martial offence. The vital importance ingrained into trainees regarding this otherwise nondescript book is demonstrated by what good shape my Dad's logbook is still in, seventy-five years later. Despite the dicey conditions it must have experienced in various troopships, barracks, duffle bags and damp Nissen huts, the logbook remains virtually unstained and undamaged.

The logbook is laid out in a logical fashion, with the left-hand page detailing the date, type of aircraft, pilot and crew, and duty carried out. The right page logs accumulated flying time, broken down into type of aircraft, and day or night hours. The right side of the page was also where his civilian (and later military) supervisors would stamp their certification, showing that his logbook had been reviewed and deemed up to date and correct.

And so, on November 10th, 1942, we find the first entry in Dad's brand new logbook, written in his neat, meticulous block printing.

YEAR 1942		AIRCRAFT		PILOT, OR 1ST PILOT	2ND PILOT, PUPIL OR PASSENGER	DUTY (INCLUDING RESULTS AND REMARKS)
MONTH	DATE	Type	No.			
—	—	—	—	—	—	— TOTALS BROUGHT FORWARD
						COMMENCEMENT OF ELEMENTARY TRAINING AT No. 6 E.F.T.S., PRINCE ALBERT
Nov.	10	Tiger Moth	4990	Sgt. Ruff	Self	1-1A-2-3-4-5-6-18-18A
Nov.	11	Tiger Moth	4990	Sgt. Ruff	Self	2-3-4-5-6-16
Nov.	12	Tiger Moth	4990	Sgt. Ruff	Self	2-3-4-5-6-7-9-(10)-15-16
Nov.	13	Tiger Moth	4990	Sgt. Ruff	Self	2-3-4-5-6-7-9
						TOTAL WEEK ENDING NOV. 15
			For CHIEF SUPERVISORY OFFICER No. 6 E.F.T.S. PRINCE ALBERT			GRAND TOTAL
Nov.	17	Tiger Moth	4990	Sgt. Ruff	Self	3-4-5-6-7-9
Nov.	19	Tiger Moth	4990	Sgt. Ruff	Self	5-6-7-9-15-16
Nov.	22	Tiger Moth	4990	Sgt. Ruff	Self	5-7-9-16
						TOTAL WEEK ENDING NOV. 22
			For CHIEF SUPERVISORY OFFICER No. 6 E.F.T.S. PRINCE ALBERT			GRAND TOTAL
Nov.	23	Tiger Moth	4990	Sgt. Ruff	Self	5-6-7-9-10-16
Nov.	23	Tiger Moth	4983	Mr. Glass	Self	CHECK
Nov.	25	Tiger Moth	4179	Mr. Russell	Self	6-7-9-16
Nov.	25	Tiger Moth	5861	Sgt. Ruff	Self	6-7-9-16
				GRAND TOTAL [Cols. (1) to (10)] 11 Hrs. 45 Mins.		TOTALS CARRIED FORWARD

At long last, after all the route marches and button polishing of Manning Depot, hours spent on tarmac duty at Air Observers School, and the academic brain strain of Initial Training School, he was finally climbing into the cockpit of a real airplane and starting the hands-on process of becoming a pilot. And what a plane he was going to learn on!

TIGER MOTH

A Tiger Moth depicted on a WWII-era cigarette card. Author's collection.

The de Havilland Tiger Moth is one of the truly beloved aircraft of the twentieth century, affectionately known to tens of thousands of who learned to fly her as the "Tigerschmitt," a laughing nod at the premier German fighter of the day, the Messerschmitt Bf 109. The Tiger Moth was a solid, easy-to-fly biplane that had been developed specifically as an entry level trainer for the RAF. Hundreds of Moths are still flying today, some eighty years after they were built, with examples decked out in wartime colours performing at airshows around the world.

Most of the Tiger Moths used by the RCAF were equipped with sliding perspex (a type of acrylic glass) canopies and were (like most RCAF training aircraft) painted a bright yellow, to aid in locating them in the event of crash in the Canadian hinterland. I am a bit skeptical about the efficacy of the canopy in keeping the pilot and student warm in the routinely minus-thirty degree Celsius prairie winter, but I guess it was better than nothing. The Moth certainly had nothing in the way of insulation otherwise—it was covered only in a fabric skin, and occupants could look down and see the aluminum tubing of the frame and the control cables running by their feet. One wrong step upon entering or exiting the cockpit, and one could put one's foot right through the wing. Communication between student and pilot was accomplished via shouting, hand gestures and hastily scribbled notes. All this may seem primitive to us today, but it got the job done, and thousands of the finest pilots in history got their start this way.

On the first page of the logbook we can see lists of numbers written in the Duty column. These codes refer to specific exercises performed, and although the codes may have varied somewhat from school to school, the explanations I provide here should be reasonably accurate.

The entry for November 10th, 1942 details a one hour and ten minute flight, with a list of nine duty codes, which consisted of tasks like familiarization with cockpit layout, preparation for flight (what a modern pilot would refer to as a pre-flight check), effects of controls (how the rudder pedals and control stick worked), taxiing, straight and level flight, and low flying. His instructor for this and his next seven flights was a Sgt. Ruff, and despite the unusual last name, I have been unable to trace him. Many instructors were combat pilots who had completed a tour of operations and were being "rested," but with a relatively low rank Sergeant, Ruff was more likely a talented student, pressed into service teaching others after earning his wings. Exercises performed over the next week got increasingly advanced as Dad grew his confidence and skills, with Ruff teaching him gliding, stalling, sideslipping, and steep turns. After another long flight on November 23rd, Dad flew with a civilian instructor, Mr. Glass, for a check on his progress.

November 25th turned out to be a red-letter day for my Dad, his solo flight, although I doubt he knew it ahead of time. On this day, another civilian, Mr. Russell, took him up for a flight, and then Sgt. Ruff took him up for his second of the day. Upon landing from this forty minute trip, Sgt. Ruff jumped out and told Dad to take the Moth up on his own and do a circuit of the airfield, then come in for a landing. With no forewarning of the coming solo flight, the student would have no time for worrying or overthinking the situation—the engine of the Moth probably wasn't even shut down. So, after almost twelve hours of dual instruction (about average for student pilots of the day) Dad was sent up on his own, and after about a ten-minute solo flight, he came in for a safe landing. He may not have officially earned his wings yet, but Dad must have been elated—he was a pilot!

YEAR 1942		AIRCRAFT		PILOT, OR 1ST PILOT	2ND PILOT, PUPIL OR PASSENGER	DUTY (INCLUDING RESULTS AND REMARKS)
MONTH	DATE	Type	No.			
—	—	—	—	—	—	— TOTALS BROUGHT FORWARD
Nov.	25	Tiger Moth	5861	SELF	—	11
Nov.	28	Tiger Moth	3882	SGT. RUFF	SELF	6-7-9-16
Nov.	28	Tiger Moth	3882	SELF	—	6-7-9-16
						TOTAL FOR WEEK ENDING NOV. 29
		signature For CHIEF SUPERVISORY OFFICER No. 6 E.F.T.S., PRINCE ALBERT				GRAND TOTAL
Nov.	30	Tiger Moth	4990	SGT. RUFF	SELF	6-7-9-10-16-17-19
Dec.	1	Tiger Moth	4156	SELF	—	6-7-9-16
Dec.	1	Tiger Moth	4156	SGT. RUFF	SELF	7-9 (CHECK)
Dec.	1	Tiger Moth	5151	SELF	—	6-7-9-16
Dec.	1	Tiger Moth	5151	SGT. RUFF	SELF	7-9 (CHECK)
Dec.	2	LINK	C2804	MacDONALD	SELF	1-2-3
Dec.	3	LINK	C2804	MacDONALD	SELF	3-4-5
Dec.	4	Tiger Moth	4990	SGT. RUFF	SELF	19
Dec.	5	Tiger Moth	4990	SGT. RUFF	SELF	19
Dec.	5	Tiger Moth	4217	SELF	—	6-7-9-16
Dec.	6	Tiger Moth	4990	SGT. RUFF	SELF	6-7-9-16 (CHECK)
Dec.	6	Tiger Moth	4984	SELF	—	6-7-9-16
Dec.	6	Tiger Moth	4984	SELF	—	6-7-9-16
Dec.	6	Tiger Moth	4990	SGT. RUFF	SELF	6-7-8-9-19
Dec.	6	Tiger Moth	4990	SELF	—	6-7-8-9
						TOTAL FOR WEEK ENDING DEC. 6

GRAND TOTAL [Cols. (1) to (10)]
25 Hrs. 30 Mins.   TOTALS CARRIED FORWARD

Over the next month, the dual and solo flights continued on an almost daily basis, with increasing intensity. For example, on December 6th, there were no less than five flights during one busy day, two of them with Sgt. Ruff and three of them solo. There was also time spent in a Link trainer, honing his skills in a safe environment. Instrument flying and navigation were introduced, and Dad's entry on December 12th includes a notation of "15 minutes map reading." Another on the 14th lists night-flying being practiced over and over during four flights that evening.

YEAR 1942		AIRCRAFT		PILOT, OR 1ST PILOT	2ND PILOT, PUPIL or PASSENGER	DUTY (INCLUDING RESULTS AND REMARKS)
MONTH	DATE	Type	No.			
—	—	—	—	—	—	— TOTALS BROUGHT FORWARD
		signature				TOTAL FOR WEEK ENDING DEC. 6
		For CHIEF SUPERVISOR OFFICER No. 6 E.F.T.S. PRINCE ALBERT				GRAND TOTAL
DEC.	7	TIGER MOTH	3882	SELF	—	6-7-8-9-15-16
DEC.	7	TIGER MOTH	4156	SGT. RUFF	SELF	7-9 (CHECK)
DEC.	7	TIGER MOTH	4156	SELF	—	6-7-9-10-16
DEC.	7	TIGER MOTH	4990	SGT. RUFF	SELF	10-12-15-16-17
DEC.	8	LINK	C2804	MACDONALD	SELF	4-5-6
DEC.	8	LINK	C2804	MACDONALD	SELF	6
DEC.	8	TIGER MOTH	5861	SGT. RUFF	SELF	20A
DEC.	8	TIGER MOTH	5861	SGT. RUFF	SELF	20A
DEC.	9	LINK	C2804	MACDONALD	SELF	6-7
DEC.	9	LINK	C2804	MACDONALD	SELF	8
DEC.	10	TIGER MOTH	4156	SELF	—	6-7-9-10-15-16
DEC.	10	TIGER MOTH	4990	SGT. RUFF	SELF	XC NAVIGATION
DEC.	11	TIGER MOTH	4948	SELF	—	6-7-8-10-15
DEC.	12	TIGER MOTH	4217	SELF	—	6-7-8-16
DEC.	12	TIGER MOTH	4990	SGT. RUFF	SELF	7-9-17-19 (15 MIN) map reading
DEC.	13	TIGER MOTH	256	MR GLASS	SELF	30 HOUR TEST -19
DEC.	13	TIGER MOTH	5942	SELF	—	12-15-16
DEC.	13	TIGER MOTH	4133	SELF	—	12-15-16
						TOTAL FOR WEEK ENDING DEC. 13
				GRAND TOTAL [Cols. (1) to (10)] **39** Hrs. **15** Mins.		TOTALS CARRIED FORWARD

On December 12th, another important milestone was reached, the crucial "30 hour test." Sgt. Glass (the examiner) flew as a passenger during a one hour flight that put Dad through his paces. In the end, he scored a respectable 66%. His test sheet shows the many different maneuvers he was expected to master, from unpowered ("gliding") landings to spinning to climbing turns. He scored low on steep turns, and there is a stern direction from Glass to "Practice!" written on the test sheet. In his summation, Glass wrote "Above average on most sequences. Needs practice, however, on low flying, side-slips, and aerobatics."

YEAR 1942		AIRCRAFT		PILOT, OR 1ST PILOT	2ND PILOT, PUPIL OR PASSENGER	DUTY (INCLUDING RESULTS AND REMARKS)
MONTH	DATE	Type	No.			
—	—	—	—	—	—	— TOTALS BROUGHT FORWARD
						TOTAL FOR WEEK ENDING DEC 13
						GRAND TOTAL
DEC.	14	TIGER MOTH	4156	SELF	—	6-7-8-9-10-16
DEC.	14	LINK	C2804	MR. MACDONALD	SELF	8-9
DEC.	14	LINK	C2804	MR. MACDONALD	SELF	6-8-10
DEC.	14	TIGER MOTH	5861	SGT. RUFF	SELF	20 A
DEC.	14	TIGER MOTH	5861	SELF	—	20 A
DEC.	14	TIGER MOTH	5861	SGT. RUFF	SELF	20 A
DEC.	14	TIGER MOTH	5861	SELF	—	20 A
DEC.	15	LINK	C2804	MR. MACDONALD	SELF	6-10
DEC.	15	TIGER MOTH	4310	SELF	—	6-7-8-9
DEC.	16	TIGER MOTH	5151	SELF	—	6-7-8-9
DEC.	17	TIGER MOTH	5940	SELF	—	7-9-20
DEC.	17	TIGER MOTH	5940	SELF	—	12-15-16
DEC.	17	TIGER MOTH	5940	SELF	—	12-15-16
DEC.	17	TIGER MOTH	4990	SGT. RUFF	SELF	7-9 (CHECK)
DEC.	18	TIGER MOTH	4156	SELF	—	10-12-15-16
DEC.	18	TIGER MOTH	4156	SELF	—	10-12-15-16
DEC.	18	TIGER MOTH	4156	SELF	—	15-16
DEC.	19	TIGER MOTH	4317	SELF	—	7-9-15
DEC.	19	TIGER MOTH	4317	SELF	—	10-12-17

D S Baker P/O
For CHIEF SUPERVISORY OFFICER
No. 6 E.F.T.S., PRINCE ALBERT

GRAND TOTAL [Cols. (1) to (10)]
53 Hrs. 30 Mins.

TOTALS CARRIED FORWARD

The final segment of the curriculum was solo navigation, and Dad set out December 27th on a one hour and forty minute solo flight, taking his Moth from Prince Albert to Kinistino, to Wakaw, and then back. The next day he was sent on two more tours, both of them two hours in duration. The first went from Prince Albert to Alvena and back, and the second from Prince Albert to Canwood, to Marcelin, and then back. On this final flight, he was accompanied by his trusty instructor, Sgt. Ruff, and they flew in Tiger Moth No. 4990, which as chance would have it, happened to be the very same aircraft he had first flown in upon arrival at EFTS back in early November. Moth 4990 came to an ignoble but sadly common end just six months later, being struck off strength and scrapped. After having facilitated the training of who knows how many Allied aircrew, suffering their ham-fisted landings and clumsy maneuvers, it seems an ungrateful fate.

YEAR 1942		AIRCRAFT		PILOT, OR 1ST PILOT	2ND PILOT, PUPIL OR PASSENGER	DUTY (INCLUDING RESULTS AND REMARKS)
MONTH	DATE	Type	No.			
—		—	—	—	—	— TOTALS BROUGHT FORWARD
DEC.	7					
DEC.	19	TIGER MOTH	4317	SGT. RUFF	SELF	19
DEC.	19	TIGER MOTH	4317	SELF	-	6-7-9-16
DEC.	20	LINK	C3504	MACDONALD	SELF	8-10-17
DEC.	20	LINK	C3504	MACDONALD	SELF	17
DEC.	20	LINK	C3504	MACDONALD	SELF	TEST (22)
						TOTAL WEEK ENDING DEC. 20
						GRAND TOTAL
DEC.	21	TIGER MOTH	4253	SELF	-	6-7-8-16
DEC.	23	TIGER MOTH	4990	SGT. RUFF	SELF	13-19-20-22
DEC.	23	TIGER MOTH	5940	SELF	-	8-9-12-16
DEC.	23	TIGER MOTH	4253	SELF	-	8-9-12-16
DEC.	24	TIGER MOTH	4990	SGT. RUFF	SELF	19
DEC.	24	TIGER MOTH	4884	SELF	-	7-9-10-15-16
DEC.	24	TIGER MOTH	4990	SELF	-	7-9-10-17-22
DEC.	26	TIGER MOTH	3882	SELF	-	7-9-10-16-22
DEC.	27	TIGER MOTH	4948	SGT. RUFF	SELF	7-9 (CHECK)
DEC.	27	TIGER MOTH	4948	SELF	-	7-9-10-15
DEC.	27	TIGER MOTH	4290	SELF	-	AXC-KIN.-WAK.- PA. NAVIGATION
DEC.	27	TIGER MOTH	5101	SGT. GLASS	SELF	60 HOUR CHECK
						TOTAL FOR WEEK ENDING DEC. 21.
						GRAND TOTAL
				GRAND TOTAL [Cols. (1) to (10)] 68 Hrs. 05 Mins.		TOTALS CARRIED FORWARD

YEAR 1942		AIRCRAFT		PILOT, OR 1ST PILOT	2ND PILOT, PUPIL OR PASSENGER	DUTY (INCLUDING RESULTS AND REMARKS)
MONTH	DATE	Type	No.			
—	—	—	—	—	—	— TOTALS BROUGHT FORWARD
DEC.	28	TIGER MOTH	5151	SELF	—	17-22
DEC.	28	TIGER MOTH	4948	SELF	—	ΔXC P.A.-ALVENA - P.A.-(NAV.)
DEC.	28	TIGER MOTH	4990	SGT. RUFF	SELF	ΔXC PA -CANWOOD- MARCELIN-P.A.
						TOTAL FOR WEEK ENDING JAN 3.
						GRAND TOTAL
					GRAND TOTAL [Cols. (1) to (10)] 72 Hrs. 40 Mins.	TOTALS CARRIED FORWARD

Having completed these three demanding exercises successfully, and with a total of 35 hours of dual and 37 hours of solo flying, Dad officially graduated Elementary Flying Training School. He was soon assigned to begin ever more complex and demanding training at the No. 4 Service Flying Training School (SFTS) in Saskatoon. Before leaving for the new School, he was granted eleven days leave, and again likely caught a train back to Provost to see his very pregnant wife for a few days.

The only memento Dad kept from his time at EFTS is a small booklet that seems to have been issued to each graduate. It is about four by six inches in size, with an Air Force blue cardboard cover, and is titled "Rhymes to Date of Class Sixty-Eight." As well as listing all the trainees and staff at the School, there is also a stanza of comic rhyme for each of the forty or so students. It is heart-warmingly naive, and reading it gives one an insight into simpler times and humbler lives.

> Bennett H. E. is the boy to see,
>
> step out on a weekend pass,
>
> With his buttons bright, his hat tilted right,
>
> the girls flock 'round en-masse.

Some of the stanzas give an idea of the disparate backgrounds the recruits were from: streetcar conductor, fireman, salesman, pharmacist, and Greyhound bus driver. Other stanzas speak of the subject's character, from "quiet, collected and calm" to "jolly, happy and free," and other lines note their ambitions, from flying a Spitfire to becoming an "ace," to "dropping one on Hitler" someday. Of course, Leading Aircraftman Coffey was not left out:

> Coffey J. R. who hails from Czar,
>
> knows aircraft from nose to tail,
>
> But wishes he knew, the person who,
>
> Sends him pamphlets through the mail.

The story behind this cryptic jibe is sadly lost, but it made me smile nonetheless when I read it.

After his leave Dad made his way back to Saskatoon and reported to the No. 4 Service Flying Training School. The School was actually the Saskatoon Municipal Airport, taken over for the duration by the RCAF. Dozens of new buildings were built, and the runways were paved as part of transforming the once quiet airfield. The SFTS was a strictly military operation, with RCAF discipline and with instructors who were experienced veterans, most having the rank of Flying Officer. The School's records for January of 1943 show that the base was staffed with 127 officers and 1135 "other ranks" to facilitate the training of 169 RCAF and twenty-four RAF recruits. The base also had four Royal Canadian Army Service Corps members (likely truck and transport drivers), four Canadian Dental Corps staff and three military police from the Canadian Provost Corps. There was one Barrack Warden, two meteorologists and 167 "other civilians," probably cooks and cleaners. There was even a contingent of the RCAF's new Women's Division (motto: "We Serve That Men May Fly"), who performed tasks as varied as telephone operators, air traffic control, and truck drivers.

The relaxed, somewhat casual and almost civilian atmosphere of the EFTS was a thing of the past. Here Dad would be learning to fly multi-engine aircraft with retractable undercarriages—modern aluminum skinned monoplanes equipped with dozens of unfamiliar controls and cockpit instruments.

The aircraft that served as Dad's main training platform was made by Cessna, and known by several different names depending on where it served. Cessna officially designated it the T-50, but to American servicemen, it was the Bobcat; to Commonwealth flyers it was the Crane.

The Cessna Crane, this particular example served in the BCATP and is preserved at the Canadian Aviation and Space Museum. Photo copyright Stuart Miller, used with permission.

The Crane struck me as a rather ugly aircraft when I first saw it, but my initial assessment has softened. I hesitate to use the word "cute," but the description does seem appropriate for this aircraft, especially in its all-yellow RCAF livery—with its somewhat bulbous nose, it looks like Walt Disney had a hand in its design.

Apparently, the Crane was no delight to fly, and the extra fuel tank that the RCAF insisted Cessna install did nothing to improve its handling characteristics. Despite the less than stellar reviews, the Canadians ordered almost a thousand of the type (the U.S. Army Air Force bought thousands more as well), and the military contracts put Cessna on the map as a major aircraft producer.

A picture of everyday life at the School is painted by the Daily Diary, which has been preserved and is available online to researchers. What struck me as I read through the Diary for the period that Dad was there was the heavy emphasis placed on recording results from various inter-service hockey games and boxing matches. Based on the evidence from the Diary, it's a wonder the students had any time for flying between sporting events!

YEAR 1943		AIRCRAFT		PILOT, OR 1ST PILOT	2ND PILOT, PUPIL OR PASSENGER	DUTY (INCLUDING RESULTS AND REMARKS)
MONTH	DATE	Type	No.			
—		—	—	—	—	— TOTALS BROUGHT FORWARD
		COMMENCEMENT OF TRAINING				No. 4 S.F.T.S. · JAN. 10
JAN.	12	CRANE I	7745	F/O GAUSS	SELF	FAMILIARIZATION
JAN.	12	LINK	L365	F/O KELLY	SELF	1-2-3-4
JAN.	13	CRANE I	7665	F/O GAUSS	SELF	6-7-8
JAN.	13	CRANE I	7665	F/O GAUSS	SELF	6-7-8
JAN.	13	CRANE I	7665	F/O GAUSS	SELF	PASSENGER
JAN.	14	CRANE I	7665	F/O GAUSS	SELF	PASSENGER
JAN.	14	CRANE I	7665	F/O GAUSS	SELF	6-7-8
JAN.	14	CRANE I	7665	F/O GAUSS	SELF	6-7-8
JAN.	16	LINK	L338	SGT. OGG	SELF	5-6
JAN.	16	CRANE I	7665	F/O GAUSS	SELF	PASSENGER
JAN.	16	CRANE I	7665	F/O GAUSS	SELF	PASSENGER
JAN.	16	CRANE I	7665	F/O GAUSS	SELF	6-7-8
JAN.	16	CRANE I	6775	F/O GAUSS	SELF	6-7-8
JAN.	16	CRANE I	6775	F/O NESBITT	SELF	6-7-8 (SOLO CHECK)
JAN.	16	CRANE I	6775	SELF	—	6-7-8
JAN.	17	CRANE I	7687	F/O GAUSS	SELF	6-7-8-13A
JAN.	17	CRANE I	7687	SELF	—	6-7-8
JAN.	17	CRANE I	7687	F/O GAUSS	SELF	PASSENGER
		M Gauss F/O		F.A. Montgomery F/L		TOTAL FOR WEEK ENDING JAN. 17
	for O.C. E FLIGHT		Officer Commanding... No. 4 SFTS RCAF Station Saskatchewan			GRAND TOTAL

GRAND TOTAL [Cols. (1) to (10)]
79 Hrs. 50 Mins.   TOTALS CARRIED FORWARD

His flight training commenced on January 12th, 1943 and, as at the EFTS, his logbook records the duty codes that show the increasingly advanced exercises and maneuvers that he had to master. The instructors certainly didn't waste any time. Four days after starting his training, on January 16th, he had no less than five training flights (plus a session in a Link), and soloed at the end of what must have been a gruelling day. It was a memorable day in more ways than one, as at some point during the same day, his wife Ruby gave birth to the first of his four sons, my eldest brother Gary.

The School's Daily Diary for January 16th gives an insight into the daily routine on the base:

> Flying all day, no night flying. R157842 LAC Miller, J. E., a student of Course 68 ceased training due to unsatisfactory progress in flying. Sports equipment was checked and issued. A wrestling and tumbling class was held in the Recreation hall and a small group took part in this sport. The senior hockey team played Flin Flon at that town and lost by a score of 7 to 2.

It seems the powers that be worked hard to keep everyone busy, and when they weren't engaged in flying or classroom work, there was basketball, hockey, badminton, volleyball, skiing, skating, boxing, and bowling to take part in. There were church parades, physical training drills, and on at least one occasion, "a bingo party was held in the Women's Division canteen for all station personnel, and an enjoyable time was had by all."

The instruction continued for week after week, the flights becoming lengthier, the maneuvers more advanced and complex. Navigation was introduced, and Dad is listed as navigator on several flights. Flying on one engine, unpowered landings, and taking off in a crosswind all had to be mastered.

A very regular notation in the Daily Diary is the recording of the names of those airmen who "washed out." It seems it was a more frequent occurrence then at EFTS. The training on the twin engine Crane was tougher, and it seems the bar was set higher—it didn't take much to be assessed as having "unsatisfactory progress in flying." The unlucky student would be sent on for retraining at Bombing and Gunnery School, or perhaps put back two or three classes to start over.

Dad had his own close call with being "washed out" on January 26th, when we can see an almost hesitant notation of "(ACC.)" written in his logbook. Coming in for a landing that morning, after a one-hour solo flight, Dad applied the brakes either too hard or too soon, and the Crane flipped over on its back on the runway. He was unhurt, but the same could not be said of poor Crane 7694. She was broken up and sent into storage and never flew again, being scrapped just after the war ended, with over three thousand hours of flying time in her log. The accident was investigated, and I remember my Dad telling me that, although he knew full well the error was his, he insisted to the investigators that the brakes had been frozen (since it was January in Saskatoon, this was not far-fetched at all) and were not working properly. Dad was grounded for what were probably three very stressful days for him, but in the end, there were no repercussions for the crash. The investigators may have had their suspicions, but no more was made of the incident—it seems it was written off as just another of the many mishaps that occurred to student pilots, and Dad carried on with his training. Perhaps the crash even had a bright side: I wonder if Dad ended up a more confident pilot, knowing he could total an aircraft and walk away unscathed!

YEAR 1943		AIRCRAFT		PILOT, OR 1ST PILOT	2ND PILOT, PUPIL OR PASSENGER	DUTY (INCLUDING RESULTS AND REMARKS)
MONTH	DATE	Type	No.			
—	—	—	—	—	—	— TOTALS BROUGHT FORWARD
JAN.	21	LINK	L-38	F/SGT. FENSKE	SELF	1-2-3
JAN.	22	CRANE I	7659	F/O GAUSS	SELF	6-7-8 -13A
JAN.	24	CRANE I	7692	F/O GAUSS	SELF	6-7-8
JAN.	24	CRANE I	7692	SELF	—	6-7-8
						TOTAL WEEK ENDING JAN. 24
			710			GRAND TOTAL
JAN.	25	LINK	L38	F/SGT. FENSKE	SELF	3-4
JAN.	26	CRANE I	7694	F/O GAUSS	SELF	6-7-8-13A
JAN.	26	CRANE I	7694	SELF	—	6-7-8-13A (ACC.)
JAN.	29	CRANE I	8690	F/Lt EDWARDS	SELF	PROGRESS CHECK
JAN.	29	CRANE I	8690	F/O GAUSS	SELF	19
JAN.	29	CRANE I	8690	SELF	—	6-7-8
JAN.	30	LINK	L38	F/SGT. FENSKE	SELF	4-5
JAN.	30	LINK	L38	F/SGT. FENSKE	SELF	5-6
JAN.	30	LINK	L38	SGT. ARMOUR	SELF	7
						TOTAL WEEK ENDING JAN. 31
			710			GRAND TOTAL

O.C. "E" FLIGHT
Officer Commanding No 2 Squadron
No 4 S.F.T.S. R.C.A.F. Saskatoon, Saskatchewan

GRAND TOTAL [Cols. (1) to (10)]
86 Hrs. 50 Mins.
TOTALS CARRIED FORWARD

Through the first two weeks of February, there were multiple daily flights, some dual and some solo, all on the Cessna Crane. On February 15th, he acted as navigator on a map reading exercise in one of the School's Avro Ansons, an aircraft he had not seen since his tarmac duty at the Air Observer School the previous year. A week later, he had four navigation tests, three dual and one solo, the second two being the start of a week of intense night flying practice. Flying in the dark, relying only on instruments to guide you, was challenging and dangerous, but it was something he was to become very familiar with over the next two years.

YEAR 1943	AIRCRAFT		PILOT, OR 1ST PILOT	2ND PILOT, PUPIL OR PASSENGER	DUTY (INCLUDING RESULTS AND REMARKS)
MONTH DATE	Type	No.			
—	—	—	—	—	— TOTALS BROUGHT FORWARD
FEB. 1	CRANE I	7913	F/O GAUSS	SELF	6-7-8-21A
FEB. 1	CRANE I	7913	SELF	—	6-7-8-21A
FEB. 1	LINK	L38	F/SGT FENSKE	SELF	7-8
FEB. 1	LINK	L38	SGT. WAY	SELF	10-11
FEB. 2	CRANE I	8661	SELF	-	6-7-8-21A
FEB. 2	CRANE I	8661	SELF	-	6-7-8-21A
FEB. 2	CRANE I	7692	SGT. COOPER	SELF	MAP READING Ex.1
FEB. 2	CRANE I	7692	SELF	-	6-7-8-21A-15
FEB. 4	LINK	L.38	F/SGT FENSKE	SELF	12
FEB. 4	LINK	L38	F/SGT FENSKE	SELF	12
FEB. 6	CRANE I	7871	SELF	-	6-7-8-21A
FEB. 6	CRANE I	7997	SELF	-	6-7-8-21A
FEB. 7	CRANE I	7924	F/O GAUSS	SELF	19
FEB. 7	CRANE I	7692	F/O COOPER	SELF	19
			F.A. Montgomery		TOTAL WEEK ENDING FEB. 7
O.C. E FLIGHT			Officer Commanding No. 2 Squadron No. 4 S.F.T.S. R.C.A.F. Saskatoon, Saskatchewan		GRAND TOTAL
FEB. 9	CRANE I	7997	F/O GAUSS	SELF	6-7-8-13-15-17-21A
FEB. 9	CRANE I	7997	SELF	-	6-7-8-13-15-17-21A
FEB. 10	CRANE IA	8751	F/L MONTGOMERY	SELF	6-7-8-15-17-20-21A
FEB. 11	CRANE I	7924	SELF	-	6-7-8-13-15-17-21A
FEB. 11	CRANE I	7924	SELF	-	6-7-8-13-15-17-21A
FEB. 11	CRANE I	7924	SELF	-	6-7-8
FEB. 12	LINK	L-18	F/O KERLY	SELF	21

GRAND TOTAL [Cols. (1) to (10)]
100 Hrs. 15 Mins.

TOTALS CARRIED FORWARD

March began with a three-hour night-time navigation exercise. Dad acted as navigator for Pilot Officer Tindall, as they flew their Crane to "P.N." (I believe this was likely Pelican Narrows, a tiny community some 400 kilometres north of Saskatoon) and back.

Year 1943		Aircraft		Pilot, or 1st Pilot	2nd Pilot, Pupil or Passenger	Duty (Including Results and Remarks)
Month	Date	Type	No.			
						Totals Brought Forward
Feb.	12	Link	L18	F/O Thomas	Self	12
Feb.	13	Crane I	7997	F/O Gauss	Self	19
						Total Week Ending Crane I
						Total Week Ending Crane IA
					Progressive	Total Week Ending Feb. 14
				O.C. E Flight		Grand Total
Feb.	14	Crane I	7721	P/O Monteith	Self	19-4-6
Feb.	15	Anson	FP808	S/P Cooper	Self	Nav. Ex. 2 Map Reading
Feb.	17	Crane IA	FJ-274	Self	-	Ht. Test
Feb.	17	Crane IA	FJ-274	F/O Gauss	Self	19-2-6
Feb.	17	Crane IA	FJ-274	Self	-	6-7-8-13-15-17-21A
Feb.	18	Crane IA	8751	Self	-	6-7-8-13-15-17-21A
Feb.	18	Crane I	8684	F/Sgt. Frudd	Self	6-7-8-13-15-17-21A
Feb.	19	Crane IA	FJ-206	F/O Gauss	Self	1-2-3-4-5-6-8-19
Feb.	19	Crane I	7665	Self	-	6-7-8-13-15-17-21A
Feb.	20	Crane I	7814	P/O Hartman	Self	Nav. Ex. 3 Map Reading
Feb.	21	Crane I	7999	Self	-	Nav. Ex. 4
						Total Week Ending Crane I
						Total Week Ending Crane IA
						Total Week Ending Anson
				O.C. E Flight		Progressive Total Week Ending Feb. 21
						Grand Total

Grand Total [Cols. (1) to (10)] 119 Hrs. 40 Mins. Totals Carried Forward

YEAR 1943		AIRCRAFT		PILOT, OR 1ST PILOT	2ND PILOT, PUPIL OR PASSENGER	DUTY (INCLUDING RESULTS AND REMARKS)
MONTH	DATE	Type	No.			
—	—	—	—	—	—	TOTALS BROUGHT FORWARD
FEB.	22	CRANE IA	FJ234	F/O WATTS	SELF	EX. I NAV. N.F. (EX22)
FEB.	22	CRANE IA	FJ234	F/O WATTS	SELF	EX. 2 NAV. N.F. (EX.24)
FEB.	23	CRANE I	7997	P/O JACOBS	SELF	6-7-8
FEB.	23	CRANE I	7997	P/O JACOBS	SELF	PASSENGER
FEB.	24	LINK	L-18	F/O KEELY	SELF	22
FEB.	24	LINK	L-18	F/O KEELY	SELF	24
FEB.	24	CRANE I	8000	P/O RAIN	SELF	6-7-8 NF.
FEB.	24	CRANE I	8000	P/O RAIN	SELF	6-7-8 NF
FEB.	24	CRANE I	8000	SELF	—	6-7-8 NF.
FEB.	24	CRANE I	8000	SELF	—	6-7-8 NF
FEB.	25	CRANE I	8000	SELF	—	6-7-8 NF.
FEB.	25	CRANE I	8000	SELF	—	6-7-8 N.F.
FEB.	25	CRANE I	8000	P/O JACOBS	SELF	6-7-8 N.F.
FEB.	25	CRANE I	8000	P/O JACOBS	SELF	PASSENGER
FEB.	26	CRANE I	8017	SELF	—	6-7-8 N.F.
FEB.	26	CRANE I	8017	SELF	—	6-7-8 N.F.
FEB.	26	CRANE I	8017	SELF	—	6-7-8 N.F.
FEB.	26	CRANE I	8034	P/O TINDALL	SELF	6-7-8 N.F.
FEB.	26	CRANE I	8034	P/O TINDALL	SELF	PASSENGER
FEB.	28	CRANE I	8034	P/O JACOBS	SELF	6-7-8 N.F.
FEB.	28	CRANE I	8034	P/O JACOBS	SELF	PASSENGER
FEB.	28	CRANE I	8034	SELF	—	6-7-8 N.F.

GRAND TOTAL [Cols. (1) to (10)]

137 Hrs. 45 Mins.

TOTALS CARRIED FORWARD

YEAR 1943		AIRCRAFT		PILOT, OR 1ST PILOT	2ND PILOT, PUPIL OR PASSENGER	DUTY (INCLUDING RESULTS AND REMARKS)
MONTH	DATE	Type	No.			
—	—	—	—	—	—	TOTALS BROUGHT FORWARD
		a Stevers F/o		N.J. Falmteau F/o		TOTAL WEEK ENDING CRANE I.
						TOTAL WEEK ENDING CRANE IA
						PROGRESSIVE TOTAL WEEK ENDING FEB. 28
						GRAND TOTAL
MAR.	1	CRANE I.	7783	P/O TINDALL	SELF	EX. 3 NAV. N.F (EX.17 AM)
MAR.	2	LINK	L-18	F/O KEELY	SELF	24
MAR.	2	LINK	L-24	SGT. PETTAPIECE	SELF	24
MAR.	3	LINK	L-24	SGT. PETTAPIECE	SELF	24
MAR.	3	LINK	L-24	SGT. PETTAPIECE	SELF	24
MAR.	4	LINK	L-18	F/O THOMAS	SELF	24
						TOTAL WEEK ENDING CRANE I.
		a Stevers F/o		N.J. Falmteau F/o	PROGRESSIVE	TOTAL WEEK ENDING MAR. 7
						GRAND TOTAL
MAR.	8	CRANE I.	8684	P/O RAIN	SELF	13-15-17-A-21A
MAR.	9	CRANE IA	FJ206	P/O RAIN	SELF	No. 10 △ INST. NAV.
MAR.	9	CRANE IA	FJ206	P/O RAIN	SELF	6-7-8-13-15-17-21A
MAR.	9	CRANE IA	8819	P/O RAIN	SELF	19
MAR.	10	CRANE IA	FJ213	SELF	-	6-7-8-13-15-17-21A
MAR.	10	LINK	L-18	F/O THOMAS	SELF	24
MAR.	10	CRANE I	FJ206	SELF	-	6-7-8-13-15-17-21A
MAR.	11	CRANE IA	FJ-213	SELF	-	6-7-8-13-15-17-21A
MAR.	11	CRANE IA	FJ268	SELF	-	6-7-8-13-15-17-21A

GRAND TOTAL [Cols. (1) to (10)]

140 Hrs. 00 Mins.

TOTALS CARRIED FORWARD

All through March, the training flights continued, sometimes as many as four in one day. Life at the School hummed along, with PT (calisthenics) drill, an official inspection by the Deputy Inspector General (who took the time to meet with the School's C.O. to "discuss various matters of importance…"), a pottery class by the hobby club, and of course, lots of hockey and basketball.

YEAR 1943		AIRCRAFT		PILOT, OR 1ST PILOT	2ND PILOT, PUPIL OR PASSENGER	DUTY (INCLUDING RESULTS AND REMARKS)
MONTH	DATE	Type	No.			
—		—	—	—	—	—
						TOTALS BROUGHT FORWARD
MAR.	11	CRANE 1A	8758	F/S. FRUDD	SELF	#2 A INST. 79-
				N J Robertson F/L		TOTAL WEEK ENDING CRANE I
				Officer Commanding No 2 Squadron		TOTAL WEEK ENDING CRANE 1A
				C. Steeves F/O		PROGRESSIVE TOTAL WEEK ENDING MAR. 14
		O.C. "E" FLIGHT				GRAND TOTAL
MAR.	15	ANSON	FP808	P/O STEEVES	SELF (1ST. NAV)	NAV #9b (1ST NAV)
MAR.	17	CRANE 1A	FS249	SELF	-	NAV. #5
MAR.	17	CRANE 1A	FS235	P/O RAIN	SELF	19
MAR.	18	CRANE 1	7687	SELF	-	NAV #6
MAR.	18	LINK	W18	F/O THOMAS	SELF	24
MAR.	19	CRANE 1A	8756	SELF	-	6-7-8-15-17-21A
MAR.	19	CRANE 1A	8733	P/O RAIN	SELF	19 (#3 CON. INST A)
MAR.	19	CRANE 1A	8756	P/O RAIN	SELF	6-7-8-13-15-17-21A
MAR.	19	CRANE 1A	8756	P/O RAIN	SELF	19
MAR.	20	CRANE 1A	8756	P/O RAIN	SELF	19
MAR.	20	CRANE 1A	8756	P/O RAIN	SELF	6-7-8-15-20-21A
MAR.	20	CRANE 1A	8756	P/O RAIN	SELF	19
MAR.	20	CRANE 1A	8756	P/O RAIN	SELF	PASSENGER
MAR.	21	CRANE 1A	FS220	SELF	-	6-7-8-15
MAR.	21	CRANE 1A	8733	SELF	-	6-7-8-15-20-21A
MAR.	21	CRANE 1	7812	P/O RAIN	SELF	PASSENGER
MAR.	21	CRANE 1	7812	P/O RAIN	SELF	LOWER LEVEL XCTY No. 19
				GRAND TOTAL [Cols. (1) to (10)] 164 Hrs. 45 Mins.		TOTALS CARRIED FORWARD

Year 1943		Aircraft		Pilot, or 1st Pilot	2nd Pilot, Pupil or Passenger	Duty (Including Results and Remarks)
Month	Date	Type	No.			
—	—	—	—	—	—	— Totals Brought Forward
		M.J. Jolentien F/L				TOTAL WEEK ENDING CRANE I
		Officer Commanding No 2 Squadron				TOTAL WEEK ENDING CRANE IA
		4 S.F.T.S. R.C.A.F. Saskatoon, Saskatchewan				TOTAL WEEK ENDING ANSON
		A. Amuson F/O				PROGRESSIVE TOTAL WEEK ENDING MAR. 21
		O.C. 'E' FLIGHT				GRAND TOTAL
MAR. 22	ANSON	8456	P/O STEEVES	F/L MOORE	NAV #12 (1ST & 2ND NAVIGATOR)
MAR. 23	CRANE I	7812	P/O RAIN	SELF	PASSENGER
MAR. 23	CRANE I	7812	P/O RAIN	SELF	20B
MAR. 23	CRANE I	7812	SELF		6-7-8-21A
MAR. 23	CRANE I	7812	P/O RAIN	SELF	6-7-8-13-15-17-21A-20-5
MAR. 24	CRANE I	8661	P/O JACOBS	SELF	20-B
MAR. 24	CRANE I	8661	F/O KAUFMAN	SELF	NAV #11 (P.N)
MAR. 25	LINK	L-18	F/O KEELY	SELF	24
MAR. 25	CRANE I	8120	SELF		6-7-8-21A
MAR. 25	CRANE I	7814	SELF	·	20B.
MAR. 26	CRANE IA	8786	SELF		20B.
MAR. 26	CRANE IA	8786	LAC. JONES	SELF	PASSENGER
MAR. 26	CRANE IA	8786	SELF	–	20B
MAR. 26	CRANE IA	8786	LAC CLEGG	SELF	PASSENGER.
					TOTAL WEEK ENDING CRANE I
					TOTAL WEEK ENDING CRANE IA
		A. Amuson F/O	_Geweleigh_		PROG. TOTAL WEEK ENDING MARCH 28
		O.C. 'E' FLIGHT	_Officer Commanding No 2 Squadron_		GRAND TOTAL
			4 S.F.T.S. R.C.A.F. Saskatoon, Saskatchewan		

GRAND TOTAL. [Cols. (1) to (10)]
176 Hrs. 55 Mins.   TOTALS CARRIED FORWARD

I was a bit mystified by the entry made on March 22nd, in which Dad listed himself as "1st & 2nd navigator." Why I wondered, would he be both? As I pondered the odd notation, I wondered if the aircraft they were flying (an Avro Anson, rather than their usual Crane) had something to do with it. My hunch turned out to be correct. Apparently, the Anson was supposed to carry up to four trainee navigators, each taking a turn at map reading and directing the pilot. The problem was that many of the Ansons purchased by the RCAF from the Avro firm in England arrived in Canada as airframes only. As the war heated up, England declined to send any engines to go with them—the RAF desperately needed them for home defence. The RCAF searched for a substitute, finally settling on an American powerplant, the Jacobs. Unfortunately, it didn't have the same power as the British engine, and so the Canadian Ansons could only carry two students at a time and hence the doubling-up.

March turned to April, and the weather must have begun to improve, as the Daily Diary notes that "arrangements were started for the organization of hardball and softball teams."

YEAR 1943		AIRCRAFT		PILOT, OR 1ST PILOT	2ND PILOT, PUPIL OR PASSENGER	DUTY (INCLUDING RESULTS AND REMARKS)
MONTH	DATE	Type	No.			
—	—	—	—	—	—	—
						TOTALS BROUGHT FORWARD
MAR.	29	CRANE I	7835	P/O JACOBS	SELF	20 B.
MAR.	29	CRANE I	7835	P/O JACOBS		PASSENGER
MAR.	29	CRANE IA	8795	SELF	-	6-7-8-15-17-21A
APR.	3	LINK	L18	P/O KEELY	SELF	24
APR.	3	CRANE I	8037	SELF	-	6-7-8-13-15-17-21A
APR.	3	CRANE IA	8795	SELF	-	NAV. EX. 8A - INCOMPLETE
APR.	3	CRANE IA	FJ-249	S/P ROWE	SELF	TEST No. 7 20 B.
APR.	3	CRANE IA	FJ-249	S/P ROWE	LAC DOBINSON	PASSENGER.
APR.	3	CRANE I	8136	SELF	-	20 B
APR.	3	CRANE I	8136	LAC KELLY	SELF	PASSENGER
APR.	4	CRANE IA	8733	P/O RAIN	SELF	20 B
APR.	4	CRANE I	7683	SELF	-	NAV. #8A
APR.	4	CRANE IA	8733	P/O RAIN	SELF	PASSENGER
						TOTAL WEEK ENDING CRANE I,
						TOTAL WEEK ENDING CRANE IA
		A. Arnason F/o O.C. E FLIGHT		Officer Commanding No 2 Squadron No. 15 S.F.T.S. RCAF, Saskatchewan		PROG. TOTAL WEEK ENDING APRIL 4
						GRAND TOTAL
APR.	5	CRANE I	8039	S/P. ROWE	SELF	6-7-13-15-16-17-21A
APR.	5	CRANE IA	FJ-252	S/P ROWE	SELF	-19-
APR.	5	CRANE IA	FJ-254	SELF	-	6-7-8-13-15-17-21A
APR.	5	CRANE IA	FJ-249	Flt. TABUTEAN	SELF	CLEAR HOOD WINGS TEST
APR.	6	LINK	L-18	P/O KEELY	SELF	25
APR.	6	CRANE IA	FJ-251	SELF	-	6-7-8-13-15-17-21A

GRAND TOTAL [Cols. (1) to (10)]

_____ 192 Hrs. 35 Mins.

TOTALS CARRIED FORWARD

On April 5th Dad completed an 80-minute flight with Flt. Lt. Tabutean, which involved a "clear hood wings test." The "test" is a bit of a mystery, as I can find no explanation in my research to explain what exactly this was. My best guess is that on many flights the student pilot would be wearing a hood that allowed him to see the aircraft's instrument panel, but nothing else. He would have to navigate and perform his maneuvers without the visual "cheat" of being able to see the horizon or ground. On a "clear hood" test, the hood was not used—the student pilot could use both instruments and his vision to fly the aircraft.

YEAR 1943		AIRCRAFT		PILOT, OR 1ST PILOT	2ND PILOT, PUPIL OR PASSENGER	DUTY (INCLUDING RESULTS AND REMARKS)
MONTH	DATE	Type	No.			
—	—	—	—	—	—	—
						TOTALS BROUGHT FORWARD
APR	6	CRANE IA	8819	S/P ROWE	SELF	BOMBING EX. 1
APR	7	CRANE IA	8784	S/P ROWE	SELF	BOMBING EX. 2
APR	7	CRANE IA	8786	S/P ROWE	SELF	19 (168)
APR	8	CRANE I	8037	S/P ROWE	SELF	BOMBING EX. 3
APR	8	ANSON	FP-809	F/SGT HARTNETT	SELF	NAV. EX. 16
APR	8	CRANE I	8684	S/P ROWE	SELF	20 B
APR	9	CRANE I	7970	SELF	LAC SCOTT	BOMBING EX. 3.
APR	9	CRANE I	7970	LAC SCOTT	SELF	PASSENGER
						TOTAL WEEK ENDING CRANE I
						TOTAL WEEK ENDING CRANE IA
		a. amason Flo.				TOTAL WEEK ENDING ANSON
		O.C. E FLIGHT		N. J. Johnleur F/L		PROG. TOTAL WEEK ENDING APR. 9
						GRAND TOTAL
APR	12	LINK	L-18	F/O KEELY	SELF	24
APR	12	ANSON	8482	P/O HARTMAN	C SMOKER	WINGS NAV. TEST
APR	13	CRANE IA	8785	SELF		BOMBING EX. 3
APR	13	CRANE IA	8785	C DICKIE	SELF	PASSENGER
APR	13	CRANE IA	8785	S/P ROWE	SELF	BOMBING EX. 4
APR	14	CRANE I	7812	P/O STEEVES	SELF	WINGS INST.
APR	14	CRANE I	7812	SELF	—	BOMBING EX. 3, 4, 5
APR	14	CRANE I	7812	SELF	—	BOMBING EX. 3, 4, 5
APR	14	CRANE I	7812	C JONES	SELF	PASSENGER
APR	15	CRANE IA	FJ274	S/P ROWE	SELF	BOMBING EX. 3

GRAND TOTAL [Cols. (1) to (10)]

208 Hrs. 35 Mins.

TOTALS CARRIED FORWARD

Reviewing the April 6th entries, I encountered another small mystery: Dad flew the first of no less than twelve "bombing exercises," some with Sergeant Pilot Rowe, and some solo.

Now, it should be noted that the Cessna Crane wasn't designed to carry any armament (despite the corny nickname the Americans gave it: the "Bamboo Bomber"). I have found no record of one ever being fitted with any kind of exterior bomb rack. So what exactly was involved in a "bombing exercise"? Again, I am left to resort to educated guesswork. Perhaps the students were given a "target" (the main intersection of a small town, city hall in Saskatoon....?) and made a flight plan and mock bombing run over their "aiming point." Was there perhaps a camera mounted in the plane, so they could snap a photo at the moment they "dropped their bombs"?

YEAR 1943		AIRCRAFT		PILOT, OR 1ST PILOT	2ND PILOT, PUPIL OR PASSENGER	DUTY (INCLUDING RESULTS AND REMARKS)
MONTH	DATE	Type	No.			
—	—	—	—	—	—	— TOTALS BROUGHT FORWARD
APR.	15	CRANE I	7958	S/P ROWE	SELF	BOMBING EX. 6
APR.	16	LINK	L-18	F/O KEELY	SELF	RADIO RANGE
APR.	17	CRANE IA	8819	SELF	–	NAV. 8B.
APR.	17	CRANE I	7873	SELF	L/C SWINBURNSON	BOMB. EX. 6
APR.	17	CRANE IA	8819	S/P ROWE	SELF	NAV. INST. NO. 14
APR.	18	CRANE I	8120	SELF	L/C KELLY	BOMB. EX. 6
APR.	18	CRANE I	8120	L/C KELLY	SELF	PASSENGER
APR.	18	CRANE IA	J235	S/P ROWE	SELF	NO. 23 LL XC
						TOTALS CRANE I
						TOTALS CRANE IA
a. amason F/o O.C. E FLIGHT						PROG. TOTAL WEEK ENDING APR. 18
						GRAND TOTALS
APR.	19	CRANE IA	J254	S/P ROWE	SELF	-19-
APR.	19	CRANE IA	J254	S/P ROWE	SELF	-19-
APR.	19	CRANE IA	J715	S/P ROWE	SELF	No. 20 NAV. INST.
APR.	20	CRANE IA	8819	S/P ROWE	SELF	-19-
APR.	20	CRANE IA	8819	S/P ROWE	SELF	-19-
APR.	20	CRANE IA	8819	S/P ROWE	SELF	-19-
APR.	20	CRANE IA	8819	S/P ROWE	L/C SWINBURNSON	PASSENGER
APR.	21	CRANE IA	J266	SELF	L/C SMITH	20-B
APR.	21	CRANE IA	J266	L/C SMITH	SELF	PASSENGER
a. amason F/o O.C. E FLIGHT						TOTAL WEEK ENDING APR. 25 CRANE IA.
						GRAND TOTALS

GRAND TOTAL [Cols. (1) to (10)]
233 Hrs. 55 Mins.   TOTALS CARRIED FORWARD

The navigation and bombing exercises continued for Dad throughout April. The rate of students "washing out" seems to have accelerated this month for some reason—it became an almost daily occurrence. Accidents increased as well, and one unfortunate LAC was given "27 days of detention" and put back two classes after running his Crane into another aircraft parked off the taxi strip. Another common accident for new students (who were used to the fixed undercarriage of the Tiger Moth at EFTS) was to belly land their Cranes, having forgotten to lower the landing gear. It was a common enough mistake that some Schools took to having a ground crew with a Very flare gun positioned at the end of the runway, ready to shoot off a red flare to warn students who were doing their runway approach "wheels up."

Humorous close calls and "fender benders" aside, deadly accidents were common—learning to fly in the time-pressured atmosphere of the BCATP was a dangerous business. We should remember that nearly a thousand young men from all parts of the world died in Canada while training.

At the very end of April, the tests and exercises were finally all successfully completed, and Dad prepared for the big day, one that he had been looking forward to for over a year, his Wings Parade, where he would be presented with the coveted pilot's wings.

Dad's final marks at Service Flying Training School were nothing to brag about: he finished 32nd out of his class of 46. Wing Commander Newcombe, the C.O. of the school, wrote this official assessment:

> A quiet hard working student who gets along well with the rest of his class mates. Works very hard to put forth a good show. Discipline is good, dress and deportment good.

The Chief Instructor of the School, Squadron Leader Edwards added:

> This students flying is average. He could be more aggressive than he is. His flying is quite accurate and safe. He (has) a tendency to over control in his instrument flying. He was an above average pupil in ground school being the quiet, studious type.

My Dad was obviously no world-beater student, but the sad truth is that even coming top of one's class did little to predict success in the nocturnal killing fields above Nazi-occupied Europe—Bomber Command aircrew had too many chips stacked against them, and blind luck played too large a role in survival.

A tragic example of this is the story of Pilot Officer David Goodwin. He was the young man who *did* finish at the top of Class 72, and was presented with a Proficiency Award at the Wings Parade. He stands out in the class photo as the only new pilot wearing spectacles, as he sits proudly beside Wing Commander Newcombe in the front row. Along with the rest of the top third of the class, he received a commission, rising automatically to the rank of Pilot Officer.

Goodwin shipped off to England some months after my Dad did, and ended up at 24 Operational Training Unit (OTU) in Worcestershire. On his final test before completing his training at OTU, he and his crew were sent to France to drop leaflets on the German occupiers, a standard OTU test that was referred to by the code name "Nickel Raid." Their Whitley bomber was hit by flak and shot down on May 22nd, 1944, all five crew members perishing.

The RCAF and the City of Saskatoon made a big deal about the Wings Parades, organizing large events attended by visiting dignitaries, one of whom would honour the graduates of class 72 by pinning their new wings onto their chests.

On April 30th, 1943 the City of Saskatoon had arranged a parade with no fewer than seven bands, and including contingents from groups as diverse as the St. John's Ambulance Brigade and the Ukrainian Great War Veteran's Association. The local paper promised those attending "an outstanding show." The parade finished up at Kiwanis Park, on the banks of the South Saskatchewan River, for the formal presentation of wings, which was performed by Air Vice Marshall T. A. Lawrence, head of Training Command for the RCAF.

Sixty students had started in Class 72 back in January, but only forty-six remained to get their wings, a washout rate of about twenty percent. Forty-two of the forty-six graduates received their wings from Air Vice Marshall Lawrence, but four of them were singled out for a special honour, having their wings pinned on by their mothers. I was delighted to see in the Saskatoon newspaper article about the day that my Dad was among these four, having his wings pinned on by my grandmother, who had travelled from Czar, Alberta for the event. Almost certainly, my Mother and baby Gary were there, too.

After the ceremony, there was a dinner at the Bessborough Hotel, where the graduates and their guests dined on roast chicken with apple jelly, au gratin potatoes, and cauliflower with "fines herbes."

With graduation came a promotion—my Dad was now Sergeant Coffey—a raise in pay (to the princely sum of $3.70/day), and an assignment. Of the forty-six graduates of Class 72, eleven were sent off to Flying Instructor School, ten went to Ground Reconnaissance School (destined for Maritime Patrol duties), three went to Air Observer School, and the British graduates were sent to the RAF's No. 31 Personnel Depot in Moncton, New Brunswick for further processing. Dad and seventeen of his comrades were ordered to No. 1 Y Depot in Halifax to await a troopship that would carry them to England.

Sgt. Coffey goes to war. Dad in another mugshot for the RCAF, this time wearing brand new pilot's wings and Sergeant stripes. Courtesy Library and Archives Canada.

The RCAF granted Dad about two weeks of leave, and he likely spent the time getting his young family settled back in Provost, Alberta, where Mom and Gary would be close to family while he was gone. It seems Mom had moved to Saskatoon to be close to Dad while he was attending SFTS, and they had rented a small house at 311 Avenue D North—the house is still there, looking somewhat dishevelled at present, but it was likely quite respectable and cozy in 1943.

Ruby and Jesse Coffey, circa May 1943. Author's collection.

After what must have been a very difficult parting from his wife and baby son, Dad made his way via train to Halifax, Nova Scotia. He reported to the No. 1 Y Depot on Windsor Street, where he was assigned a billet while he awaited news on when and on which ship he would be leaving.

Y Depot was really more of an organization than a place, a kind of holding company as it were. It kept track of all the RCAF personnel awaiting transport to Europe, assigning them billets in Halifax and generally keeping them organized.

There were two ways for troops to get to England and both involved trying to get past the wolfpacks of German U-boats prowling the North Atlantic. The first was by convoy, a system that relied on the principle of "strength in numbers" to get through. Dozens of cargo and troopships would leave port the same day, assemble into a formation and sail together, protected by a phalanx of destroyers, frigates and corvettes. The convoy might make nine or ten knots at best, perhaps a knot or two faster that a submerged U-boat could manage.

The second method involved going it alone, in a ship that was deemed fast enough to be relatively safe travelling solo. A speedy ship travelling on its own was a difficult target for the U-boats to even find, let alone chase down and attack. There was easier prey for the submarines to focus their efforts on.

Dad was originally scheduled to depart Halifax on May 27, 1943 on a troopship that was part of Convoy HX 241, made up of forty-three ships with their escorts. For whatever reason, Dad "missed the boat," literally and figuratively, and departed the next day (along with 4,500 other troops) on the SS Pasteur, which was going it alone across the Atlantic. She was an ocean liner, built just before the war, equipped with four propellers and powerful engines that generated 50,000 horsepower. The Pasteur could plow through the water at twenty-six knots in a pinch, more than three times the speed a submerged U-boat could manage. They made the crossing in a remarkable six days, arriving in Liverpool some five days ahead of the convoy that had left Halifax the day before them. The Pasteur was a fine ship that served the Allies well, ferrying some 300,000 troops in various theatres during the war. She served as a passenger liner for various companies for thirty-five years after the war, but had reached the end of her service life by 1980. I am happy to report that, while being towed to a scrapyard in Taiwan, she decided she had had enough and listed to her side and sank to the bottom of the Indian Ocean, where she is now enjoying a dignified and well-deserved rest.

Dad entered a new stage of his Air Force experience from the moment the SS Pasteur left Halifax harbour—up to that point, the risk to life and limb had been through accident. For the next eighteen months or so, whether it be via U-boat, night fighter, flak, or flying bomb, there would be other young men actively trying to kill him.

CHAPTER THREE:
INTO THE FRAY

JUNE 1943 TO FEBRUARY 1944

Dad arrived safely in Liverpool on June 4th, 1943 and the powers that be wasted no time in getting him off the S.S. Pasteur and on his way to his assigned post. Newly arrived aircrew and ground crew were placed under the charge of a Draft Conducting Officer (often a retired British Army officer). He would shepherd them through the Liverpool docks and onto a train and then accompany them south to ensure they made the journey without mishap. It must have been a disorienting experience for the young Canadians—blackouts, strange accents, odd customs, and rationed food. The next day he arrived at the RAF's main hub for processing new Commonwealth air force arrivals, the No. 3 Personnel Receiving Centre in Bournemouth, on England's south coast.

The former seaside holiday centre of Bournemouth had essentially been commandeered by the military for the duration, and all the hotels and guesthouses were used for billeting airmen. It was thus a tempting target for the Germans, and just ten days before Dad and his comrades arrived, twenty-six Luftwaffe FW190 fighter-bombers had dashed across the channel from their airfield near Caen in Occupied France, each armed with a 500 kg bomb. They took the city completely by surprise and scored direct hits on several hotels, killing over a hundred people, including eleven newly arrived Canadian airmen. They strafed the streets with cannon and machine-gun fire and then roared back out over the channel, pursued in vain by hastily scrambled RAF Spitfires. It was a devastating raid and the evidence of the destruction would still have been clearly visible when Dad and his fellow Canadians arrived on June 5th, making it clear to them that they were in a real shooting war now.

The Personnel Receiving Centre must have been an absolute hive of activity, with hundreds of new arrivals showing up every day, and hundreds more getting their postings and leaving for their new assignments. Young men from places as diverse as South Africa, Australia, Canada, America, New Zealand, Barbados and India would be mingling and taking stock of their new surroundings. According to the Personnel Receiving Centre's official records, Dad was among a group of some 1220 airmen who arrived there that day, ranging from "Officer Pilots" to "Airmen Groundcrew," with Dad being one of 304 "Sergeant Pilots." They were assigned billets and had their pay sorted out, and for the next three weeks, until a posting was determined for him, Dad and his fellow airmen would cool their heels in Bournemouth. They would be attending lectures by combat-experienced aircrew, church parades (mandatory), exploring the city, enduring yet more medical tests and performing the odd bit of light duty such as air raid watch from a rooftop. Dad also attended the stores depot and was issued his flying gear and battledress uniform in preparation for his first posting.

While many new arrivals (such as ground crew trades like engine fitters and armourers) might be sent directly to an operational squadron to begin their work, pilots were another story. Dad still had a lot to learn before he was ready to be thrown at the Germans, and on June 29th, he boarded a train and reported to the No. 11 (Pilot's) Advanced Flying Unit in Shawbury, Shropshire.

Although Dad arrived in England proudly wearing pilot's wings, he was in reality still a babe in the woods—months of intensive training were still ahead of him. For one thing, flying conditions in England were a far cry from the clear, friendly, uncrowded skies of the Canadian prairies; he was now in an environment of atrocious weather, thick fog, barrage balloons, and itchy-fingered Allied anti-aircraft gunners whose attitude was often "shoot first, ask questions later." The skies over Britain were crowded with thousands of bombers, fighters, and training aircraft, and even the occasional Luftwaffe intruder looking for an easy kill. Navigation at night would be another new challenge—my Dad's logbook shows he had a grand total of only twenty-three hours of night flying under his belt by this point in his training, and half of that was as second pilot. The very nature of night flying would be different in England: the well-lit towns of Canada were gone - here he would be flying in strictly enforced wartime blackout conditions.

RAF Shawbury was a well-established airbase, built before the start of the war. Accommodations were likely quite comfortable in comparison to the hastily constructed bases that Dad would find waiting for him at Tholthorpe and Gransden Lodge in the year to come.

The Airspeed Oxford, or "Oxbox". Original WWII-era cigarette card. Author's collection.

His training platform at Shawbury would be the Airspeed Oxford, a twin-engine aircraft specifically designed to get pilots ready to fly the multi-engine bombers they would be taking into combat. It was (somewhat unkindly, I think) referred to as the "Ox-box," but perhaps the nickname was affectionate, as the Oxford really was a fine aircraft, perfectly suited for its task. The goal of his eight weeks at the (P.)A.F.U. was to get Dad confident and competent flying an aircraft in what was, in reality, a war zone.

On July 4th Dad spent several hours in his old friend the Link trainer, and on the following day flew for the first time in England, and for the first time in an Oxford, accompanied by Flying Officer Sedgewick. Three days and four dual flights later, Dad soloed with the Oxford on July 8th.

Year 1943		Aircraft		Pilot, or 1st Pilot	2nd Pilot, Pupil or Passenger	Duty (Including Results and Remarks)
Month	Date	Type	No.			
—	—	—	—	—	—	— Totals Brought Forward
						Commencement of Training - No. 11 (P) A.F.U.
July	4	Link	L-5	Sgt. Innes	Self	Ex. 1
July	4	Link	L-5	Sgt. Innes	Self	Ex. 1 + 2
July	5	Oxford	W5164	F/o Sedgewick	Self	Map Reading
July	6	Oxford	AB762	P/o Little	Self	7A, 8A, 9A, 1, 1A, 2, 3, 4A, 4B, 5, 6
July	7	Oxford	E-17	4/Sgt. Wood	Self	8A, 8B, 9A, 9B, 9C.
July	7	Oxford	AB654	4/Sgt. Drew	Self	Nav. Ex. 2
July	8	Oxford	W6648	4/Sgt. Wood	Self	7, 9c, 9a, 9b, 9c
July	8	Oxford	W6648	Self	-	12
July	8	Oxford	W6648	4/S Wood	Self	1F, 8a, 9a
July	7	Link	L-3	Sgt. Bonfield	Self	Ex. 3 + 4
July	8	Oxford	AB654	Sgt Godfrey	Self	Nav. Test Ex
July	9	Oxford	MP286	4/S. Wood	Self	10A, 10B.
July	9	Oxford	MP286	Self	-	10, 10A
July	9	Oxford	V3461	Self	-	8a, 9a.
July	9	Link	L-1	Sgt. Wright	Self	Ex. 4
July	11	Link	L-5	Sgt. Tucker	Self	Ex. 4
July	11	Oxford	AB686	4/S Wood	Self	11F (A-F)
July	11	Oxford	AB68	Self	-	15a
July	12	Oxford	V4165	4/S Wood	Self	11F, 17, 18, 15A.
July	12	Oxford	V4165	Self	-	15a, 18
July	12	Oxford	V4165	Self	-	15A.

Grand Total [Cols. (1) to (10)]
249 Hrs. 20 Mins.

Totals Carried Forward

As at Elementary Flying Training School and Service Flying Training School, the codes in Dad's logbook refer to specific exercises and maneuvers to be mastered. Beginning with "familiarity with cockpit layout," he advanced flight after flight, mastering skills like "Gliding turn – flaps up," "spinning," "engine failure," and "low flying at high speeds."

On July 12th, he did a solo test, consisting of an almost two-hour cross county navigation exercise, and by July 19th was deemed proficient enough to move on to the No. 1534 Beam Approach Training Flight, a "subsidiary" as it were, of the Advanced Flying Unit.

Beam Approach was a method used to allow a pilot to find, approach and even land his aircraft on a runway in dense fog or complete darkness, when his vision was of little or no use. Airfields would broadcast a series of continuous, audible signals (dots and dashes, for example), and the pilot could home in on them, calculating his flight path based on the sounds.

As a non-pilot, I have difficulty picturing how the system worked; it must have taken a lot of skill and practice (and nerve!) to get proficient with it. During training, the student would wear a hood to prevent him from seeing outside the cockpit, and would (under the supervision of his instructor) bring the aircraft within feet of the runway, or even in some cases land it, using only the beeps and tones to guide him.

It was a skill that could well save his life and the lives of his crew one day. Landing in an English fog, dense as proverbial pea soup, must have been a terrifying experience, and the Beam Approach method gave pilots in such situations a fighting chance to land safely.

After successfully completing the B.A.T. portion of his training, Dad returned to the Advanced Flying Unit for another five weeks of training, which emphasized navigation (note the two long "XCTY" cross-country night flights) and included something called an "F-Comm Test" (flight communications perhaps?) on August 2nd. Starting August 4th, Dad performed six "F.P.L." flights, which I believe stands for "Flare Path Landing." Landing an aircraft in the dark was obviously a handy skill for an aspiring bomber pilot, and the flare path made the job a lot less hazardous. A flare path was a method of lighting the approach and runway's edges. The lights involved may have been electric (carefully shaded so they would only be visible to the friendly aircraft approaching to land, and invisible to enemy aircraft flying overhead), or paraffin goose-neck lamps, burning a wick. Dad practiced three of these landings with an instructor on the 4th, then did three more solo. On the 7th, he did two more with Flying Officer Bengree beside him, then did six on his own.

YEAR 1943		AIRCRAFT		PILOT, OR 1ST PILOT	2ND PILOT, PUPIL OR PASSENGER	DUTY (INCLUDING RESULTS AND REMARKS)
MONTH	DATE	Type	No.			
—	—	—	—	—	—	— TOTALS BROUGHT FORWARD
July	12	OXFORD	V4165	SELF	-	No. 1 X CTY
July	13	OXFORD	BF933	S⁄G. COLDRICK	SELF	15, 1/F
July	13	OXFORD	BF933	SELF	-	15, 4b, 18
July	14	OXFORD	V3680	SELF	-	18, 10A, 10b.
July	15	OXFORD	LW735	SELF	-	7a, 8a, 9a, 10b, 18
July	16	OXFORD	BF933	⅓ ROSS	SELF	9b, 1/F
July	16	OXFORD	BF933	SELF	-	9a, 10b, 10a, 15a
July	16	OXFORD	V3680	SELF	-	15a, 18, 9c
July	17	OXFORD	AB639	S⁄G. COLDRICK	SELF	1/F (E-N)
July	19	OXFORD	MP404	S⁄G. COLDRICK	SELF	1/F, 15a, 4b, 10B
July	19	OXFORD	LB424	SELF	-	10a, 10b, 18
July	19	OXFORD	E9	SELF	-	7a, 8a, 9a, 18, 4b
					COMMENCED	TRAINING No. 1534 B.A.T
July	20	OXFORD	DF333	¾₀ KRAMER	SGT. CARMICHAEL SELF	EX. 1
July	20	LINK	B.A.T.	SG⁄T. GOSHAWK	SELF	EX. 2
July	21	OXFORD	DF473	¾₀ CRAMER	SGT. CARMICHAEL SELF	EX. 1 & A
July	21	OXFORD	DF473	¾₀ CRAMER	SGT. CARMICHAEL SELF	EX. 2 & 3.
July	21	LINK	B.A.T	SG⁄T. GOSHAWK	SELF	EX. 3
July	22	LINK	B.A.T.	SG⁄T. GOSHAWK	SELF	EX. 4
July	22	OXFORD	X572	¾₀ CRAMER	CARMICHAEL SELF	EX. 3
July	22	OXFORD	S531	¾₀ CRAMER	CARMICHAEL SELF	EX. 4

GRAND TOTAL [Cols. (1) to (10)]

268 Hrs. 40 Mins.

TOTALS CARRIED FORWARD

Year 1943		Aircraft		Pilot, or 1st Pilot	2nd Pilot, Pupil or Passenger	Duty (Including Results and Remarks)
Month	Date	Type	No.			
—	—	—	—	—	—	— Totals Brought Forward
July	28	Oxford	MP286	SELF		No. 2 X Cty Nav.
July	29	Oxford	W6585	SELF	·	16, 46, 18, 10b
July	28	Link	L-1	St. Bonfield	SELF	EX. 12
July	28	Link	L-4	F/Lt. Martin	SELF	EX. 12.
July	29	Oxford	AB705	St. Bullock	SELF	D/N.
July	31	Link	L-1	St. Innes	SELF	EX. 1
July	31	Link	L-2	Sgt Sowder	SELF	EX. 11
Aug.	1	Oxford	AB639	F/O Selby	SELF	
Aug.	1	Oxford	V4165	SELF	St. Jackson	Q.D.M.s
Aug.	2	Oxford	AB762	F/S. Plane	SELF	No. 5 X Cty
Aug.	2	Oxford	AB639	P/O Macaulay	SELF	D/N
Aug.	2	Oxford	F-9	F/Lt. Donald	SELF	F² Comm. Test
Aug.	4	Oxford	C-19	Sgt. Todd	SELF	3 F.P.L.
Aug.	4	Oxford	C-19	SELF	·	3 F.P.L.
Aug.	7	Oxford	F-30	F/O Bengree	SELF	2 F.P.L.
Aug.	7	Oxford	F-30	SELF	·	6 F.P.L.
Aug.	8	Oxford	F-2	P/O Turton	SELF	C/S.
Aug.	9	Oxford	F-14	SELF	·	4 F.P.L.
Aug.	9	Oxford	C-25	SELF	—	C/S
Aug.	10	Oxford	C-21	St. Bullock	SELF	B.X.C.
Aug.	10	Oxford	C-21	SELF	·	B.X.C.
Aug.	13	Oxford	F-21	SELF	·	C/S
Aug.	14	Oxford	F-24	SELF		4 F.P.L.

GRAND TOTAL [Cols. (1) to (10)]
297 Hrs. 05 Mins.   Totals Carried Forward

The meanings of the duty codes "C/S" and "D/N" have eluded me thus far, but "Q.D.M" was a type of navigation exercise involving requesting a distant airfield for a bearing, and then following it in.

Dad graduated the (P.)A.F.U. course at the beginning of September 1943, and after two weeks of leave, arrived at RAF Wellesbourne, an airfield in the English Midlands, to begin the next phase of his training at the No. 22 Operational Training Unit. It was here that a team was formed, one that would stick together for the next fourteen months of training and combat.

Bomber Command had an interesting and very effective (and I think one that showed clever insight into human psychology) method of sorting dozens of pilots, navigators, wireless operators, air gunners and bomb aimers who were all strangers to one another (with occasional exceptions, as we will see), into teams. They simply gathered them together into a cavernous aircraft hangar and, after a roll call, an officer would quiet them down and instruct them to "sort themselves out" into crews and report to him when they had done so.

The method was the polar opposite of the system experienced by American aircrews, who were assigned into crews by a senior officer, who ensured that the pilot, co-pilot, bombardier, and navigator were all officers and the other trades were enlisted men. On and off the ground, rank structure was adhered to, and it seems there was little fraternization in the USAAF.

The British method was far more egalitarian, and I think the bonds formed between the young men must have been tighter, as they chose each other rather than being assigned to a team arbitrarily.

It must have been quite a sight inside the huge hanger in Wellesbourne that day, with the hundred or so young Commonwealth airmen looking around at each other self-consciously, probably wondering where even to start. Pilots were self-evident from the wings they had sewn on their tunics. Each of the other trades had single-winged brevets ("N" for navigator, "AG" for air gunner, "BA" for bomb aimer and "WAG" for wireless operator/air gunner) on the left breast of their battledress blouses —there must have been much brevet reconnaissance going on as they tried to put together a full crew of five. Did my Dad take charge, as he was the pilot and thus would be the "skipper" of the crew and the one, regardless of rank, who would be in charge in the air? Something tells me not. My Dad's essential character was introverted—personable and friendly, but introverted nonetheless. I don't think he would have been the catalyst in an awkward, unfamiliar situation like "crewing up." For that, you need an extrovert: a confident, talkative people-person. It is pure conjecture, but I bet Teddy made the first move.

Warrant Officer Raymond "Ted" Rutherglen was from Nelson, British Columbia, a small town in BC's rugged Selkirk Mountains. Ted was born with a common (and temporary) birth condition called lanugo, a covering of fine hair all over his body. His mother thought he looked like a Teddy bear, and the nickname stuck—he was universally known as Ted or Teddy for the rest of his life. Teddy's father had been a soldier (a Hussar in the Boer War) and a policeman (in Nairobi, Kenya) before settling in Canada and marrying. Apparently, the senior Rutherglen couldn't stomach domesticity after a life of adventure: he abandoned his wife and four children and headed for America. They never saw him again, although years after returning from overseas, Ted received a letter from him which, after glancing briefly at its contents, he tore up in front of his own young son.

Ted and his three siblings were raised by their mother, a strong woman who was apparently a force to be reckoned with, being known within the family as "the Sergeant Major." Ted grew up loving the outdoors, and for the rest of his life was happiest when in the forests and high country of British Columbia. After graduation from High School, he joined the British Columbia Regiment (Duke of Connaught's Own) in June of 1940 and served as a "rifleman." It seems the Army didn't suit young Ted, as a year to the day of joining up he was given a discharge "upon enlistment into RCAF."

Ted progressed along the same BCATP conveyor belt as the rest of his crew, being earmarked as a wireless operator/air gunner (or WAG for short) while at Manning Depot.

The role of the WAG on a bomber crew was critical, but it is one of the least understood (and appreciated) of the aircrew trades. There was nothing glamorous about the work Ted did, but it was vital to the crew's success—without him they were literally deaf, unable to hear orders from base or from the Master Bomber over the target during a raid. He would keep their navigator advised of the latest reported wind speed and direction information as it was broadcast from England. If they had to ditch in the English Channel or the North Sea on their way home, it was Ted who would continuously broadcast their position so rescue boats could attempt to find them. The WAG was a jack-of-all-trades in a way, trained in navigation, air-to-air gunnery, bomb aiming, and first aid, as well as radio and Morse code communications. When he had any free time, and when they were near or over the target, he would stand up and position his head in the perspex astrodome bubble at the back of the cockpit canopy, keeping watch for enemy fighters or other hazards. When possible, he would scan the airwaves and try and find the frequency being used by the Germans that night. He could then turn on a special microphone and broadcast the sound of one of the Lancaster's roaring Merlin engines, hopefully blocking communication between ground controllers and night fighters, at least temporarily.

To acquire all the necessary skills for this multi-faceted task, Ted was sent first to Wireless School, then on to Air Observer School, Bombing and Gunnery School, and finally Central Navigation School, totalling more than a year of intensive training in Canada.

When I received a copy of Ted's logbook from his son, I was amazed to read about the close calls that Ted had had while training. In brief, matter-of-fact notations, Ted relates near-death experiences with the understatement typical of his generation:

"Engine failure – emergency landed Prince Albert"

"One engine cut over Lake Winnipeg. Force landed #5 Air Observer School Winnipeg"

"Force landed at Neepawa. (Heavy icing)."

"Crash landed near Mcgregor, in ploughed field. Ceiling zero[2] – starboard engine out - radio unserviceable. Out of petrol"

"Test flight -ceiling zero on take off – made four overshoots – nearly into control tower."

"let down through cloud and missed Wheatland grain elevators by 10 feet (ceiling zero)"

There are other similar notations, and reading them gives one a sense of the dangers faced by all students and instructors as they tried to accomplish their training as quickly as possible regardless of the weather.

Ted finished his training, and he and Dad ended up at Y Depot in Halifax at the same time, my Dad embarking for England a few days after Ted arrived in Halifax. They may have passed each other in the street, or perhaps even met casually, not knowing fate would bring them together again in a few months.

After arriving in Liverpool and spending a month at the Personnel Receiving Centre in Bournemouth, Ted boarded a train for the No. 4 (Observer) Advanced Flying Unit at RAF West Freugh in a remote corner of Scotland. Here he would hone the basic skills he had learned in Canada up to current RAF standards—things like words per minute of Morse code, night navigation, photography, and operating a powered gun turret would all be tackled.

After six weeks here, Ted was posted to the No. 22 OTU, and it is here we return to that hanger full of strangers, looking about to find the makings of a crew.

---

2   Meaning thick cloud right down to ground level.

It seems logical that Ted would want to find a pilot first, so perhaps he collared my Dad quite quickly. They might have found some common ground in that they both had recently lived in British Columbia, and I'm betting Ted was a good (and swift) judge of character and just liked what he saw. They say opposites attract, and the effusive extrovert and the quiet, studious introvert may have liked each other immediately. At any rate, the next trade on the shopping list was to find a navigator, and they were indeed fortunate to land a young man from Ontario who was to develop into one of the best navigators in Bomber Command, **Flying Officer Robert Bayne**.

Bob Bayne had grown up in Ottawa, and like Ted, had been raised by his mother after his father left the family. He had graduated from Ottawa Tech High School (where he was a basketball player of some renown) and joined the Royal Canadian Army Service Corps. However, again like Ted, Army life had not agreed with him, and he joined the RCAF on June 1st, 1942. After Manning Depot (and, like all the other crew, a stint on tarmac duty at a Service Flying Training School) Bob went on to Initial Training School, where the powers that be decided he would be a navigator.

From ITS, it was on to Air Observer School, where he graduated with the rank of Sergeant. From there he should have taken the next usual step and attended the Central Navigation School in Rivers, Manitoba. However, Bob Bayne's training took an unusual turn: after arriving at the Personnel Receiving Centre in Bournemouth, he was chosen, along with about two hundred other airmen from the P.R.C., to attend the RAF's Aircrew Officer School located in Sidmouth, a small town on the coast of Devon. Graduating three weeks later a newly minted Flying Officer, he was then assigned to the No. 5 Air Observer School on the Isle of Man, which offered a far more intense and advanced curriculum in navigation than its Canadian equivalent.

It seems Bob was able to put his considerable basketball skills to work in between training flights on the Isle of Man. He recalled that he organized a game with a group of Polish airmen—they played on some open ground at the docks and were watched by a large crowd of locals. The Poles won, and Bob commented, "they couldn't speak a word of English, but how they could play ball!" Bob graduated from the A.O.S., and shortly after he found himself in the big hanger at the No. 22 Operational Training Unit along with a dozen or so other navigators looking for a crew to join.

The job of navigator in a Bomber Command aircrew was an absolutely critical one. For an entire bombing operation, up to nine hours, Bob Bayne would be ensconced in his curtained-off cubicle behind the pilot's seat, carefully and continuously plotting their course and current location. He had to account for the continually shifting wind speeds and direction, as well as the precisely specified dog-leg turns that were part of their assigned route. He had to keep track of their timing to the minute—if they were running late (or ahead of schedule), he had to feed my Dad a course alteration that would make sure they arrived over the target at exactly the assigned time, to the minute. If Dad had to take evasive action for some reason, Bob's charts and tools would go flying, and when the rollercoaster ride was over, he would have to try and work out a course to get them back on track. He had to be able to take a reading from the stars using a sextant (an ancient maritime technique), as well as using sophisticated modern electronic navigation aids like Gee, Oboe, and H2S. All in all, there is no doubt that Bob's task was the most technically exacting and challenging of all the trades, and the Coffey crew were lucky indeed to have a navigator who was at the top of his game.

Once Bob was buttonholed as the new navigator, there were two more spots to fill on the nascent crew, that of rear gunner and bomb aimer, and as fate would have it, they had already found each other. It may have been the bomb aimer who was brought into the crew first, and once he was on board, he quickly made off to find his buddy, whom he likely sold to his new crewmates as the finest tail gunner in the RCAF!

Sergeants **Robert McWhirter** (rear gunner) and **Malcolm Dingwall** (bomb aimer) were both from the same rural area of Saskatchewan, and knew each other well. During the roll call that day, they were astonished to hear each other's names called out, and there was no question that they would stick together once they found each other in the big hanger. Since the Coffey crew needed exactly these two trades, it was a perfect fit.

Malcolm Dingwall was the oldest of the crew, about twenty-nine years old when they met at OTU. His advanced age and the fact he was married caused the crew to sometimes jokingly refer to him as "Grandpa," but he was known as "Ding" most of the time. Malcolm had grown up in rural Saskatchewan on a small farm near the village of Asquith. In his late teens, he left the family farm and made a seriously impressive bicycle journey some hundred miles north to Shellbrook to look for work. Malcolm settled in Shellbrook, finding work where he could, including running a "cream route," picking up from small farms all around the area and delivering their milk to the central dairy. He met Edith Storey at the local cafe, where she worked in the family business, and they soon married.

Like it did to millions of others, the war interrupted whatever plans the newlyweds may have made for building a life together.

When he joined the RCAF in the spring of 1942, Malcolm was likely hoping to be a pilot. In common with so many Depression-era youth, he lacked a high school diploma and was told by his superiors that he was needed elsewhere, and put into the bomb aimer stream.

The bomb aimer on a Bomber Command Lancaster or Halifax could arguably be called the most important member of the crew: all the other six crew members were there solely to get Malcolm safely to the right spot, at precisely the right time, so that he could do his job. Once the aircraft started its bomb run over the assigned target, Malcolm was effectively in command of the aircraft. As they approached the aiming point, he gave precise course corrections to my Dad that had to be followed to the letter (a standard Bomber Command joke was about a bomb aimer who instructed his pilot "… steady, steady, left a bit… steady… back a bit… !"). Only when Malcolm was satisfied that they were perfectly positioned would he "press the tit" (the slang term for the bomb release button) and send their bomb load cascading down, and speak those welcome words "bombs gone!" over the intercom to the rest of the relieved crew. It was entirely within the bomb aimers' rights to call a "dummy run" if he was not satisfied. The pilot would be required to turn around, fly back the way they had come, enter the bomber stream a second time and try again. Obviously, with flak bursting around them and the risk of collision, this was something to be avoided, and everyone endeavoured to get it right the first time!

After Manning Depot, "Ding" was sent to No. 7 Initial Training School in Saskatoon and was actually there at the same time as my Dad, although in a different class. From ITS, he went to No. 2 Bombing and Gunnery (B&G) School in Mossbank, Saskatchewan. Bomb aimer training was rudimentary at the time and involved dropping eleven-pound practice bombs from an Avro Anson onto a target floating in a lake or sitting in an empty field. The "bombs" emitted a puff of smoke when they hit, allowing observers on the ground to give the students a paper plot of how accurate they had been.

As well as dropping bombs, Malcolm would have learned gunnery, as in the Wellington, Halifax, and Lancaster, the front gun turret was his responsibility, although in practice, these guns were rarely used. To master the art of air-to-air firing, Malcolm was taken up in an obsolete Fairy Battle, where he blasted away with an equally obsolete Vickers drum-fed .303 machine gun at a canvas target (or "drogue") being towed by another Battle.

All in all, I think it is safe to say that "Ding" gained the majority of his substantial bomb-aiming skills while in England, as opposed to this training in Canada. Of all the crew, it appears that his schooling in the BCATP bore the least resemblance to what he was actually to face in real combat.

After B&G School, "Ding" was sent to No. 7 Air Observer School in Portage La Prairie, Manitoba, where he learned the same navigation and map reading skills that had been taught to Dad, Bob Bayne, and Ted Rutherglen. After graduating A.O.S. he had to say goodbye to wife Edith and their brand new baby daughter Diana, and board a train for Y Depot in Halifax. There he cooled his heels for a month before boarding a troop transport in July of 1943 for the crossing to England. After a time at the Personnel Receiving Centre in Bournemouth he was posted to the No. 22 Operational Training Unit, and it is there he found himself meeting an old friend far from home: Bob McWhirter.

Sergeant Robert McWhirter had grown up on his stepfather's farm in rural northern Saskatchewan. Bob followed the path of thousands of other youngsters in the Great Depression, withdrawing from school after completing Grade Eight in order to work the family farm full time. He was doing a man's work from an early age and in tough conditions: by the time he was a young man, threshing grain for twelve hours a day or cutting and splitting wood in a winter bush camp were part of his routine. One winter, he and a hired hand dug a thirty-foot well by hand on the family's farm, hauling the dirt and rocks up hand-over-hand with a bucket.

This background of hard and sometimes tedious work, completed regardless of the cold or heat or wet, was to serve him well in his assigned trade of air gunner. The ability to stay focused on the task at hand despite discomfort and fatigue was better preparation for combat than almost anything the Air Force was to teach him. One other valuable skill the farming life likely taught him was hunting: there is no doubt the hunter's skills of leading a moving target and of calculating deflection were just as useful in downing a Ju 88 night fighter as they were in bagging a duck for dinner!

The job of rear gunner—or "Tail End Charlie" as they were nicknamed—was one of the most straight-forward of the aircrew, but at the same time, one of the most vital and challenging. If Ted Rutherglen was their ears, Bob McWhirter was their eyes: hour after hour he (and later, Ken Hart in the mid-upper turret) was continuously scanning the pitch dark skies looking for a telltale movement that could signal an imminent night fighter attack. Bomber Command air gunners were trained to shoot only if it would be effective, as the tracer rounds arcing out from their four Browning machine guns could give their presence away and draw other night fighters. It was better just to keep the enemy in sight and maintain a constant running commentary with one's pilot, letting him know when to take evasive action. A well-timed and executed "corkscrew" maneuver could usually shake off a night fighter, and a bomber crew was paid to get to the target and bomb it, not to engage in aerial dog fights with enemy fighters. It didn't help that their .303 calibre machine guns were no match for the night fighter's 20 mm cannons, either in range or in stopping power. Getting into a shooting match with a Junkers Ju 88 or Messerschmitt bf110 was usually a losing proposition, so stealth was the watchword, and air-to-air combat avoided whenever possible.

The rear gunner worked in miserably uncomfortable and acutely dangerous conditions. Isolated from the rest of the crew in his cramped turret, he could expect no help if their bomber was set on fire or mortally wounded. His parachute was located inside the fuselage of the aircraft: if he needed to bail out and couldn't reach the exit door, he had to open the doors of the turret, grab the chute, clip it on and then rotate the turret so the doors faced out into the slipstream. Then he could fall out backwards into the night. If the aircraft's hydraulics were damaged and the turret would not turn, he could be trapped.

The temperature at 20,000 feet could easily dip to minus forty centigrade, and Bob had only his electrically heated flying suit to protect him. All in all, it was the most tedious, uncomfortable, and dangerous job on the aircraft, and to do it well required a special kind of courage.

Bob McWhirter joined the RCAF in the fall of 1942 (much against his parents' wishes, who knew he could have easily gotten a deferment as the only son on the farm) about the same time my Dad was making his first flights in a Tiger Moth at EFTS.

Bob was quickly earmarked for air gunner training while at Manning Depot, and was posted to #1 Air Gunner Ground Training School in Quebec after a stint on tarmac duty at the SFTS in Souris, Manitoba. The air gunner ground school lasted six weeks and got him intimately acquainted with the Browning .303 machine guns that would be the tools of his trade for the next two years. He learned to take them apart, clean them, and put them back together—while blindfolded and wearing gloves (there could be no bare hands when he was at 20,000 feet trying to clear a jammed Browning at minus 40C)! His instructors were combat veterans, and the curriculum was no-nonsense. For now, it was all ground-based, but it was a necessary preliminary before climbing aboard an airplane for air-to-air firing.

After graduating, Bob went on to the No. 9 Bombing and Gunnery School in Mont-Joli, Quebec. It was here he would take to the skies, his first taste of flying. The aircraft he trained in was the obsolete Fairy Battle, an RAF light bomber that had turned out to be completely outmatched by the Luftwaffe fighters in the Battle of France and had been shot down in large numbers. Pulled from frontline service, the remaining Battles were sent overseas as training aircraft. They were equipped with a single Vickers K machine gun mounted in the open cockpit facing the rear, an arrangement that any Royal Flying Corps Observer in 1916 would have been familiar with. Bob and his fellow students had to start somewhere, I suppose!

Taking to the skies above the St. Lawrence river, Bob and his pilot met up with a Noorduyn Norseman, which was towing a canvas sleeve (or "drogue") at the end of a long steel cable. When I spoke to Bob in 2016, he laughingly recalled how his pilot made sure to keep well back from the Norseman, as he was well acquainted with rookie air gunners and their wild aim. The bullets in Bob's Vickers machine gun were coated in bright paint, so later when everyone had landed, he could assess his accuracy by looking at the telltale colour around the holes in the drogue.

As well as air-to-air firing and aircraft recognition exercises, there was also a mock turret on the ground, in which students could practice their aim on the images projected onto a movie screen. There was also a live firing range on the ground, with a powered gun turret equipped with the .303 Brownings he would be using in combat.

After twelve weeks of air gunner training, Bob was promoted to Sergeant, and proudly sewed the one-winged AG brevet to the left breast of his battledress blouse.

From Mont Joli, he went directly to Halifax and, like my Dad, made a fast solo crossing to Europe aboard the Queen Mary, arriving in Greenock, Scotland, after about four days at sea. Like all the others, he spent some time at the Personnel Receiving Centre in Bournemouth. From there he travelled to the No. 22 Operational Training Unit, where we now return to that big hanger, and Bob being press-ganged into the Coffey crew by his old friend Malcolm Dingwall.

So here we have the original five crew members assembled as a team for the first time. Such a casual way to pick the other young men into whose hands you would be entrusting your life! Was this tall skinny pilot any good? Was that little tail gunner[3] a good shot? Was his night vision any good? They must have all asked themselves questions like this, and one of the main purposes of the OTU experience was to bond these five into a team who had rock solid confidence in each other's skills and reliability. In his fine book, No Moon Tonight, Lancaster pilot Don Charlwood wrote about his first flight with his new comrades at an Operational Training Unit, saying, "We were not a crew, we were a planeload of bewildered individuals."

The OTU would meld these "bewildered individuals" into a tight, efficient team.

---

3   The irreverent Teddy Rutherglen christened diminutive Bob with the nickname "Button"!

RAF Wellesbourne, the home of the No. 22 Operational Training Unit, had been built in 1941 with the express purpose of preparing Commonwealth aircrew for battle: the "Operational" portion of its name says it all. The six weeks they spent there would be intense, focused… and dangerous: our crew were to have a very close brush with death only a week before completing the course.

The aircraft they would be flying at OTU was their first taste of a truly modern combat aircraft—the Vickers Wellington Mk III. The "Wimpy" (the nickname came from the Popeye character J. Wellington Wimpy) was another beloved aircraft, having a reputation among those who flew her as reliable and tough - she would bring her crews home despite suffering horrific damage. The key to the Wimpy's strength was the unique geodetic aluminum airframe designed by Roy Chadwick, who went on to develop the bouncing bomb used in the famous Dambuster's raid. Dad would have his hands full adapting to this new aircraft: although it was a twin-engine monoplane like the Oxford, its empty weight was four times as great.

The Vickers Wellington. Original WWII press photo. Author's collection.

The Wellington had been the backbone of Bomber Command since 1939, but with the introduction of the new four-engine "heavies" (the Stirling, the Halifax, and the Lancaster), she started to play a lesser role, although she remained in front line service right up to the end of the war.

The Wimpy was no beauty to be sure—she has a sad, Basset Hound look about her to my eye (especially on the ground sitting on her stubby undercarriage), but she was a fine aircraft and beloved by her crews.

YEAR 1943		AIRCRAFT		PILOT, OR 1ST PILOT	2ND PILOT, PUPIL OR PASSENGER	DUTY (INCLUDING RESULTS AND REMARKS)
MONTH	DATE	Type	No.			
—	—	—	—	—	—	— TOTALS BROUGHT FORWARD
						ATTACHED No. 22 O.T.U - SEPT. 7
SEPT.	28	WELLINGTON	DF·594	P/O CROSSE	SELF & CREW	C. & L. O/S,
SEPT.	29	WELLINGTON	DF·594	P/O UNTERSEHER	SELF & CREW	C. & L. O/S, S.E.F.
SEPT.	29	WELLINGTON	DF·594	P/O UNTERSEHER	SELF & CREW	C. & L. O/S, S.E.F.
SEPT.	30	WELLINGTON	DF·594	P/O CROSSE	SELF & CREW	C. & L. O/S, S.E.F.
SEPT.	30	WELLINGTON	DF·594	P/O CROSSE	SELF & CREW	C. & L. O/S, S.E.F.
SEPT.	30	WELLINGTON	DF·594	SELF	CREW	C. & L. O/S, S.E.F.
SEPT.	30	WELLINGTON	HF·631	SELF	CREW	C. & L. O/S, S.E.F.
OCT.	2	WELLINGTON	HF·760	P/O UNTERSEHER	SELF & CREW	EX. 5 - DUAL BOMBING
OCT.	2	WELLINGTON	HF·760	SELF	CREW	EX. 6 - SOLO BOMBING
OCT.	3	WELLINGTON	HF·647	P/O CROSSE	SELF & CREW	EX. 8 - DUAL CROSS CTY.
OCT.	9	WELLINGTON	HF·760	SELF	CREW	EX. 9 - SOLO CROSS CTY.
OCT.	10	WELLINGTON	HF·639	SELF	CREW	EX. 10 - SOLO CROSS CTY.
OCT.	13	WELLINGTON	HF·631	SELF	CREW	EX. 11 - SOLO CROSS CTY.
OCT.	16	WELLINGTON	HF·631	SELF	CREW	EX. 13 - SOLO CROSS CTY.
OCT.	17	WELLINGTON	HF·644	SELF	CREW	EX. 14 - "GEE" CROSS CTY.
OCT.	18	WELLINGTON	HF·647	SELF	CREW	EX. - "GEE" CROSS CTY.
OCT.	18	WELLINGTON	HF·647	SELF	CREW	SOLO BOMBING
OCT.	22	WELLINGTON	HF·647	SELF	CREW	SOLO BOMBING
OCT.	22	WELLINGTON	DF·560	SELF	W/O MARTIN CREW	FIGHTER AFFILIATION.
OCT.	24	WELLINGTON	DF·560	SELF	W/O MARTIN CREW	FIGHTER AFFILIATION

GRAND TOTAL [Cols. (1) to (10)]
352 Hrs. 35 Mins.

TOTALS CARRIED FORWARD

The crew's first flight was on September 28th, 1942, when they were taken up in a Wellington Mk III equipped with twin Hercules engines, this particular aircraft coded DF594. Their pilot for this introduction to the Wimpy was Pilot Officer Crosse, who, like most other instructors at the OTU was an experienced combat veteran. He took them up for a quick fifteen-minute flight, including some circuits and landings ("C&L" in the logbook), and at least one overshoot ("O/S"). Overshoots involved simulating an aborted landing by touching down on the tarmac and then pouring on the throttles to lift off again as if one were going to "overshoot" the end of the runway.

The next day, September 29th, they got straight into it, completing two training flights, each over two hours long, overseen by Flying Officer Unterseher.

Training rookie aircrew at the Operational Training Units was a dangerous business—No. 22 OTU lost almost a hundred Wellingtons during the war, with over three hundred aircrew killed (some 240 were

Canadian), and many of those killed were instructors. Flying Officer Emil Unterseher was a Canadian from Hilda, Alberta who had already flown a tour of operations with 404 Squadron flying the Bristol Blenheim.

Unterseher ("Undie" to his friends) walked away from a Wellington that crashed on take-off about six months after he helped train the Coffey crew, but sadly was killed in June of 1944. The student pilot of the Wellington he was in crashed into the top of a mountain in England's Lake District during a night training flight. All eight aboard were killed.

The two flights on the 28th seemed to be mostly for Dad's benefit, involving circuits and landings, over-shoots, and single-engine flying ("S.E.F." in the logbook). On September 30th, they repeated the two flights, this time under the watchful eye of Pilot Officer Crosse.

Dad must have adapted to the Wellington without issues, as after these five flights he was cleared to solo, taking his new crew up for two flights on September 30th, repeating the pattern of circuits and landings, overshoots, and single-engine flying.

On October 2nd, Malcolm Dingwall finally got a chance to practice his trade, as the crew performed a one hour and fifteen minute "dual bombing" exercise. Pilot Officer Unterseher guided Dad to the bombing range (the mudflats in the Bristol Channel were often utilized, as well as designated farmer's fields sur-rounding Wellesbourne), where they likely dropped twelve-pound practice bombs. Just like at Bombing and Gunnery School back in Canada, the bombs were inert, but did produce a puff of smoke when they hit the ground so the aim could be assessed.

The crew repeated the exercise later the same day, this time with Dad flying solo. On the 3rd, it was navigator Bob Bayne's time for a workout—they flew "Ex. 8", an almost five hour cross-country navigation exercise, with Pilot Officer Crosse sitting in the instructor's seat.

Over the next two weeks, the cross-country flights continued, with a new twist thrown in on October 17 and 18, when Bob Bayne used the new GEE navigation equipment for the first time in the air. He had been training with it in the classroom since they had arrived at OTU, but this time was for real. GEE was the code name for a system that used three transmitters placed around Britain to send out signals that receivers on aircraft could pick up. The receiving box precisely measured the distance from the transmitters, and thus the navigator could plot a very accurate position of where he was on his chart. The system got less accurate the farther one was from the transmitters, and the Germans could easily jam the signals, so GEE was less effective over Occupied Europe, but it could literally be a lifesaver for Allied aircraft in Great Britain. Just how useful GEE could be was to become very clear to the crew in about four weeks' time, as we shall see.

On the 18th and 22nd, there was more solo bombing, and on the afternoon of the 22nd, tail gunner Bob McWhirter finally got a chance to test his mettle with a "fighter affiliation" exercise.

A fighter affiliation exercise must have been an exhilarating experience for the air gunner and the pilot, but everyone else on board was probably just holding on and wishing for it to be over! Somewhere over Warwickshire a Spitfire or Hurricane would "bounce" them, coming in out of the sun and attempting to "shoot them down," often armed with a gun camera and the real guns on "safe." Bob McWhirter, in the tail turret, could be equipped with a cine camera as well, and this "duel to the death" would sometimes be documented in black and white.

Meanwhile, in the front of the Wellington, Dad was getting instruction from Warrant Officer Martin on how to perform the standard evasive maneuver used in Bomber Command, the "corkscrew." Putting the Wimpy into a steep turning dive to the port or starboard, Dad would plunge the aircraft downwards for several hundred feet, then pull the stick back and go into a power climb in the opposite direction. Repeat as required! The maneuver must have placed a tremendous strain on the aircraft, but it was highly effective in throwing off a pursuing night fighter's aim or losing him altogether in the dark. The whole time, of course, the rear gunner would be blasting away at the fighter and giving the pilot a running commentary of the fighter's movements. The urgent call over the intercom of "fighter incoming! Corkscrew port go!" would be obeyed by the pilot without hesitation or question. The rest of the crew would be hanging on for dear life.

A debate has raged for some eighty years as to which fighter, the Hawker Hurricane or the Supermarine Spitfire, was the superior aircraft. Each side has its valid points, but for Bob McWhirter, there was no contest. In 2016, while recalling the affiliation exercises, he grew animated, his eyes twinkling as he told me "…we could hold our own against the Hurricane… but oh those Spitfires… !", laughing and shaking his head ruefully at the memory, "…they really made us work for it!"

On October 24th, they repeated the exercise, and two days later, on the 26th, they began a critical new phase of their training: night flying.

From October 26th to November 5th, the crew flew seven night-training flights ranging in length from thirty minutes to almost two and a half hours, practising circuits and landings, overshoots and single-engine flying, over and over.

Year 1943		Aircraft		Pilot, or 1st Pilot	2nd Pilot, Pupil or Passenger	Duty (Including Results and Remarks)
Month	Date	Type	No.			Totals Brought Forward
Oct.	26	Wellington	DF-594	P/O Underseher	Self & Crew	Local C&L, O/S, S.E.F.
Oct.	26	Wellington	HF-631	P/O Underseher	Self & Crew	" " " "
Nov.	2	Wellington	DF-594	P/O Tompkins	Self & Crew	" " " "
Nov.	2	Wellington	DF-594	Self	Crew	" " " "
Nov.	3	Wellington	HZ-107	Self	Crew	" " " "
Nov.	3	Wellington	HZ-103	Self	Crew	" " " "
Nov.	5	Wellington	DF-586	Self	Crew	" " " "
Nov.	7	Wellington	HF-647	P/O Fisher	Self & Crew	Dual Bombing
Nov.	7	Wellington	HF-647	Self	Crew	Solo Bombing
Nov.	8	Wellington	HF-237	P/O McKay	Self & Crew	Ex. 9 Dual Cross Cty.
Nov.	9	Wellington	HF-761	Self	Crew	Ex. 10 Solo Cross Cty.
Nov.	10	Wellington	HF-761	Self	Crew	Ex. 11 Solo Cross Cty.
Nov.	11	Wellington	HF-761	Self	Crew	Wendling - Base
Nov.	11	Wellington	HF-647	Self	Crew	Ex. 12 Solo Cross Cty.
Nov.	12	Wellington	HZ-103	Self	Crew	Ex. 13 Solo Cross Cty.
Nov.	15	Wellington	DF-735	Self	Crew	Solo Bombing
Nov.	17	Wellington	DF-739	P/O Forbes	Self & Crew	Wellesbourne - Pershore
Nov.	17	Wellington	DF-789	Self	P/O Forbes & Crew	Fighter Affiliation
Nov.	17	Wellington	DF-789	P/O Forbes	Self & Crew	Pershore - Wellesbourne
Nov.	18	Wellington	HF-761	Self	Crew	Night Flying Test
Nov.	18	Wellington	HF-761	Self	Crew	Operation (Nickel) - Nantes
					No. 22 O.T.U Course Totals —	
					Grand Totals —	

Grand Total [Cols. (1) to (10)] 420 Hrs. 25 Mins. Totals Carried Forward

November 7th was a busy night, with a two-hour dual bombing exercise, immediately followed by a solo bombing flight. The next night Flight Lieutenant Fisher guided them through an almost four hour navigation exercise, and the following night they completed and even longer flight on their own. Perhaps Dad and his crew were becoming confident now, having completed so many solo flights without incident, but the following night disaster almost struck.

On the night of November 10th, the crew took off in Wellington HF761 (coded DD-P), the same aircraft they had flown the night before on a four-and-a-half-hour solo night cross-country exercise. Tonight, they were assigned an exercise labelled "Ex. 11 Solo Cross Cty," and it was to be a long, stressful night for them all.

Normally, Operational Training Unit aircraft avoided the eastern portions of England, as this was known as "Bomber Country," dotted with dozens of busy Bomber Command and USAAF airfields. The skies above counties like Yorkshire and Norfolk were crowded with Lancasters, Halifaxes, and B-17s and were no place for a "sprog" (meaning "rookie") Wellington crew. Normally, OTU crews stuck to flying over the Irish Sea or Wales, all to the west and north, leading me to believe that the Coffey crew's navigation went astray not long into their flight. At the end of four hours, they found themselves lost over The Wash, an estuary of multiple rivers flowing into the North Sea, far to the east of where I think they should have been. The weather was atrocious that night, with zero visibility due to fog and cloud, and on top of this, Bob Bayne's GEE set malfunctioned, leaving him without his most important navigation tool. They flew for two hours blind in the dark, trying to find a break in the cloud so they could get a bearing on where they were, but without luck. Dad dared not descend too low without knowing where they were: his altimeter might show them at 2,000 feet above sea level for example, but if they were over a mountainous area without realizing it, they could easily slam into a 2,500-foot mountainside. They were now becoming seriously short on fuel, and Dad ordered Ted Rutherglen to begin sending a mayday distress call, as well as ordering the crew to put their parachutes on in preparation for abandoning the aircraft. It was expected of the pilot that he would fly the Wellington straight and level while all his crew bailed out, then try and make his own way out. If they were over the ocean, bailing out would almost certainly be a death sentence—survival time in a flying suit in the frigid North Sea would be brief.

Things had reached this desperate state of affairs when a voice out of the darkness came to their aid.

The United States Army Air Force's 392nd Bombardment Group had arrived in England from Arizona only three months previously and had been assigned to the most northerly of the USAAF bases, the airfield at Wendling in Norfolk. There they had set up a very modern, well-equipped bomber station, with an extensive system of landing lights along all its reinforced concrete runways. However, the Group was still in training, and its B-24 Liberators and crews had not started combat missions yet.

They may not have been operational yet, but someone at Wendling was certainly on the ball that night. The base responded to Ted's mayday calls: a course was given, landing lights were turned on, and Bob Bayne guided them out of the North Sea, into the skies above Norfolk and on to a safe landing at Wendling. And just in the nick of time—the Wellington's engines by then were running on fumes.

The five exhausted but relieved Canadians were given a warm welcome and a billet for the night. The Americans made a call to Wellesbourne to let the No. 22 OTU Commanding Officer know that one of his missing crews was safe, and then topped up the Wellington's empty fuel tanks. In the morning, they got a hearty American breakfast—I recall Dad telling me he was astonished at the quantity and quality of the food available, especially the pitchers of fresh orange juice!—and then took off to make the fifty-five minute flight back to Wellesbourne.

It seems the powers that be at No. 22 OTU embraced the philosophy of getting right back in the saddle after a setback, as that very night our crew took off again, this time successfully completing a five hour and twenty-five minute cross-country exercise, and followed it up the next night (November 12th) with an even longer one. A solo bombing exercise followed the next night, and this was to be their final night exercise—three nights hence, Dad would be writing the somewhat ominous word "Operation" for the first time in his logbook.

In the meantime, it was time again to play tag with a fighter and to give Dad and tail gunner Bob McWhirter a chance to test their mettle. On November 17th, Flying Officer Forbes accompanied them to RAF Pershore, about twenty-five miles east of Wellesbourne, and home of the No. 1681 Bomber Defence Training Flight. During the short flight, he likely instructed the crew on maneuvers and tactics to employ in the event of a fighter attack. The No. 1681 was one of several units tasked with training both new and experienced bomber crews in how to defend themselves against fighter attacks. Flying Hurricanes, Spitfires, and Tomahawks equipped with gun cameras, they did their best to "shoot down" their RAF comrades.

After landing at Pershore, they likely met their "adversary," set up a flight plan and had Bob's rear turret set up with his own cine camera to record his "hits." The flight itself was only fifty minutes long, but it must have been a long fifty minutes for Ted Rutherglen and Bob Bayne, who were just along for the (likely unpleasant) ride. Malcolm Dingwall, their bomb aimer, may have had some fun, however, as the Wellington was equipped with a front gun turret, although it was of little use in real combat, as night fighters rarely attacked head-on.

"You *never saw* us! . . ." "*I shot you* down! . . ." "*You weren't within a mile!* . . ."
"*Oh, pull your finger out!* . . ." Etc.

A humorous take on fighter affiliation by the beloved wartime cartoonist Bill Hooper. Original WWII-era TeeEmm magazine, author's collection.

They landed again at the airfield at Pershore and perhaps had the chance to debrief and to view the film taken to see how they had done—I am sure there was a lot of good-natured bragging between the crew and the fighter pilot as to who had bested who! That afternoon they were home at Wellesbourne again—the next night, they would fly over German-occupied territory for the first time.

A "Nickel" was Bomber Command code for a propaganda leaflet, and Nickel raids were a standard "final exam" for most Operational Training Unit aircrews. The preparation and execution of the raid were no different than a normal Bomber Command raid (right down to the one hour "night flying test" on the afternoon before the raid), only the payload differed: instead of bombs, the crew would be dropping thin newsprint propaganda leaflets. Many aircrew shook their heads at the need to risk their lives to deliver what they considered to be "bumpf" (basically toilet paper) to the Germans, but the idea of a Nickel raid did make sense in some ways.

Nickel raids were almost always against what were relatively lightly-defended targets like cities in France or Belgium. It gave the crew the chance to experience a real operation, but against what we might call a "soft" target. It also kept the German defences on constant alert, as they had no idea whether or not the appearance of a single bomber might be the precursor of a major raid. However, a Nickel raid was not without its risks, as the sad fate of Flying Officer Goodwin and his crew, related earlier, attests.

The No. 22 OTU records relate that seven Wellingtons were dispatched on Nickel raids that night, each going to a different French city. Dad and crew were dispatched to Nantes, a major city on the Loire river. It was near the German submarine base at St. Nazaire, which was most assuredly no "soft" target, so I am betting their assigned course kept them well clear of it. Although Nantes was a major port and transportation hub, it had drawn little attention from Bomber Command thus far in the war, and it's defences were likely relatively light. Still, it would give the Coffey crew a real taste of flak and searchlights, a foreshadowing of things to come.

One odd fact about that night's raid has mystified me and eluded explanation thus far: the unit's records indicate that four of the seven raiders carried "ordinary Nickels," while the remaining three (including our crew) carried "a special load." The meaning of this cryptic notation is unknown. Based on zero evidence (I readily admit) my best guess is that the leaflets in the "special loads" may have contained some kind of coded message for the French resistance.

An example of the leaflet (which Dad saved in his mementos) survives, and it is easy to see why the aircrew dismissed them as "bumph." Written in German, obviously intended for Nantes' occupiers, it is boring, pointless, and laughingly inept as propaganda. Telling German soldiers in the autumn of 1943 that everyone, including Hitler, knew they had "lost the war," and giving them assurances of fair treatment from the likes of Stalin should they surrender must have made them guffaw.

Leaflet dropped on German occupiers of Nantes, France by the Coffey crew.
Germany has lost the war — we know it, Hitler knows it. Author's collection.

At any rate, all seven of the Operational Training Unit's Wellingtons made their way safely home after delivering this knockout blow to the Wehrmacht's morale. The four-hour and five-minute flight was the last time Dad ever flew a Wellington, as their time at the OTU was now over. They had passed their tests, completed their training and been melded into a tightly knit, efficient team. Dad's official records contain a summary evaluation of him and his crew from the Officer Commanding the No. 22 OTU, who wrote:

> This Advanced Flying Unit trained Pilot is well above the average, and has a very good crew. The Navigator and W/OP are the best of the Course, and the whole crew is strongly recommended for P.F.F. An extremely able captain, who is recommended for a Commission.

The Coffey crew must have made a strong impression indeed to be recommended for Bomber Command's elite Pathfinder Force (PFF) at this early stage.

At almost the same time our crew were packing their bags, preparing to move to the next stage of their training, another young man was arriving at Wellesbourne to begin his time at OTU.

London, Ontario native **Sgt. Ken Hart** arrived at the base on November 15th, and began flying as a rear gunner for various crews. It seems he was a "spare bod," (slang for an airman not assigned to any one particular crew) for some reason. For Ken, his time at the OTU was more of a refresher course, as he had completed his air gunner training back in 1942, about the same time Dad was learning to polish boots to RCAF standard at Manning Depot in Edmonton. Ken had shipped overseas and crewed up at the very same No. 22 OTU (perhaps in the very same hanger) he was now returning to. After completing training at the No. 22 OTU in August of 1942, he had been assigned to 405 Squadron (based at RAF Beaulieu in Hampshire on England's south coast) and had flown a number of anti-submarine patrols as the mid-upper gunner on a crew skippered by Flight Sergeant Stovel.

A horrific accident had occurred on his first operation, and several weeks later, Ken was court-martialed and grounded. Ken Hart's story is one of resilience and courage, and we will return to it in due course because Ken was destined to become one of "our" crew in the near future.

By this time, Dad, Ted, Malcolm and the two Bobs must have been chomping at the bit to get to an Operational Squadron and begin their work. After their six weeks of OTU and their successful Nickel raid, they were likely brimming with confidence in themselves and each other, anxious to be let loose on the Germans. However, the Bomber Command training regime still had two more hurdles for them, the first of which bore a name that sounds like the title of a pulp fiction novel: "Battle School."

Battle School is a seldom mentioned sidebar in the training regimen of most wartime RCAF aircrews. When it is remembered, it is usually with disdain: when I asked Bob McWhirter about his Battle School memories, a look of almost comical disgust crossed his face.

"What a waste of time!" he exclaimed.

Well, waste of time or not, almost every Canadian aircrew spent a month at Battle School, so someone obviously thought it was important. In theory, Battle School was a sort of mini-commando course, teaching aircrew skills in escape and evasion and hand to hand combat. There was calisthenics and what was referred to as "general toughening up" exercises, completed outdoors in the Yorkshire mud and rain. The students were sent on mock commando assaults, complete with tear gas, and weapons drills with Sten gun, Lee Enfield .303 rifles and the Webley .45 calibre revolver. The last was a weapon that was available for aircrew to take with them on Operations if they wished—few did.

The instructors at Battle School were seconded from the RAF Regiment, a force created early in the war and tasked with defending RAF airfields from ground and air attack. In theory, aircrews completing the training would be well prepared to evade capture and escape from Germany if they had to bail out, and to incapacitate anyone who stood in their way. In practice, most aircrews found it a miserable experience, with rustic living conditions, poor food, and exhausting drill in foul weather.

The No. 6 Battle School was situated at RAF Dalton in Yorkshire, on the edge of the high, lonely Yorkshire Moors. Dad and crew arrived on December 4th, the same day as seventeen other crews who dribbled in from various locations up until midnight, keeping the airfield's Motor Transport staff busy well into the night.

Someone with a sense of humour wrote the School's Operational Record Book (the O.R.B. was a sort of daily diary of events), and the notes are often tongue-in-cheek and lighthearted. On one day, sandwiched between notations about new arrivals and postings out, the following "Anecdote" is found:

Scene: A Group Captain's Office.

Group Captain: 'I find you guilty of this offence. You are sentenced to 2 months Battle School at Dalton'

Accused faints, and when he recovers, petitions the King!

Group Captain to Adjutant: 'That is the severest punishment I can give – What is this Battle School, anyway?'

The Battle School course obviously enjoyed wide "renown" among Air Force personnel!

The Coffey crew spent their first day at Battle School just settling in, taking stock of their new surroundings. The real fun began the next day when an "epidemic of minor ailments" was reported, mostly head colds. The weather was atrocious, cold and damp, and "some students were so cold they used the blackboard pegs as firewood" as coal was in short supply.

Over the new two weeks, the students engaged in all sorts of commando-type exercises, from target practice on the rifle range to route marches across the moor. All-day mock "assaults" were carried out, on at least one occasion while wearing gas mask respirators ("tear gas and smoke was used with good effect" reported the Daily Diary). On another occasion, the mock combat took place in thick fog, and the O.R.B. praised the aircrew for the "keenness shewn" as they charged across water-filled ditches and skewered straw-filled dummies with their bayonets. The school did their best to engage their students' imagination, and on one exercise, the young men were divided into "guerrillas" and "Gestapo"—at the end of the day, it was declared the attackers had been "repulsed by the brave Gestapo"!

Map reading was taught, both in the classroom and the field, a skill that might actually have come in handy in an escape or evade-type situation. As part of their escape and evasion training, some unfortunate crew was regularly picked at random and loaded up in the back of a truck (wearing blindfolds) and driven miles out into the Yorkshire moors. There they were dropped off in the dark and told to find their way back to the base and not get "caught" by the Home Guard, who had been made aware of their whereabouts and were on the "hunt" for them. It was one of the two vivid memories Bob McWhirter had of Battle School, and it was not a pleasant one. He recalled the experience with disdain, finding it a complete waste of time (his other vivid recollection was that the Commanding Officer of the school was very tall, had fiery red hair, and was called "The Turkey" by the young Canadian airmen—not to his face of course!).

In my mind's eye, I can picture my Dad, the ostensible "skipper" of his crew (at the age of twenty-two), doing his best to play the leadership role by encouraging Bob, Malcolm, Bob, and Teddy to play along and get in the spirit of the thing. It must have been a lost cause as they trudged, tired, cold, and hungry through the moors.

I have to admit, when I first learned about Battle School and its aims, I was skeptical about the concept of downed Allied aircrew fighting their way out of Occupied Europe with miraculously acquired Sten guns, but maybe I missed the point. I think perhaps the course attempted to teach teamwork and self-confidence, which were probably two of the most important attributes an airman would need if he were to survive (whether it be a tour of operations, evading capture after bailing out, or life in a prisoner of war (POW) camp).

After four weeks of this, "Coffey's Commandos" graduated and were likely glad to put the cold mud of Dalton behind them, and move on to a form of training that was more up their alley: they were posted to a Heavy Conversion Unit, where they would learn to fly the four-engine Handley-Page Halifax bomber, the aircraft they would be flying into combat two months hence.

After two weeks of leave, they arrived back in Yorkshire, reporting to the No. 1664 Heavy Conversion Unit at RAF Dishforth, just down the road from the Battle School barracks they had recently left.

The Heavy Conversion Unit took an already well-trained medium bomber aircrew and "converted" them, by giving them advanced instruction on flying a four-engine heavy bomber—and increasing the crew's number by two, a flight engineer and a mid-upper gunner.

Up until now, Dad had handled the aircraft on his own, but with the additional size of the aircraft (the loaded weight of the Halifax was just over double that of the Wellington), and the addition of two more engines to look after, he would now be getting some help. Early in the war, every crew had a second pilot, but this was deemed wasteful, and the RAF created the position of flight engineer. The flight engineer was the pilot's right-hand man, figuratively and literally, sitting on a fold-down jump seat in the cockpit and assisting the pilot in maintaining control of the aircraft at take-off and landing especially. In a four-engine bomber, there was simply too much going on for one man to handle. During flight, the flight engineer constantly monitored the engines, fuel consumption, and all the mechanical, hydraulic, and electrical systems on the aircraft, affecting repairs when necessary. The flight engineer assigned to the crew was **Sgt. Wilfred Porter**, an Englishman whom I have been unable to find out much about—he was not with the Coffey crew for very long, as we shall see.

Their new mid-upper gunner was the young man we met briefly in November at No. 22 Operational Training Unit: **Sgt. Ken Hart.**

Kenneth Alger Hart had a not untypical upbringing for a Canadian kid of the era, born in 1922 into a loving, solidly-middle class family in London, Ontario. Ken's father ensured the family's financial stability by working at a number of jobs during the Depression, including owning a butcher shop where young Ken worked for a time. Ken was a strapping young man by the sounds of it, played football in high school, and like many teenage boys, loved cars. He and his friends bought an old Model T Ford, which they turned into a hot rod, and Ken's brother recalls that the jalopy could be "heard all over south London!"

The war, however, changed everything. Ken's uncles and beloved older brother Bev had already joined up, and in the summer of 1941, Ken enlisted in the RCAF with ambitions, like so many other young men, of becoming a pilot. For whatever reason, his hopes were dashed, and after a short time at the No.

4 Elementary Flying Training School, the powers that be decided he could better serve his country as an air gunner.

After graduating from the Bombing and Gunnery School in Fingal, Ontario, Ken shipped out from Halifax and arrived in Bournemouth, England, on May 1st, 1942, where his training continued. In October 1942 (about the time my Dad was starting his flight training back in Saskatchewan), Ken joined 405 Squadron, which was technically part of Bomber Command, but was temporarily "on loan" to Coastal Command to fight the German U-Boat menace.

405 Squadron was based at RAF Beaulieu in Hampshire, and Ken arrived there as mid upper gunner assigned to a Handley-Page Halifax skippered by Flt. Sgt. Clifford Stovel. Their job was to fly long, lonely patrols into the Bay of Biscay, searching the sea and attacking German U-Boats, which generally travelled on the surface, submerging only to attack.

On November 6th, 1942 Ken and his crew took off for their first operational patrol, and a tragic accident occurred shortly after. Although Ken continued to fly with the crew on several more combat patrols, an investigation was begun into the incident. Before the end of the month he was grounded and informed he would be facing a court martial. Eventually Ken was convicted of an offence—he was demoted, placed in detention and grounded for the next fifteen months.

When Ken first met his new crewmates at the Heavy Conversion Unit, they must have been curious about his background and experiences, and no doubt been surprised when he told them about being grounded. But when pressed for details, Ken simply told the other members of the Coffey crew he didn't want to talk about it and that he would tell them the whole story when they finished their tour.

I can understand Ken's inner conflict when meeting his new crew—he must have been worried about their reaction. Joining the Coffey crew was, after all, his second chance: a chance to prove himself, to put the horrible accident behind him and show he could do the job he had been trained for. But what if he told them what had happened and they refused to fly with him? And then what if word got around to other crews and the authorities had second thoughts about letting him fly again at all? All these nagging worries must have been on his mind, but Ken Hart was a young man of character, and lying to his new comrades was not an option. So he took the only route he could that honoured both his privacy and his honesty: "Guys, I don't want to talk about it now, but I will explain everything when we are done."

And when they were done, he did.

Now that there was a full crew of seven, the next step was to convert them into a heavy bomber crew, and the aircraft they would be flying is rather difficult to summarize. The Handley-Page Halifax is one of those aircraft that had to go through several iterations before it hit its stride. Once they completed their conversion and made it to an operational squadron, they would be flying the Halifax Mark III, as fine an aircraft as any that flew in WW II. However, at the Heavy Conversion Unit (HCU) they would be training on the older Mark V, a woeful footnote in the Halifax's otherwise stellar history. Underpowered, clapped-out veterans of countless maritime patrols, the Mark Vs at the HCU were hand-me-downs from Coastal Command that were unfit for bomber operations, having been equipped with weak undercarriages that wouldn't support a full bomb load. Their odd, almost triangular-shaped rudder fins had proven to be prone to locking up, with potentially lethal results. All in all, flying the Mark V Halifax probably left Dad longing for a Wellington!

The curriculum at the Heavy Conversion Unit was very similar to the one at the Operational Training Unit: lots of circuits and landings, Standard Beam Approach practice, and flying and landing with one or two engines shut down. For the first week of the two-week course, it doesn't seem there was a lot of action for the air gunners, navigator or bomb aimer; it was mostly for the benefit of Dad and his new flight engineer, Sgt. Porter, allowing them time to forge a close working rapport (unsuccessfully, as we shall see).

One week into the training, two flights were made by the Coffey crew that involved the full attention of all aboard: sea searches.

YEAR 1944		AIRCRAFT		PILOT, OR 1ST PILOT	2ND PILOT, PUPIL OR PASSENGER	DUTY (INCLUDING RESULTS AND REMARKS)
MONTH	DATE	Type	No.			
—	—	—	—	—	—	TOTALS BROUGHT FORWARD
	Jan 3	ATTACHED No. 1664 Con. Unit. R.C.A.F. Dishforth.				
Jan.	20	Halifax V	ZU-Y	F/O Baldwin	Self & Crew	Familiarization, C & L
Jan.	23	Halifax V	ZU-Y	F/O Baldwin	Self & Crew	C & L.
Jan.	25	Halifax V	DH-X	F/O Baldwin	Self & Crew	2 & 3 Engine Flying
Jan.	26	Halifax V	DH-X	S/L. Peterson	Self & Crew	C. & L.
Jan.	26	Halifax V	DH-X	Self	Crew	C. & L.
Jan.	28	Halifax V	ZU-Y	S/L Peterson	Self & Crew	Check Dual
Jan.	28	Halifax V	ZU-Y	Self	Crew	C. & L., Local Flying, S.B.A.
Jan.	29	Halifax V	ZU-Y	S/L Peterson	Self & Crew	3 Engine Landings
Jan	29	Halifax V	DH-Y	F/O Baldwin	Self & Crew	Dual C. & L. - Night
Jan.	29	Halifax V	DH-Y	Self	Crew	Solo C. & L. - Night
		Halifax V	DH-E	Self	Crew	Sea Search
		Halifax V	ZU-D	F/L Bissett	Self & Crew	Sea Search
Feb.	2	Halifax V	DH-Y	F/L Bissett	Self & Crew	Fighter Affiliation
Feb.	2	Halifax V	DH-Y	Self	Crew	Fighter Affiliation
Feb.	2	Halifax V	ZU-K	Self	Crew	Cross Cty. & Bombing
Feb.	3	Halifax V	ZU-A	Self	Crew	Bullseye
		ASSESSMENT - Above Average				SUMMARY for 34 Co. A/C UNIT - 1664 Con. Unit.
		H.V. Peterson		S/LDR. O.C. "A" Flight		DATE - 5-2-44
						SIGNATURE - F/S Coffey J.R.
			Wg. Cmdr. C.I. 1664 C.N.			

GRAND TOTAL [Cols. (1) to (10)]   440 Hrs 00 Mins   TOTALS CARRIED FORWARD

On the night of January 30th, 1944, Bomber Command had made another massive attack on Berlin, part of the so-called Battle of Berlin. 534 Lancasters, Halifaxes and Mosquitoes were sent, and the force was hit hard by the defences, losing thirty-three aircraft. One of the downed Lancasters was skippered by Pilot Officer K. Kirkland, an Aussie flying with 106 Squadron. He and his crew had taken off from RAF Metheringham for Berlin but had not returned—the plane may have had mechanical problems or been hit by flak, but for whatever reason, the crew reported they were going down in the North Sea.

On the morning of January 31st, a large, coordinated search was begun for the crew. At least four aircraft from No. 1664 HCU took part, including Dad and crew, who took off with instructions to fly a specified grid over the North Sea, with hopes of finding the Kirkland crew alive in their life raft. It was likely four sombre crews who took off from Dishforth that morning, as the day before, they had lost seven of their comrades. The McLeod crew has taken off the night before on a cross-country navigation exercise, the same one the Coffey crew would be embarking on in less than forty-eight hours. Pilot Officer McLeod and his crew had gotten lost, and had descended through the thick cloud to try and find where they were. Miles off course, the unfortunate Halifax and her crew were over higher ground than they knew, and all were killed when the plane slammed into Ilkley Moor.

There was no time to brood about the loss, however, and the search aircraft from No. 1664 HCU took off to fly to their assigned areas the next morning. If a search aircraft successfully found a downed aircrew, it would circle them, radio their location back to base and shortly thereafter, an RAF Marine Rescue high-speed launch would arrive to load them up and take them home.

The search lasted two days but was unsuccessful: the crew perished and none were ever recovered, save for Pilot Officer Kirkland, whose body washed ashore two months later on the Frisian Islands, just off the Dutch coast.

Dad and crew had spent some twelve fruitless hours over the two days scanning the waves and were likely glad for a break on February 2nd, when they took part in two fighter affiliation flights, each over an hour long. It was a busy day for the crew, as that night they took part in a five-hour cross-country and bombing exercise.

February 3rd was their final day of training, and the exercise they were assigned was one that tried to be as realistic as possible and was referred to as a "Bullseye."

The Bullseye exercise was in effect a mock Bomber Command operation staged against an English city. The city in question (London and Bristol were popular choices) would be alerted ahead of time, and it was an excellent way for their Anti-Aircraft defences to practice their techniques as well. Multiple aircraft from the HCU would take off, following a specific route and time schedule. There would be frequent dogleg changes in the course, just like on a real "op," and the gunners would have to be on the lookout for "enemy" night fighters, as Mosquitos or Beaufighters could be assigned to harass them. If a "Mossie" could get into an attack position without being spotted, it would turn on its navigation lights as a way of saying "bang, bang... you're dead!" to the shocked (and likely embarrassed...) air gunners on board its prey.

Once over the target city, the Halifax would complete its bomb run, and the bomb aimer would take a picture of the aiming point (which might be lit up with an upwards-facing flashlight) as a test of his accuracy. All the while, the city's searchlights would be trying to "cone" them by concentrating all their lights on one hapless aircraft—it was a very unpleasant experience for a bomber crew, whose lives depended on staying hidden in the dark.

It was about as realistic as it could get, just short of live ammunition and explosives, and it gave every member of the crew a real workout.

Upon landing after their five-hour and ten-minute "attack," the Coffey crew completed their training at the Heavy Conversion Unit, and were now considered a fully trained aircrew, ready for Squadron operations. They didn't have long to wait or far to go: they were immediately posted to the RCAF's 420 "Snowy Owl" Squadron, flying out of Tholthorpe, just ten miles south of Dishforth.

They were going into combat.

The Coffey Crew in
Great Britain
1942 - 1944

V1 "Doodlebug"

Greenock

Edinburgh

Middleton St. George

Isle of Man

Dalton

Dishforth

Tholthorpe

York

Liverpool

The Wash

Shawbury

Wendling

Aberystwyth

Warboys

Coltishall

Gransden Lodge

Thorpe Abbots

Avro Anson

Wellsbourne

Stormy Down

★ LONDON

Beaulieu   Tangmere

Bournemouth

St. Eval

U Boat

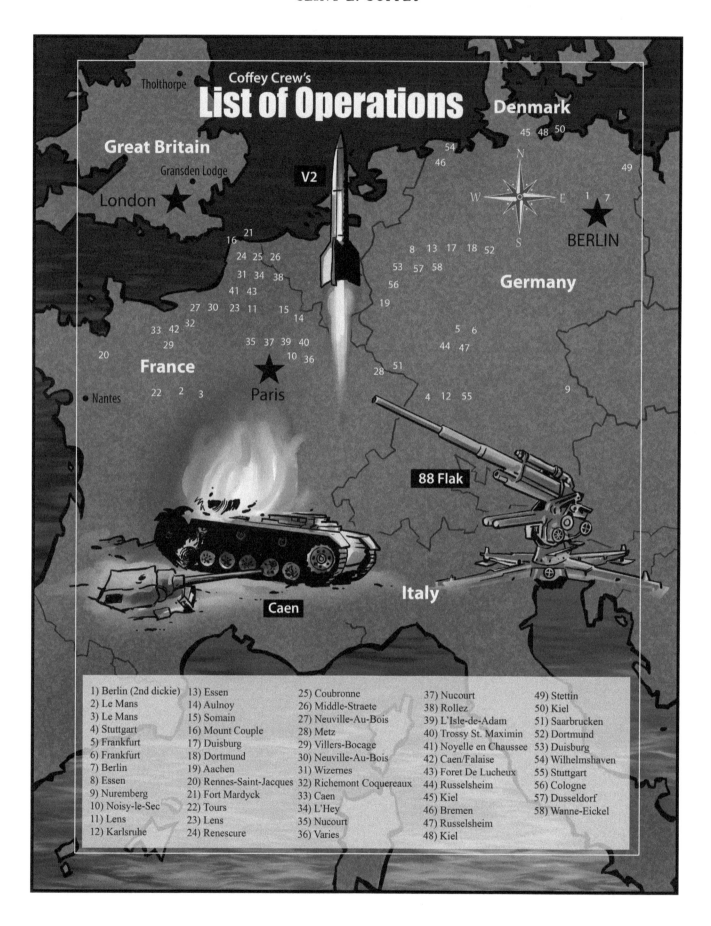

Coffey Crew's List of Operations

1) Berlin (2nd dickie)
2) Le Mans
3) Le Mans
4) Stuttgart
5) Frankfurt
6) Frankfurt
7) Berlin
8) Essen
9) Nuremberg
10) Noisy-le-Sec
11) Lens
12) Karlsruhe
13) Essen
14) Aulnoy
15) Somain
16) Mount Couple
17) Duisburg
18) Dortmund
19) Aachen
20) Rennes-Saint-Jacques
21) Fort Mardyck
22) Tours
23) Lens
24) Renescure
25) Coubronne
26) Middle-Straete
27) Neuville-Au-Bois
28) Metz
29) Villers-Bocage
30) Neuville-Au-Bois
31) Wizernes
32) Richemont Coquereaux
33) Caen
34) L'Hey
35) Nucourt
36) Varies
37) Nucourt
38) Rollez
39) L'Isle-de-Adam
40) Trossy St. Maximin
41) Noyelle en Chaussee
42) Caen/Falaise
43) Foret De Lucheux
44) Russelsheim
45) Kiel
46) Bremen
47) Russelsheim
48) Kiel
49) Stettin
50) Kiel
51) Saarbrucken
52) Dortmund
53) Duisburg
54) Wilhelmshaven
55) Stuttgart
56) Cologne
57) Dusseldorf
58) Wanne-Eickel

CHAPTER FOUR:
THE MIGHTY NOISE

FEBRUARY 1944 — APRIL 1944

I am neither scholar nor historian, but after years of research and contemplation about my Dad's RCAF experience, there are a few things about which I have developed strong opinions. One thing became crystal clear to me as I began the task of trying to understand my Dad's time in Bomber Command: it would be impossible to appreciate the small day-to-day picture of what he and his crewmates did if I didn't try to grasp at least the basics of the big picture in which they operated.

There have been times when I have regretted this epiphany, like the day that William Manchester's remarkable book The Arms of Krupp arrived in the mail, and I held its massive thousand-page bulk in my hands, thoroughly intimidated. I had ordered it simply because I had noted from his logbook that Dad and his crew had visited the German city of Essen on several occasions—I wanted to understand why the city in general, and the Krupp complex in particular, were such important targets for Bomber Command.

On another occasion, I found myself wondering about the French city of Caen and why Bomber Command had been ordered to intercede in the ground battle raging there after D-Day. I ended up spending weeks educating myself about the weapons, units (especially the Waffen SS), tactics, and strategies that were at play in the ground war in France in the summer of 1944.

It seems to me that all history is interrelated at some level, and that if one were to claim to have any kind of expertise in only one specific aspect of something as huge as the Second World War without gaining an understanding of the overall picture... well I think one would be seriously missing the mark. It would be like attempting to study the Sistine Chapel with one eye through a rolled-up tube of paper. As this insight became clear to me, I decided to set a rule for myself: if any questions, no matter how arcane, came up in my mind as I read my Dad's logbook, I would jot them down and take the time to try and find out the answer, even if it meant getting "sidetracked" for a bit, studying a subject that might, at first blush, seem unrelated.

Although following this rule turned out to be very rewarding, I also found that, in a cruel twist of fate, the process of finding an answer often led to another question! At any rate, as I went through Dad's logbook line by line, my reading list expanded. I began to learn about subjects like the Battle of the Atlantic and the German U-Boat wolfpacks, Hitler's V weapons program, the almost chess-like move and counter-move by German and British radar scientists, the life of Sir Arthur Harris, the history of aerial bombing, the science of high explosives and other pyrotechnics, the history of several major German cities, the system of food rationing in wartime Britain, and so on, and so on.

So, being mindful of this insight that one has to have an appreciation for the big picture if one is going to understand the details, (and emphasizing again that I am a layman, not a historian, and that this book is meant as a tribute, not a history), we are going to leave Jesse, Bob, Malcolm, Ken, Ted, Wilfred, and Bob Bayne for a time and explore the campaign they were joining—a bit of its background and what it was trying to accomplish.

In 1940, Britain had escaped invasion by the skin of her teeth—the famed Few of the RAF's Fighter Command had defeated the Luftwaffe in the Battle of Britain and made a Nazi invasion of England improbable, at least for the time being. Hitler, however, seemed unstoppable—invincible even (at least on the ground), and Britain was on her "back foot," with precious little in the way of manpower or resources to try and strike back. It seemed just a matter of time before the Nazi empire would defeat Britain, whether through starvation or invasion. Britain's army had been kicked off the Continent, barely escaping annihilation at Dunkirk, her powerful Royal Navy was of limited use against Hitler's Fortress Europe, and Hitler's U-boat wolfpacks roamed almost at will in the North Atlantic, decimating the Allied convoys bringing supplies to England. The future of a free Britain looked bleak indeed.

Prime Minister Winston Churchill saw the dilemma clearly, and also saw the only possible solution: after the Battle of Britain was won and the threat of imminent invasion averted, he wrote that "the fighters have been our salvation, but the bombers alone provide the means to victory." This conviction hardened even further as the months wore on, and later the same year, he wrote that what was needed if the Allies were to defeat Hitler was "an absolutely devastating, exterminating attack by very heavy bombers from this country upon the Nazi homeland."[4] Strong stuff.

The trouble was that the RAF's Bomber Command had been neglected for years and was nowhere near ready to take on the task of hitting back at Germany with any effectiveness, although they certainly tried. In the early part of the war, small formations of outdated twin-engine light and medium bombers would fly toward the German coastline in daylight (and without fighter escort) to try to find suitable targets to bomb. They were hamstrung by politicians whose prohibitions prevented them from bombing anything other than German warships (and then only when they could hit them without the possibility of hitting anything else—some British politicians actually fretted that hitting German private property would be "illegal!").

In those early days, the RAF's daylight raids against Germany proved to be something akin to suicide, as the modern Luftwaffe fighters armed with heavy cannon and machine guns decimated the supposedly impenetrable bomber formations.

There had been confident pronouncements among some influential aerial warfare pundits that "the bomber will always get through"—perhaps they were right, but at what cost? It became clear to the RAF that unescorted daylight raids into Germany were cost-prohibitive, to use a rather heartless mercantile phrase that does no justice to the courage and sacrifice of thousands of young airmen. The leaders of the United States Army Air Force were to insist on learning this painful lesson for themselves in 1943, supremely confident that they could succeed at daylight bombing where the RAF had failed. American aircrew would pay a heavy price for this confidence (or was it hubris…?), the odds only evening up for them when long-range fighter planes began escorting the formations of B-17 Flying Fortresses in early 1944.

It is clear that the RAF took to the night skies early in the war by necessity. They eventually developed expertise in it, pioneering advanced navigation and target marking technology and techniques, but progress was slow. In those early days, crews continued to try to find their way to their target by "dead

---

4   Both Churchill quotations found in The Right Of The Line by John Terraine

reckoning," using map, compass, and chronometer—and, if visibility was good, what little they could see of the ground—to find their aiming point.

The issue of the morality of the WWII bombing campaign is a controversy that has raged since the Second World War began, and it is another one of those issues about which I have, over time, developed a strong opinion.

It is easy (and I think an all too common error) to look back on history with 20/20 hindsight and to see nothing but "mistakes" by those who came before us, to wonder how they could have possibly done or believed "that" (whatever "that" happens to be for us). We look back on the Allied commanders in WW II from our world of GPS satellite navigation and laser-guided smart bombs, and the Allied Bomber Campaign may seem crude and even cruel from our vantage point. It takes real effort to put ourselves in the shoes of British leaders in 1941, who looked across the English Channel at Fortress Europe and an all-conquering Nazi empire and desperately looked for a way of defending themselves or, better yet, of striking back.

I have found that reading the words of those who were there, written at the time it happened, helps put one into the shoes of those who made hard decisions.

One such man was Sir Arthur Harris, who was Bomber Command's leader from 1941 until the end of the war, and whose book (titled Bomber Offensive) coolly and clearly lays out the options that Britain had in 1941:

1) Surrender

2) Accept a stalemate for the present and prepare for an inevitable invasion, or to be eventually starved into submission as Hitler cut off their supply lines across the Atlantic.

3) Strike back with the only means at her disposal, a bomber offensive.

No one had ever attempted to wage war solely with airpower before, and no one knew if it would work, but "Bomber" Harris believed to his core that it would work if he marshalled the resources he needed.

Nazi Germany certainly had no qualms about legality or morality—the Luftwaffe had been bombing civilians and undefended cities since the infamous attack on the Spanish town of Guernica in 1937. They had area-bombed the Polish city of Wielun on the first day of the war, and went on to do the same to Warsaw and Rotterdam. The razing of Rotterdam's city centre was the final straw for Churchill, who then took the restraints off the RAF's Bomber Command and authorized them to attack German cities.

On the night of December 28, 1940, Air Vice-Marshall Arthur Harris stood on the Air Ministry's rooftop in London watching a Luftwaffe raid in progress. It was part of Germany's bombing "Blitz" on Britain, which lasted some eight months. The raid that Sir Arthur watched was one of the most devastating, involving both high explosives and incendiaries, which caused massive fires.

Harris watched the destruction and coolly took note of the tactics employed by the Luftwaffe, and their results. I am willing to wager that more was going on for him than dispassionate assessment: there must have been a hardening in his heart as well, a longing to hit back at the enemy. There was nothing he could do about it that night, but I think Sir Arthur Harris was a man who would have completely understood the old saying, "revenge is a dish best eaten cold."

Just over a year later, Harris was appointed by Churchill as Bomber Command's new Air Officer Commanding. He would work tirelessly and relentlessly until he had transformed the force into the most powerful and effective offensive weapon the world had ever seen.

He made no secret of his goals, telling the British people in a newsreel:

> The Nazis entered this war under a rather childish illusion that they were going to bomb everyone and nobody was going to bomb them. At Rotterdam and London, Warsaw and half a hundred other places, they put this rather naive theory into operation.
>
> They sowed the wind, and now they are going to reap the whirlwind.
>
> There are a lot of people who say that bombing can never win a war... well my answer to that is that it has never been tried, and we shall see...[5]

Harris's appointment to lead Bomber Command was one of those moments when all the stars aligned: he was the perfect man for the job, arriving at the perfect time. He was a career military man who had flown in combat on the Western Front as a fighter pilot in the First World War, as well as flying against the German Zeppelin airships when they bombed London.

Harris was absolutely relentless in his prosecution of the mandate he had been given, which was one that he believed in with all his heart: strike Germany hard from the air and destroy her capacity to wage war. He browbeat, demanded, and cajoled everyone he thought could assist him, never taking "no" for an answer, never resting, always calling for more aircrew, bigger planes, more aircraft production, more resources of every kind for Bomber Command. Harris was selfless in his pursuit of increased resources for his command, never worrying that by getting "in the face" of his superiors or those in powerful positions, he might limit his own career prospects.

One of the first orders of business he turned his razor focus on was getting rid of all the twin-engine light bombers in Bomber Command. He relegated them to training or other duties, replacing them all with the new "heavies," the four-engine Halifaxes, Stirlings and especially Lancasters, that were beginning to roll off the assembly lines in larger and larger numbers.

Slowly, but with increasing confidence, the force grew, and in 1943, by scraping together every available aircraft, including crews still in training at Operational Training Units, Harris was able to mount the first 1,000 plane raid against Germany, striking a devastating blow against the city of Cologne. Things accelerated after that, with production of the Lancaster hitting its stride, new navigation technology coming on stream, new pyrotechnics (like flares and target markers) becoming available, and new tactics being used. One such tactic was the "bomber stream:" instead of each bomber flying on its own, the take-off times for Squadrons across England were coordinated, so that the whole force could form a "block" of aircraft, some ten miles wide and perhaps fifty long. This wasn't formation flying, but it did serve to overwhelm the German defences, as there were too many aircraft in too short a time passing over for them to focus on any one of them effectively.

Another effective new tactic was the use of *WINDOW,* the code name for bundles of aluminum foil strips that were hurled out of aircraft, forming clouds of billowing metal that drifted slowly to earth—German radar reflected off these metalized "clouds," rendering their radar screens useless.

---

5   Viewable on YouTube.

By the spring of 1944, when the Coffey crew arrived at their new Squadron in Yorkshire to begin operations, Bomber Command was approaching the peak of its powers. Harris was able to send out multiple forces each night, including "spoof" raids, which were small forces that either turned back before reaching the enemy coast in order to draw away night fighters, or staged "nuisance" raids to keep the defenders busy while the real attack was taking place miles away.

Each operation was organized to the last detail by Harris and his senior officers at High Wycombe, his rural Headquarters. Time on target, bomb loads, routes, flying heights, the colour of target markers—everything was pre-planned. The HQ's teletypes would send out their coded orders in the morning and all across England bomber stations would begin the frantic work of preparing for that night's operation.

And here is where we come to a hard truth. By necessity, the targets were often cities—Germany's ability to wage war was enabled by the factories that produced everything that a war machine needs, and those factories were in cities. The Ruhr Valley, to take but one example, was packed with factories, power stations, workshops, steel mills, and coal mines from end to end—it wouldn't be much of an exaggeration to say you couldn't throw a stone in Essen in 1944 without hitting some legitimate military target. And here we find another hard truth. As cruel as it may sound, the logic was coldly inescapable: the workers in those factories (and their homes) were deemed legitimate targets too—"Bomber" Harris wrote in his book, *Bomber Offensive*, that they were "active soldiers in my mind."

The Allied bombing campaign was cold and ruthless industrial warfare, unlike anything seen before in history - there really seemed no alternative if the Nazi empire was to be defeated.

The wartime leaders of the United States Army Air Forces often claimed they engaged in "precision" bombing, but really, it seems to me this was pure marketing hyperbole: stating that a particular factory in a certain city was the target of an attack, and then actually hitting that factory (and nothing else) were two entirely different things. The USAAF's famed Norden bombsight couldn't see through cloud any better than the British Mark XIV bombsight could, and ninety percent of the time, the American crews (and they were every bit as courageous and skilled as their counterparts in Bomber Command) found their aiming point using the same methods as their night-bombing allies, with equal accuracy. In WW II, that meant bombing a carefully targeted area to destroy everything that was in it. The claim that the Norden bombsight could make it possible to put "a bomb in a pickle barrel from 20,000 feet" was pure fantasy, but it is a piece of a propaganda storyline that can still be found today in newspaper articles, books, and documentaries: "the RAF carpet-bombed cities, the USAAF precision-bombed factories" goes the fiction.

The RAF's night bombing campaign was effective in several ways. The actual destruction it caused was one, flattening factories, railyards and shipyards, collapsing coal mines, and generally reducing Germany's potential industrial output. What wasn't destroyed had to be ferociously defended at great cost, or alternatively, dispersed far and wide, sometimes in underground factories, a costly and inefficient enterprise.

The campaign forced Germany to divert critical resources away from the Eastern Front and the Atlantic Wall to defend the Reich against the "bomber boys:" at the height of the Bomber Campaign an estimated 1,000,000 Germans were involved in the defence, manning Flak batteries, night fighters, searchlights, and radar facilities. The lion's share of 88 mm cannons and twin-engine fighter planes (both items were formidable tank destroyers when used in that role) that rolled off the assembly lines were diverted to home defence, and away from the Eastern Front, where they could well have stalled the Red Army's advance.

Repairing the damage inflicted by Bomber Command was also a significant drain on Germany's resources. Tens of thousands of workers (and forced labourers) were involved in repairing and rebuilding, and countless thousands of tons of precious concrete and steel were used to build air raid shelters and flak gun towers. I sometimes wonder what the Allied soldiers storming the Normandy beaches on the morning of June 6th, 1944 would have faced if Hitler could have redirected all those 88 mm guns, all that concrete, and all those workers to reinforcing his Atlantic Wall coastal defences.

88mm Flak gun. Imagine this beast mounted in a turret on a mobile chassis — that was a Tiger tank. Original wartime German snapshot. Author's collection.

Bomber Command's campaign had another effect that is not mentioned often enough: the morale boost for the British people. The long-suffering population of Britain must have looked to the skies every evening and seen the waves of bombers heading east towards their enemy and been proud and heartened. And not just the British… just after the end of the war Sir Arthur Harris received a letter from a Dutch civilian who wrote:

> We shall never forget the nights when your squadrons passed us in the dark on the way to Germany. The mighty noise was like music for us and it told us about happier days to come. Your passing planes kept us believing in coming victory, no matter what we had to endure.[6]

---

6   Quoted in *Bomber Harris: His Life and Times* by Henry Probert

There is no doubt the Bomber Campaign was having a real effect on Germany's war machine, with the RAF hitting by night and the USAAF Flying Fortresses (wisely, the formations of B-17s were now being escorted by scores of long range fighter planes) attacking their targets by day. The campaign had finally reached critical mass, with the right equipment, tactics, numbers, and training to really begin striking knock-out blows. The losses they were suffering were harsh, averaging about three to six percent of aircraft sent each night, but the factories were rolling out Lancasters and Halifaxes with increasing speed, and the training programs were churning out replacement aircrew for the thousands of young men who were being killed.

So, on that sombre note, let's return to February 7th, 1944, and to Jesse Coffey, Bob McWhirter, Malcolm Dingwall, Teddy Rutherglen, Ken Hart, Wilf Porter, and Bob Bayne, who we find jumping off the back of a transport truck and onto the tarmac of their new home, RAF Tholthorpe in Yorkshire.

The airfield at Tholthorpe had been built just before the start of the war, and had originally been equipped with grass runways suitable for the light bombers stationed there. It had recently been handed over to 6 Group, the all-Canadian bomber group, and had been extensively expanded, with new buildings and three new concrete runways. Just a month or two prior to Dad and crew arriving, the base had become the new home to 420 Squadron, which had up to that point been in North Africa, flying Wellingtons. Along with 425 Squadron (also newly arrived from North Africa), they were now converting to the Handley-Page Halifax Mark III, one of the finest heavy bombers of the war.

I visited the remains of Tholthorpe airfield in 1982, on a damp, gloomy early spring day. I was a few months into a bicycle tour of Ireland and the U.K., and was making a point of trying to visit some of the places Dad had spent time so many years before. While I walked the broken remains of the tarmac, a local farmer named Geoff approached in his muddy Land Rover. After finding out why I was there (I was no doubt trespassing) he kindly offered to show me around and, after loading my bike into the back of his Defender, we drove the perimeter track and looked at a few forlorn Nissen huts and brick buildings that still remained. Geoff had grown up in the area and was a youngster during the war—he had fond memories of the Canadian flyers and held them in high esteem.

At the time the Coffey crew reported for duty with 420 Squadron, its commander was Wing Commander Daniel McIntosh, a Canadian from Regina who had joined the RAF just before the start of the war. McIntosh rose through the ranks quickly and was an experienced combat pilot, having flown many "ops" on Wellingtons.

He must have been a "hands-on" type of leader, as on February 7th, their first day at Tholthorpe (note Dad's mistake in his logbook, recording the date as February 3rd), he personally took them up in the new Halifax III (coded PT-B, an aircraft they would soon call their own) for a thirty-minute orientation flight. McIntosh landed, hopped out, and Dad climbed into the pilot's seat to take his crew up himself for an hour and forty minutes of circuits and landings, probably relishing the power and handling of the Mark III, with its powerhouse Hercules engines, sturdy undercarriage, and redesigned rudder fins; compared to the tired old Mark Vs he had flown at the Heavy Conversion Unit, it must have seemed like a whole new aircraft.

YEAR 1944		AIRCRAFT		PILOT, OR 1ST PILOT	2ND PILOT, PUPIL OR PASSENGER	DUTY (INCLUDING RESULTS AND REMARKS)
MONTH	DATE	Type	No.			
—	—	—	—	—	—	— TOTALS BROUGHT FORWARD
						420 SQUADRON THOLT H
FEB.	2	HALIFAX III	B	W/R McINTOSH	SELF & CREW	CIRCUITS & LANDINGS
FEB.	2	HALIFAX III	B	SELF	CREW	CIRCUITS & LANDINGS, LOCAL
FEB.	9	HALIFAX III	F	SELF	CREW	CIRCUITS & LANDINGS, LOCAL
FEB.	11	HALIFAX III	LW595	SELF	W/O RUTHERGLEN	LINTON TO EAST MOOR
					SGT. PORTER	
					SGT. DINGWALL	883 ON (45 LOST) (INCL'D DIARIES)
FEB.	15	HALIFAX III	"K"	W/O AYJOLFSON	CREW & SELF	"OPS." BERLIN (BASE-MID. ST GEO)
FEB.	29	HALIFAX III	B	SELF	CREW	CROSS COUNTRY
Summary for FEB. 19.44					1. HALIFAX III	SUMMARY FOR FEB.
Unit 420 SQDN		Aircraft			2. HALIFAX III	
Date February 29d		Type			3.	GRAND TOTAL
Signature C. Coffey P/O					4.	Lamedenn S/L O.C. "A." FLT.
MAR.	2	HALIFAX III	"B"	SELF	CREW	CROSS COUNTRY
MAR.	3	HALIFAX III	"F"	SELF	CREW	FIGHTER AFFILIATION
MAR.	3	HALIFAX III	"K"	SELF	CREW	BULLSEYE-TARGET-LONDON
MAR.	4	HALIFAX III	"H"	SELF	CREW	PRACTISE BOMBING
MAR.	5	HALIFAX III	"H"	SELF	CREW	PRACTISE BOMBING AND AIR TO SEA FIRING
FEB.	24	LINK		SGT. WILSON	SELF	REVISION, B.A. FIG 8

GRAND TOTAL [Cols. (1) to (10)]
471 Hrs. 00 Mins.   TOTALS CARRIED FORWARD

There were more circuits and landings and local flying on February 9th, and then an odd entry on February 11th, which so far has eluded a confirmed explanation. In the late afternoon of that day, Dad and three of his crew (Ted Rutherglen, the wireless operator, Wilf Porter, the flight engineer, and Malcolm Dingwall, the bomb aimer) took off in a Halifax Mark III, not from their assigned base at Tholthorpe, but from another airfield at Linton-on-Ouse, which was located only a few miles away. They took off at 1640 hours and made a fifty minute hop, landing at a third RCAF base at RAF East Moor, home to 432 Squadron. The distance between the two airfields is very short, and it shouldn't have taken almost an hour, so I am betting Dad took the opportunity to have some fun with his new aircraft, taking the "scenic route," as it were, to RAF East Moor, which was close to the village of Sutton-on-the-Forest, only about ten miles away from where they took off. Curiously, another crew from Tholthorpe (skippered by Sgt. H. Hardy) made the same flight that day, Hardy making the trip in fifteen minutes according to the logbook of his flight engineer that day, Sgt. Digby Willoughby (a young Jamaican we will be meeting shortly).

The purpose of the flight was initially a head-scratcher, but a little research turned up the fact that 432 Squadron was in the process of converting to the Halifax Mk III in February of 1944, and I think it likely Sgt. Coffey and Sgt. Hardy were pressed into service to deliver two of their new aircraft to them at RAF East Moor. It's a plausible theory, and I think the fact that Dad lists the aircraft's serial code number (LW595) rather than just the identification letter in his logbook is significant.

How or when the two crews made it back to Tholthorpe is unclear, and the next entry in Dad's logbook, on February 15th, places him at yet another RCAF airfield, this time Middleton St. George. It turned out this entry was a real test of my research skills, as it presented a headache-inducing, multi-level puzzle.

The first question I asked myself was why was my Dad a passenger on another crew? And then, why was he flying in a Halifax Mk. II, when I knew 420 Squadron was newly equipped with Mk. IIIs? And thirdly, why was he flying out of Middleton St. George, some forty miles away from Tholthorpe? And finally, who was "W/O Ayjolfson?" There was no such officer listed in the 420 Squadron records.

It was Bob McWhirter, the crew's tail gunner, who finally set me on the right track to explain the entry. When I asked him about the small mystery during an interview in 2016, he remembered that, like all new Bomber Command pilots, Dad had been sent on a "second dickie" trip.

The second dickie trips were an opportunity for a new pilot to learn from an experienced crew on a real operation. The "sprog" pilot would stand behind the real skipper for the whole trip, watching, listening, and learning. He would see the teamwork, hear the intercom chatter, experience the flak, and searchlights, and hopefully come home with a feel for how a successful bomber crew functioned. Obviously, he would also face the same risks as the crew he was with, and those risks were very real—the Coffey crew had in fact been posted to 420 Squadron to fill the spot of one of three crews whose pilots had been sent on second dickie trips on January 27th and had failed to return.

Thirteen pilots from Tholthorpe had been sent off that night to fly "second dickie" to Berlin with other crews, and Pilot Officer Proud, Flying Officer Baker, and Sergeant Patterson had not come home. The crews they left behind were now "headless" and therefore useless to the Squadron—all eighteen men were shipped back to an Operational Training Unit to find new skippers and start over.

Bob McWhirter, recalling the night of February 15th some seventy years later, couldn't remember why Dad was sent away to Middleton St. George for his second dickie trip, but he did tell me that while my Dad was gone, the rest of them sat at Tholthorpe, "sweating bullets," hoping he would return in one piece. I am sure most of the concern was out of genuine affection for their skipper, but I am also certain that avoiding the fate of the Proud, Baker, and Patterson crews was also on their minds. Having come all this way, to then have to return to an Operational Training Unit to start the process of team building all over again with a new pilot was surely an unpleasant prospect. There was not even a guarantee that the remaining members of the crew would be kept together—they might well be split up, and all sent to various places to form entirely new crews.

Now that I knew what Dad was doing that night, the 420 Squadron's records cleared up the other part of the mystery, that is, who he was flying with. Since 420 Squadron had only recently arrived from North Africa, the night of February 15th was actually their very first real operation in their new Halifax bombers, thus they had no experienced crews for Dad to fly with. Therefore, he was driven the forty-some miles to 419 Squadron at Middleton St. George to fly with Warrant Officer "Cliff" Eyjolfsson (note Dad's misspelling) and his crew for their night's operation. Eight other new pilots from Tholthorpe went with him, all making their second dickey trips—and this would be no Nickel raid against a soft target: they were going to Berlin. Talk about learning to swim by being thrown in the deep end of the pool!

The February 15th operation against Berlin was part of "Bomber" Harris's strategy for ending the war; his plan was to force the Germans to surrender by destroying their capital city—cutting off the head of the snake, as it were. Berlin was an economic/industrial powerhouse, and it was also the home of the Nazi governing apparatus—Harris was convinced that destroying it would end the war and make a costly invasion of Europe unnecessary. I am not qualified to pass judgment on the merits of his plan, but in the end it failed, as Berlin turned out to be a nut too hard to crack.

Part of the problem was geography: Berlin was at the far end of Bomber Command's range, increasing the amount of fuel they needed and thus decreasing the bomb load they could carry. It was also a vast city, spread out over a wide area, making concentration of bombing difficult. Worst of all, it was heavily and ferociously defended. Night fighter airfields and successive rings of searchlight and anti-aircraft batteries defended the approaches to Berlin, and at three points in the city, Hitler had built Flak Towers. These monstrous (and quite medieval looking) concrete edifices were over a hundred feet tall, with walls ten feet thick. They doubled as air-raid shelters for civilians, but their primary purpose was as fortress-like platforms for heavy and medium anti-aircraft guns, which were mounted on their roofs. All in all, Berlin was the most heavily defended metropolis in the world, and aircrews referred to it as "The Big City"—it was a target they dreaded seeing when the curtain was pulled back during their pre-operation briefings.

A Flak tower in Berlin in a photo taken just after Germany's defeat in 1945.
Author's collection

February 15th attack on Berlin that Dad was about to take part in was the biggest of all the attacks that made up the four-month long Battle of Berlin, involving almost 900 bombers, most of them Lancasters, Bomber Command's star "heavy."

Dad climbed aboard Halifax "L for Lucky" in the early evening of February 15th, and took his place crouched behind Warrant Officer Eyjolfsson (who was by all accounts a fine pilot, bringing his crew home safely from thirty operations and returning to Canada with a DFC at the end of the war). They took off in the early evening and joined the almost thousand strong bomber stream heading for Germany. Bomber Command staged a "spoof" raid against Frankfurt-on-Oder to try to draw the German defences away from Berlin, but the night fighter controllers were not fooled, and the attackers faced a hot reception over Berlin. In his post-raid interview, Eyjolfsson reported a "tremendous flak barrage sent up at aircraft."

I can't imagine what an experience it must have been for Dad, seeing for the first time the awesome spectacle of a major Bomber Command attack: the searchlights, the red glow of the burning city through the low cloud, the sudden ripple of a 4,000-pound bomb (known as a "cookie") exploding, the slowing descending flares dropped by the Pathfinder Force, the flak exploding all around, the Lancasters and Halifaxes falling from the skies in flames—forty-three aircraft were lost this night, representing over three hundred young men—it must have been a hellish and awe-inspiring (and likely terrifying) experience.

Almost eight hours after taking off, Eyjolfsson and crew landed at Bury St. Edmunds (an American bomber base in Suffolk), along with most of the rest of his squadron's aircraft, as their home airfield at Middleton St. George was fogged in.

How exactly Dad made it back to Tholthorpe is unknown (and I am happy to report that all the second dickie pilots who went with him returned safely to their crews), but when he arrived I am certain he got a grilling from his crew about his Berlin experience!

It appeared at first that the Coffey crew may have been granted two weeks leave at this point, as the next entry in Dad's logbook is fourteen days later (noting a five-hour daytime cross-country training flight on February 29th), but then I saw the small afterthought on the bottom of the logbook page. Dad did two training sessions in a Link, one on the 14th and another on the 24th. He was also hospitalized briefly around this time with a bout of bronchitis—an unsurprising ailment considering he was living in a damp Nissen hut in Yorkshire in February.

The crew's cross-country flight on February 29th seems to have been routine, but for another 420 Squadron crew, the day's training flight ended in tragedy. Flight Sergeant Harry Hardy and crew had taken off in the evening from Tholthorpe for a cross-country exercise, and while practising corkscrew maneuvers over Wales, their Halifax suddenly plunged out of control into the ground. Only two crew members survived, one making an absolutely miraculous escape from the stricken aircraft. After recovering from his injuries, **Sergeant Digby "Jimmy" Willoughby** (the crew's flight engineer) was to become the final member of the Coffey crew. We will return his story shortly.

The next entry in Dad's logbook is another cross-country flight, this time at night, lasting five hours and ten minutes, on March 2nd. The following day was a busy one. The crew took part in a fighter affiliation exercise in the late afternoon, then took off in the early evening to "bomb" London, during an almost six-hour nighttime "bullseye" exercise.

More trips to the bombing range followed on the 4th and 5th, with the latter one being spiced up a bit with some air-to-sea firing. I have to say I wondered at the need for Bomber Command gunners to practice firing into the sea, but I supposed it all helped hone their skills, and in fact the Germans did make extensive use of flak ships off the Dutch coast, so the possibility of a low flying bomber finding itself in a brief shooting match with a floating enemy wasn't so far-fetched.

At any rate, Bomber Command had set up a few target ranges for crews to use for firing at a stationary target on the sea. The designated area would be set up with an anchored target that would be accessible at low tide, and covered it with heavy canvas that would record "hits." It must have been a fun exercise for the crew, with Dad getting a chance to roar around the target at low level, and the gunners getting to blast away with live ammunition at an "enemy" who couldn't fight back! The range they were at was likely RAF Donna Nook, on the coast of Lincolnshire, which has been in use as a bombing and gunnery range since 1926. It was thrilling for me to find a modern video on YouTube of a NATO A-10 strafing the range with cannon, knowing that seventy years previously, Dad and crew had been in the same spot, doing the same thing.

The March 5th exercise turned out to the Coffey crew's final flight as a crew-in-training: the next time they took off, it would be the real deal, a combat operation.

The March 7th operation against Le Mans, France was not only the first real operation for Dad and his crew, it was also the opening blow in a new campaign that the RAF and USAAF had been assigned, the Transportation Plan.

Allied plans for the invasion of Europe were firmly in place, and Bomber Command was about to play a crucial role in ensuring the invasion's success—"Bomber" Harris was tasked with destroying the German's ability to move men and materials against the Allied landing zones and beachheads.

The marshalling yards and railway systems of Germany and Occupied Europe were vital to the Wehrmacht if they were to quickly transport their tanks and troops to meet the expected Allied invasion of France, wherever it might arrive. The German Army had always been short of truck transportation, using horse-drawn wagons extensively throughout the war, and tanks broke down more frequently when forced to travel long distances under their own power, not to mention the phenomenal fuel consumption. These factors made every locomotive, every rail car, and every mile of railway track precious to the German military if they were to respond effectively to any Allied invasion. This also made the disruption and destruction of these targets equally vital to the success of the upcoming Operation Overlord, the invasion of Normandy—every hour of delay imposed on the Wehrmacht in getting their reinforcements to the landing beaches could prove crucial.

Hitler's coastal defences, the vaunted Atlantic Wall, were also pummelled by Bomber Command, with targets up and down the French coast carefully selected so as not to give any hints as to the actual location of the upcoming invasion.

Despite the obvious merits of the Transportation Plan, Winston Churchill had grave misgivings about bombing the transportation targets as he was skeptical that Bomber Command aircrews had the skill to hit railway yards in urban areas of France and Belgium without killing tens of thousands of friendly civilians. He wanted invading Allied troops to be viewed as liberators, not as enemies. Indeed, the French civilian population did pay a heavy price, although nowhere near as heavy as Churchill had feared, due mostly to the advances Bomber Command had made in target marking and tactics, and to the skill and training of its aircrews.

YEAR 1944		AIRCRAFT		PILOT, OR 1ST PILOT	2ND PILOT, PUPIL OR PASSENGER	DUTY (INCLUDING RESULTS AND REMARKS)
MONTH	DATE	Type	No.			
						TOTALS BROUGHT FORWARD
MAR.	7	Halifax III	"B"	SELF	F/O BAYNE	"OPERATION" - LE MANS .
					Sgt. DINGWALL	H.E. 6 x 1000
					W/O RUTHERGLEN	9 x 500
					Sgt. PORTER	1450 GALS.
					Sgt. HART	A/C MISSING - NIL
					Sgt. McWHIRTER	
MAR.	10	Halifax III	"B"	SELF	F/O BAYNE	BULLSEYE
					Sgt. DINGWALL	TARGET - LONDON
					W/O RUTHERGLEN	
					Sgt. PORTER	
					Sgt. HART	
					Sgt. McWHIRTER	
MAR.	13	Halifax III	"B"	SELF	F/O BAYNE	"OPERATION" - LE MANS
					Sgt. DINGWALL	H.E. 6 x 1000
					W/O RUTHERGLEN	9 x 500
					Sgt. PORTER	1450 GALS.
					Sgt. HART	A/C ON - 280
					Sgt. McWHIRTER	A/C MISSING - 3
MAR	15	Halifax III	"B"	SELF	CREW + Sgt. RUSSELL	AIR TEST

GRAND TOTAL [Cols. (1) to (10)]
488 Hrs. 32 Mins.   TOTALS CARRIED FORWARD

Crews were told that accuracy was paramount on these raids into France and that they were only to drop their bomb load if they were confident of the aiming point. Rather than bomb when there was any question of accuracy, many crews put their lives at increased risk by bringing their bomb loads home, something they would never consider had they been bombing over Germany. Master Bombers, controlling the raid via radio instructions while flying above the main force, would sometimes pause or call off an attack if dust and smoke obscured the aiming point.

Inevitably, however, with thousands of tons of high explosives raining down from 10,000 feet, some bombs went astray. Some Allied soldiers (after D-Day) and many French civilians lost their lives during Bomber Command's campaign in support of the D-Day invasion.

As part of the strategy for this campaign, both the American and British air forces were temporarily placed under the direct command of the Supreme Commander of Operation Overlord, Dwight D. Eisenhower. It was a bitter pill for "Bomber" Harris to swallow—he sincerely believed that the best way to ensure success on D-Day was to have his men continue to pound Germany's industrial heartland. However, he was a soldier to the core, and once he was given his orders, he followed them, despite his frustration at what he considered a distraction from his real work.

Far removed from these big-picture strategies, the Coffey crew climbed into a bombed-up Halifax for the first time, and began their pre-flight checks and routines. At 6:35 p.m. they lifted off the runway at Tholthorpe, the first time Dad had taken off in a fully-laden Halifax. Aircraft B for Baker was carrying six 1,000-pound and nine 500-pound bombs, and they were part of a 304 strong force from a multitude of squadrons across England sent to destroy the railway marshalling yards at Le Mans. Other squadrons across Britain were taking off around the same time to attack other railway yards at Trappes, Amiens, and Laon. The force attacking the Le Mans yards arrived on target about 9 p.m. local time, and the raid was a success, with over 300 bombs hitting the yards, destroying track, vital workshops, six locomotives, and 250 railcars. It was a five-hour round trip and, remarkably, not a single one of the raiders failed to return to their bases safely—it was an auspicious start to the campaign and to the Coffey crew's tour of operations.

Two years of training had come to fruition—the crew were warriors now, but I can't help but wonder how they felt upon landing safely back at Tholthorpe—did they feel elation and pride, or were their feelings more subdued? One "op" down, twenty-nine more to go to complete the required first tour… it must have seemed a daunting prospect.

The Halifax III they had flown to LeMans was coded B for Baker, and this aircraft was now assigned as "theirs"—unless it was unserviceable for some reason, they would always fly in this particular plane. As was traditional, they had to give "her" a name and add some artwork to the nose.

Airplane nose art in WW II was common in almost all air forces, and ranged from aggressively militaristic, to sexually suggestive, to ridiculously comic. Dad and his crew ended up naming their plane "Maisye," and when I asked my Dad (when I was a teenager) where the name came from, he said he thought it was "something the ground crew had come up with." It wasn't until I met Bob McWhirter in 2015 that I got a fuller explanation.

The name "Maisye" was inspired by none other than "Teddy" Rutherglen, the crew's outgoing and gregarious wireless operator, who I think may have played such a pivotal role in bringing the crew together at the Operational Training Unit. Bob McWhirter recalled, during an interview in 2015, that Ted always carried a guitar with him and would serenade the crew frequently. Bob told me, chuckling with delight at the memory, that he thought Ted "fancied himself a cowboy." Apparently, one of the songs Teddy often regaled them with was "Mairzy Doats," a novelty song made popular in 1944 by the Pied Pipers. From "Mairzy" came "Maisye," and a bomber got its name.

Along with the name came the nose art, and Maisye was adorned with Bomber Command's unofficial mascot, a gremlin.

These fictional little green creatures were very mischievous and were blamed for every mechanical and electrical fault that happened on the aircraft, whether on the ground or in the air. Perhaps the Coffey crew's ground crew (universally known as "erks") thought that having a gremlin painted on the aircraft would appease the little devils and prevent problems. If so, they were undoubtedly on the right track, as not once in fifty-nine combat operations did the Coffey crew have to turn back due to any kind of equipment malfunction, a remarkable record and a testament to the diligence and skill of their ground crew.

Original snapshot from author's collection.

The gremlin on Maisye's nose was shown gleefully astride a 500-pound bomb and firing a .303 Browning machine gun. A tiny flag flutters at the back of the bomb displaying Dad's initials ("J. C."), and the gremlin's mount had a bomb bay of its own, with small bombs dropping out, one for each operation completed.

The weather was atrocious for the next several days, and there was little flying done by either squadron at Tholthorpe, but on March 10th, Dad and crew took part (along with two other crews from 420 Squadron) in a Bullseye exercise against London that lasted just short of five hours.

As I read over 420 Squadron's Operational Record Book for March, one name caught my eye: on March 9th it is noted that Flt. Lt. W. C. Vanexan of 425 Squadron was assigned to investigate an accident that had occurred recently. I knew I had seen Vanexan's name somewhere before, but it took a while for me to connect the dots. 420 Squadron and 425 Squadron shared the airfield at Tholthorpe, and I don't know whether he and my Dad had ever crossed paths before, but it turns out they were fated to bump into each other in an unfamiliar place in the very near future…

"Ops" were back on three days later (March 13th), when they made another sortie against the marshalling yards at Le Mans to finish the job and disrupt any repair work that had been done.

Two hundred and thirteen Halifaxes arrived over the marshalling yards a little after midnight, where they found relatively clear skies with some ground haze that still allowed for details on the ground to be seen. Crews reported that the Mosquitoes of the elite Pathfinder Force had arrived "bang on time" and had marked the two aiming points with bright red and yellow flares using a technique that involved an advanced and highly accurate navigation aid called Oboe.

Oboe consisted of two radio beams (code-named "Cat" and "Mouse") broadcast from stations on the south coast of England. Simply put, the fast, high flying Mosquitoes would fly along one beam into the target area, and when they intersected the second beam, they were perfectly positioned over the aiming point. Due to the curvature of the earth, the beams were much less effective over longer distances, but over France, the system worked extremely well and resulted in deadly accurate target marking.

Opposition over the French city was reported as light, with some heavy flak and "very slight" fighter activity. It's likely that the Luftwaffe had not yet caught on to the Transportation Plan and had not yet begun to respond by bringing reinforcements of flak, searchlight batteries, and night fighters from Germany. Only one of 213 attackers failed to return, and Dad and crew, in Halifax LW419, landed safely back at Tholthorpe at 0401 hours (note that in his logbook Dad wrote 280 aircraft on the raid, with three missing—perhaps the information came from the BBC wireless news, but it is slightly inaccurate). The raid was another success, destroying more track, fifteen locomotives, and hundreds of rail cars.

The Coffey crew received a special honour for their night's work: a "target token" award. Bomber Command's all-Canadian 6 Group was the only Group to give out these awards, which was presented to each member of a crew whose bombs fell closest to the aiming point. I had not heard of the award before, and was delighted to learn about it from mid-upper gunner Ken Hart's daughter, who kindly made me a copy of her father's award. Malcolm Dingwall's family still has his copy safely among his mementos, but it seems the others have been lost over the years.

Target token awarded the Coffey crew. Courtesy of Susanne (Hart) Thrasher.

The following day, March 15th, the crew took Maisye up again on a sunny spring day for an "air test," an hour and a half flight that ensured the Halifax was in good shape for that night's operation. Along for the ride was one of the most important members of the Coffey crew (although he seldom left the ground), their ground crew chief, Sgt. Russell.

GPU.6319D
BOMBING-UP FOR A RAID ON GERMANY
A W.A.A.F. driving a bomb-load to a Halifax bomber while mechanics check-over the engines.

Original wartime press photo. Author's collection.

Bomber Command ground crew were a vital part of any squadron's success, and the Herculean task they performed during the Second World War has never been given its proper due.

Almost no front-line squadron had hangars big enough to accommodate a four-engine bomber, so all the work was performed outdoors, on each aircraft's assigned dispersal pad; these were spread out around the perimeter of the airfield. In every type of weather imaginable, from blazing heat to sub-zero cold, from pouring rain to gusting winds to snow, the "erks" laboured to keep the aircraft flying. Constantly under pressure for time, they grabbed sleep and food as they could, often setting up rudimentary shacks near their assigned aircraft to save time going back and forth to the barracks.

Armourers, riggers (airframe mechanics), fitters (engine mechanics), instrument "bashers"—they all pored over their assigned aircraft from end to end daily, ensuring everything was functioning smoothly. Perspex would be polished, gunsight lightbulbs changed, Browning machine guns cleaned, instruments tested, ammunition tracks inspected, autopilot oil sump checked, bombs fused and winched into the bomb bay, engines gone over and tested—the list was endless, as was the work. In charge of the LACs and Corporals who made up Maisye's groundcrew was their "Chiefie," Sergeant Russell. Tight bonds formed between air and ground crews, and these two groups of young men were very much a close-knit team.

After the hour and a half test flight, Maisye landed at about noon and was ready for that night's operation. The final part of the air test was for Sgt. Russell to hand my Dad the RAF's infamous Form 700, which every pilot had to sign, acknowledging that the aircraft was in good shape, and that they were accepting responsibility for it until they returned it to its rightful owners, the ground crew!

During the pre-operation briefing, all the aircrews on "ops" that night would learn their destination. At the front of the briefing room was a large map, behind a curtain. When all were assembled the curtain was drawn, showing the "target for tonight" and the route. On this night, March 15th, twelve crews from 420 Squadron would be heading for Stuttgart, a major industrial city in the heart of Germany. The briefing would include the expected weather, routes to take there and back, heights at which to fly, time to be on target, colours of target indicators being used, opposition expected, and so on.

After the briefing was the traditional pre-operation egg meal— almost everyone else in Britain was eating powdered eggs, but Bomber Command aircrews ate fresh eggs, a small perk for these young men whose every meal might very well be their last.

Next came changing into their flying clothes, testing their oxygen hookups and being issued a parachute (the standard joke from the Women's Auxiliary Air Force (WAAF) riggers who packed and handed out the 'chutes was "bring it back if it doesn't work"). After that the crew would either ride their bikes or climb into a transport truck to be driven to the dispersal pad and their waiting Halifax.

Our crew's Halifax was loaded exclusively with incendiaries this night: inside their bomb bay, they carried twelve Small Bomb Containers (SBC), each loaded with a variety of potent fire-making incendiary bombs. Note the error in Dad's logbook, where he reverses the order of his bomb load notation: it reads "6x4x90" when it should read "6x90x4," meaning six SBCs, each containing ninety four-pound incendiaries. The second line is correct: 6x8x30, or six SBCs, each containing eight thirty-pound incendiaries.

The Small Bomb Container was an ingenious tool for the efficient and safe packaging, transporting, loading and deployment of small bombs, especially flares and incendiaries. The armourers packed each container with its designated load, and then the container was winched up into the bomb bay of the aircraft. When triggered by the bomb aimer over the target, the SBC opened, releasing dozens or even hundreds of incendiaries on the unfortunate city below. The SBC returned with the aircraft to be used over and over again.

The incendiaries themselves were ingenious and devastatingly effective. Bomber Command had researched the science of destruction extensively and had developed the tactic of using high explosive at the start of the raid to blow apart roofs and windows to expose the interiors of buildings to a rain of incendiaries that followed shortly after. It was a ruthlessly effective way of destroying any built-up area.

The four-pound incendiary bomb was dropped by the millions during WW II, and its magnesium body and the thermite pellets it contained would burn for about ten minutes after it hit the ground.

The thirty-pound Type J was even more deadly—after it fell free of the SBC, a parachute would deploy, which allowed the bomb to hit the ground relatively gently, after which its thermite contents were ignited. The interior soon reached 300 p.s.i., at which point a jet of superheated, horizontal flame fifteen feet long and two feet wide shot out of the base. The jet could last for over a minute, and the RAF named the Type J the "Superflamer" for good reason—in tests, the jet of flame was said to be able to crumble a brick wall.

The Coffey crew took off from Tholthorpe just before 7 p.m. and climbed to 20,000 feet to join the bomber stream, 863 heavies strong. The Pathfinders arrived over the city first, at around 11 p.m., but their marking was reported as scattered, perhaps due to strong winds. The Germans had also started decoy fires on the ground, which likely tricked some of the newer crews. At any rate, the raid was not considered concentrated or particularly effective, although crews did report they could see the glow of the burning city from a hundred miles away as they made their way home.

Attempts to trick the German Nachtjagd controllers failed. The attacking crews were met over Stuttgart by a strong force of Junkers Ju 88 and Messerschmitt bf110 night fighters, and combat was reported all along the return route, even over the English Channel. Thirty-seven crews failed to return from Stuttgart. The Coffey crew (along with five other crews from Tholthorpe) were diverted to the RAF fighter base at Tangmere in West Sussex, perhaps due to bad weather in Yorkshire. The six crews landed at about 3 a.m., and after grabbing some fitful sleep (in whatever space the fighter base could find for their unexpected guests), they took off and returned to Tholthorpe later the same day.

YEAR 1944		AIRCRAFT		PILOT, OR 1ST PILOT	2ND PILOT, PUPIL OR PASSENGER	DUTY (INCLUDING RESULTS AND REMARKS)
MONTH	DATE	Type	No.			
—	—	—	—	—	—	— TOTALS BROUGHT FORWARD
*MAR.	13	HALIFAX III	"B"	SELF	F/O BAYNE	"OPERATION" - STUTTGART
					SGT. DINGWALL	INC. 6×8×30
					W/O RUTHERGLEN	6×4×90
					SGT. PORTER	2038 GALS.
					SGT. HART	A/C ON - 788 LANDED TANGMERE
					SGT. McWHIRTER	A/C MISSING - 40
*MAR.	19	HALIFAX III	"F"	SELF	F/O BAYNE	"OPERATION" FRANKFURT
					SGT. DINGWALL	INC 9×8×30
					W/O RUTHERGLEN	6×4×90
					SGT. PORTER	1808 GALS.
					SGT. HART	A/C ON - 778 (LANDED
					SGT. McWHIRTER	A/C MISSING - 22 THORPE ABBOT
*MAR.	22	HALIFAX III	"B"	SELF	F/O BAYNE	"OPERATION" FRANKFURT
					SGT. DINGWALL	INCEN. 8×8×30
					W/O RUTHERGLEN	7×4×90
					SGT. PORTER	1808 GALS.
					SGT. HART	A/C ON - 832
					SGT. McWHIRTER.	A/C MISSING - 33
				GRAND TOTAL [Cols. (1) to (10)] 509 Hrs. 45 Mins.		TOTALS CARRIED FORWARD

Two non-flying days followed, and then on the night of March 19th, the crew took part in a massive raid on Frankfurt, deep in the heart of Germany. A force of almost 850 heavies took part in the attack against this major industrial city, some of them on diversionary raids and some laying mines in the Heligoland Bight, off the coast of Germany, in hopes of confusing and dividing the Luftwaffe's night fighters.

This operation was only our crew's fourth together, and only their second into Germany, so they were still new at the game (a "sprog crew"), and this inexperience, especially my Dad's, would lead to an embarrassing accident before the end of the night.

Take off that night was just after 7 p.m., and their Halifax was once again loaded with four-pound and thirty-pound incendiaries. The bomber stream, 846 strong, crossed the coast of Holland and made straight for Berlin before turning sharply and heading south to Frankfurt, Dad and crew arriving over the target and bombing at 10:05 p.m. from 22,000 feet.

The raid went well for Bomber Command—the Pathfinders had marked the target well, and the bombing was accurate and concentrated. Frankfurt was heavily damaged, with thousands of homes and hundreds of factories destroyed.

The trip home from Frankfurt did not goes as planned for Dad and crew. For some reason they were diverted to a USAAF base in Thorpe Abbotts, Norfolk, some 200 miles south of Tholthorpe. They were likely running short of fuel for some reason, as all nine of the other aircraft from 420 Squadron landed safely back at their base. At least one other aircraft from Tholthorpe, a Halifax from 425 Squadron, was in the same fix as the Coffey crew and was also approaching the American B-17 base at Thorpe Abbotts, home of the 100th Bombardment Group.

In 2015, I received a package from the Government of Canada that consisted of a disc containing some 300 pages of documents related to my Dad's time in the RCAF. Some of the documents, like dental records, for instance, were of only passing interest, but there were also many that surprised and some that shocked: an accident report (the magisterial sounding "REPORT ON FLYING ACCIDENT OR FORCED LANDING NOT ATTRIBUTABLE TO ENEMY ACTION") from April of 1944 was one of the latter.

My Dad had told me about crashing the Cessna Crane during his pilot training, but as far as I knew, that was the only accident he had ever had during his time as a pilot. Either the accident he was involved in at Thorpe Abbotts this night was not a memorable event for him, or (much more likely) he was embarrassed by the incident and chose to leave it out of the stories he told me. When I asked Bob McWhirter about the accident in 2016, he recalled it immediately, but didn't seem to consider it a particularly memorable event—but it might have stuck out more boldly in his memory if he had been in the tail turret of the other Halifax involved in the incident!

Landing at an unfamiliar airfield at night after a stressful five hour operation into Germany could not have been easy, gut both of the Tholthorpe Halifaxes set down safely and were taxiing to their assigned parking spots when the trouble began. In my Dad's own words, from the accident report:

> Upon receiving a red signal from taxiing truck, I came to a full stop, some 25 yards behind the nearest aircraft, and applied the parking brakes. After approximately one minute of idling the motors at 1000 r.p.m., the engineer notified me that the engines were ready for shutting down. I reached downwards and exercised the blower, watching the boost pressure gauges to ensure they registered a charge and when I looked up again we were only a few feet from the aircraft ahead. I applied full brake and throttled right back but it was too late to avoid a collision.

The technical details of what Dad was doing are beyond me, but the bottom line is he was distracted long enough for a near disaster. Halifax LW 419 taxied into the rear of the aircraft ahead of it, the whirling propellers of Maisye's starboard outer engine tearing into the other aircraft's tailplane. The Halifax on the receiving end, LW 391, was skippered by Flt. Lt. Vanexan, whose tail gunner (Sergeant J. St. Goddard) must have been terrified as he saw Maisye's spinning props ripping into the rudder and tailplane, just a few feet away from turning him into mincemeat. It must also have been a memorable trip for Flight Sergeant Irvine, who was flying his second dickie trip with Vanexan—a harrowing combat op to Frankfurt, a diversion to a strange airfield, and then being crashed into on the ground by another aircraft, all in one night!

In the end, no one was hurt (contrary to the telegram sent by the Americans to Tholthorpe telling them of the incident and noting that my Dad had "slight injuries"), but both of the Halifaxes were rendered unflyable. In the day's final humiliation for Dad, a Halifax from Tholthorpe had to be dispatched to pick up both crews—Flight Sergeant Lucas Holoway loaded them up in Halifax PT-E, and they made the one hour and ten-minute flight back to Tholthorpe.

Wing Commander G. A. McKenna who, within weeks, would be appointed 420 Squadron's Commanding Officer, conducted an investigation into the incident, standard procedure in the case of any accident, and his findings seem fair and frank. Although Dad insisted that he had applied the parking brake, McKenna doubted that they could have been "engaged fully." He noted that it was moonless and pitch dark at the time of the accident and that the American airfield had "incomplete" lighting, only a row of small red lights along one edge of the perimeter track. He felt the inadequate lighting "certainly had a bearing" on what happened, but that my Dad bore the brunt of the responsibility by displaying a "lack of airmanship." Ouch.

One aspect of the accident nags at me: the role played by Sgt. Wilfred Porter, the crew's flight engineer and the pilot's right-hand-man (literally as well as figuratively) from the time they climbed into the aircraft to the time they left it, especially at takeoff and landing. Where was Sgt. Porter, and what was he doing while my Dad was distracted? Why hadn't he noticed the Halifax was straying? It is pure conjecture, and I have no desire to shift the responsibility for the accident onto Sgt. Porter, or to question his competence, but I can't help but wonder if my Dad didn't resent Porter for his role in the embarrassing incident. After all, the reason they had to land at the unfamiliar airfield in the first place was that they were running short of fuel, and monitoring fuel consumption was the flight engineer's responsibility. Did these grievances (whether valid or not) connect with the personnel changes that were to unfold a few nights hence?

Two nights later, on March 22nd, the crew made a return trip to Frankfurt, part of an 816 strong force whose goal was to finish the job they had started three nights before. In order to fool the German night fighters, several diversion raids were staged, and the route the main force followed jinked suddenly south after crossing the Dutch coast. The ruses seemed to work, as the Germans predicted that Hanover was Bomber Command's intended target and directed their forces there, sparing the bomber stream from being mauled as badly as it might have been.

Maisye arrived over Frankfurt at about 1:30 a.m. and dropped her load of incendiaries onto the unfortunate city, which was devastated in the attack. Almost 1,000 were killed and over 100,000 left homeless. Just two days later, a force of 200 American B-17s who had been unable to find their primary target instead bombed Frankfurt, their secondary target. The city never suffered another major raid during the war—there was no need, as there was little left standing to bomb.

After one day off, the crew learned on the morning of March 24th that they were "on" for that night. Based on the fuel loads ordered for the eleven 420 Squadron Halifaxes taking part, this would be no short trip to France, but likely another trip deep into Germany.

At the briefing that afternoon, the curtain was pulled back, and the red ribbon traced a lengthy, intimidating route across the North Sea, Denmark, and then down to the "Big City," Berlin. This trip would be

Dad's second to Berlin (the first had been his second dickie trip with the Eyjolfsson crew in February), but for the rest of his crew, it would be their first time to the much-feared destination.

The March 24th raid on Berlin was destined to be the last time that Bomber Command's Main Force of heavies would visit Hitler's capital, and it was not a successful finale to what some had dubbed the Battle of Berlin. The operation would go down in Bomber Command history as the Night of the Big Winds—Dad would record it sardonically in his logbook as "Operation Berlin… and all points west."

Bomber Harris was keen to get one last crack at Berlin before the shorter nights of spring and summer would prevent long trips deep into Germany. He was also well aware that within weeks, Bomber Command would come under the control of General Eisenhower and that his targets would henceforth be selected for him, based on the needs of the upcoming Normandy invasion.

Year 1944		Aircraft		Pilot, or 1st Pilot	2nd Pilot, Pupil or Passenger	Duty (Including Results and Remarks)
Month	Date	Type	No.			
						Totals Brought Forward
Mar.	24	Halifax III	"B"	Self	F/O Bayne	"Operation" - Berlin (All Points West)
					W/O Rutherglen	Inc. 6x90x4
					Sgt. Dingwall	6x8x30
					Sgt. Porter	2038 Gals.
					Sgt. Hart	A/c on - 808
					Sgt. McWhirter	A/c Missing -23 Landed Coltishall
Mar.	25	Halifax III	"B"	Self	Crew	Coltishall - Base
Mar.	26	Halifax III	"B"	Self	F/O Bayne	"Operation" - Essen
					W/O Rutherglen	Inc. 7x90x4
					Sgt. Dingwall	8x8x30
					Sgt. Porter	1808 Gals.
					Sgt. Hart	A/c on 652
					Sgt. McWhirter	A/c Missing 9
Mar.	30	Halifax III	"B"	Self	F/O Bayne	"Operation" - Nürnberg
					W/O Rutherglen	Inc. 7x8x30
					Sgt. Dingwall	5x90x4
					Sgt. Willoughby	2038 Gals.
					Sgt. Hart	A/c on - 811
					Sgt. McWhirter	A/c Missing - 96
				Grand Total [Cols. (1) to (10)] 532 Hrs. 15 Mins.		Totals Carried Forward

As was often the case with Bomber Command operations, weather played a decisive role. The forecasters warned that Berlin was likely to be covered in cloud this night, but Harris gambled and ordered the attack to proceed. Another weather-related factor that came into play that night was a complete unknown, a wild card that is today a well-understood phenomenon; we call it the "jet stream." These rivers of rushing air, sometimes travelling at 250 m.p.h., typically occur at heights above 25,000 feet, so in 1944 they had only very rarely been encountered, and little understood or studied. On this night, they were to play a pivotal role in events.

Loaded down with thousands of pounds of incendiaries (and for the first time, Dad began writing the load notation correctly—perhaps he had been corrected by the officer reviewing his logbook) and aviation fuel, Maisye took off from Tholthorpe at 6:50 p.m. She joined over 800 other heavy bombers beginning to form into a stream on their way to the Big City.

Spoof (diversionary) raids were staged on several European targets at the same time to try and fool the night fighters, a tactic that was often at least partially successful, although the Germans were becoming very skilful at seeing through Bomber Command's ruses.

Once the attacking force reached their cruising height over the North Sea, the trouble began.

The jet stream winds roaring out of the north at 120 m.p.h. began pummelling the Lancasters and Halifaxes, blowing them south and scattering the compact bomber stream. Selected navigators (designated "windfinders") began radioing their bases to report the power and speed of the wind, but the numbers were considered impossible, and they were arbitrarily lowered to something more "realistic" before being re-broadcasted to the main force navigators. The result was mass confusion, with some crews using the numbers given them, despite their own observations, and some (usually the more experienced and self-confident crews) sticking with the numbers their navigators were experiencing first hand. The compact five-mile by seventy-mile bomber stream disintegrated into a shambles, with crews arriving over Berlin at different times and from different directions. The Coffey crew overshot Berlin by fifty miles, and they had to turn and make their way back to their aiming point flying into a brutal headwind.

Berlin turned out to be covered in cloud, and the Pathfinders were forced to resort to "skymarking," the least accurate method of marking, involving the use of flares dropping on parachutes (code- named *Wanganui*). In the strong winds, the flares quickly drifted away from the aiming point and then disappeared into the thick cloud. One of the Pathfinder skippers was designated the Master Bomber. He and his crew (who obviously put themselves at enormously increased risk) orbited the Big City throughout the attack, giving direction and encouragement to the rest of the force via radio. He must have felt extreme frustration this night as he watched the raid turn into a fiasco. Hours later, at their post-raid debriefing, several 420 Squadron crews "reported their resentment of the language used" by the Master Bomber (one can only imagine!). Uncoordinated as the attack turned out to be, no city can have some 2500 tons of high explosives and incendiaries dropped on it and emerge unscathed. The damage inflicted was substantial; however, it was nowhere near the knockout blow Harris had hoped to achieve.

As the raid finished, it was time for the scattered bomber force to try and make it home—their night was far from over. At this stage of the war, the Luftwaffe's Nachtjager (night fighter) force was at the height of its numerical strength and tactical sophistication. They were quick to exploit the opportunity this night afforded them. The jet stream winds had scattered the bomber force across Germany, off course and running low on fuel, sitting ducks for the night fighters stalking them.

Some crews (including the Coffey crew, despite the best efforts of Bob Bayne, their navigator) had wandered so off course that their quickly dwindling fuel forced them to abandon the designated route and make for home in a straight shot over the highly defended Ruhr Valley. Even with this risky route, the crew barely made it across the English Channel and had to make an emergency landing at RAF Coltishall, a Fighter Command base some 200 miles south of Tholthorpe.

They weren't the only ones—at least two other 420 Squadron Halifaxes were in the same fix and landed at Coltishall as well. Exhausted after their eight-hour and twenty-minute flight, the seven members of the Coffey crew likely grabbed a few hours of fitful sleep in the Sergeant's Mess at Coltishall and later that morning made the fifty-minute flight back to Yorkshire.

By this time, Dad and crew must have been feeling somewhat at home at Tholthorpe, as much as they could be at "home" 5,000 miles away from their families. Daily life at the base had a rhythm to it, and I am fortunate to have gained some insight into this daily routine from one who was there, Bob McWhirter, the crew's tail gunner.

I spoke with Bob on several occasions before his passing, and he also gave me a copy of his brief but fascinating autobiography, from which I will quote directly.

Aircrew were divided into Officers and Other Ranks and their accommodations and messes were separate. Most of our crew bunked together in one of the ubiquitous Nissen huts. Invented by Major Nissen during WW I, the Nissen hut was a prefab corrugated metal structure used as a quick way of housing troops. Bob described them as:

> … a round roofed, metal building with a cement floor, something like our present
> day Quonset. Most of the buildings on the base were of this type. They were cold
> and damp most of the year, heated by a small, flat topped iron stove and fuelled by a
> low-grade coal called "coke." Our housekeeping was done by a "bat lady," who also
> polished shoes and buttons and pressed uniforms. One of the good things about
> the Air Force was we always had a good bed to come home to. It included sheets,
> unlike the Army…

Personal hygiene was attended to at an ablution hut, as there was no running water in the Nissens. The Sergeant's mess where they ate was likely of the same construction. The food they were provided was as spartan as their accommodation. Sausages that consisted primarily of breadcrumbs (Bob recalled that they "flew apart when you tried to cut into them with a knife"), cottage pie (mostly root vegetable and little meat) and heaps of locally grown Brussels sprouts. Macaroni and mutton were staples as well and were often served "cold and clammy," according to Bob.

RAF Tholthorpe was a large, sprawling affair (designed this way to make it a difficult target to destroy). Travel about the airfield was usually done by walking or by using one of the many bicycles. The squadron records note that on April 17th, 1944 a shipment of 130 more bicycles arrived on the base, bringing the total number at Tholthorpe to about 1300. Any photo taken at a Bomber Command base in WW II is likely to include a bicycle somewhere in the shot—they were everywhere!

There were hundreds of support staff on the base to look after every imaginable task, from packing the parachutes to preparing the food to driving the tractors that pulled trolleys full of bombs to the waiting

Halifaxes. There were medical staff, meteorologists, stores clerks, paymasters, perimeter guards and of course, the hundreds of hard-working ground crew, the "erks" whose tireless efforts kept the aircraft flying.

All these hundreds of support staff were there to ensure that the aircrew had nothing to distract them from the one duty they needed to focus on: bombing the enemy.

Actually, there *were* some distractions provided to keep morale up, in the spirit of the old saying "all work and no play…"

There was a makeshift cinema on the base, as well as a gymnasium. Games (both inside the gym and outside when the weather permitted) were organized, and groups like E.N.S.A. (the Entertainment National Service Organization) toured around Britain putting on shows. Dances were held on the base, arranged by the YWCA, and villagers from the surrounding area were sometimes invited.

The airbase and the young men stationed there enjoyed a good relationship with the local village of Tholthorpe, and the locals were proud of the work being done there and did what they could to support it. As the base expanded, there were times when housing shortages became acute, and the villagers opened their homes to the Canadians, billeting them in spare bedrooms until space became available on-base. One local man (Geoff Wood, the kind farmer who had given me a tour of the airfield in 1982), recalling the war years some seventy years later to a newspaper reporter, said that the Canadians sometimes allowed local boys to use their gym and that the pommel horse was an especially loved novelty.

They also appreciated the chewing gum and Pepsi the Canadian airmen generously handed out—I remember my Dad laughing when he told me about the refrain "any gum chum?" that he and his comrades heard frequently from English children.

Our crew had two days off, and then on the morning of March 26th, they got the word that they were "on" for that night. At briefing, they learned their target would be Essen, in the heart of what experienced aircrews sardonically referred to as "Happy Valley," the Ruhr.

> Oh, there was flak, flak, all that you pack,
>
> in the Ruhr, in the Ruhr,
>
> oh, there was flak, flak, all that you could pack,
>
> in the valley of the Ruhr,
>
> oh, there were fighters, fighters, bags of bloody fighters,
>
> in the valley of the Ruhr.
>
> My eyes are dim they cannot see,
>
> the searchlights they have blinded me…

So went a song, set to the tune of "The Quartermaster's Stores," that was sung in Bomber Command messes during the war. "Happy Valley" was a place that inspired cold sweats among crews that had survived a visit. But I wonder what a newly arrived "sprog" crew thought when they first heard the term—"…*oh well, Happy Valley doesn't sound so bad, eh guys…?*"

Happy Valley would become familiar to the Coffey crew in the next six months, as they would survive some eight trips there, two of them to the city of Essen, the epicentre of Nazi Germany's industrial output.

The scope of industry contained in the eighty-mile long Ruhr Valley was astounding. The area was crammed end-to-end with armaments factories, workshops, coal mines, coke ovens, synthetic fuel plants, steel mills, power stations, brickworks—the list is endless. No wonder the Ruhr was such a prime target for Bomber Command throughout the war, and so ferociously defended by the Germans.

By far, the most impressive feature in the Ruhr was the massive Krupp factory complex, which took up a good portion of the Essen city core. In business for some 400 years, the Krupp family had built up an industrial (and mainly armaments-focused) complex unrivalled in the world.

I had always thought of Berlin, or perhaps Nuremburg, as the heart and soul of Nazi Germany, but really, it was here—in the middle of the Ruhr Valley—Hitler and his regime would have been non-starters without the Krupp's family business, which was essentially the Nazi war machine's financier and armourer. In the words of Wing Commander Guy Gibson, leader of the famed Dambusters raid in 1943, the Ruhr was "the place that had unleashed so much misery on the world."

A WWII-era postcard depicting part of the Krupp complex circa 1900. Author's collection.

Alfried Krupp, the firm's wartime head, became a devoted Nazi early on and an enthusiastic advocate of slave labour. By 1944, there were some fifty-five slave labour camps in Essen alone, "employing" around 100,000 unfortunates, who were worked and starved to death, and then replaced. Krupp would requisition more slaves from the big concentration camps like he was ordering boots for his workers. At the end of the war, Alfried was arrested, tried, and sentenced to prison for war crimes, but in a sadly all-too-common story, he was pardoned after a few years and released, primarily due to Cold War politics. Apparently, his business acumen was deemed indispensable in the fight against Communism—he returned to head the firm that bore his name and died one of the richest men in Europe.

Weighed down yet again with thousands of pounds of incendiaries, Maisye lifted off the tarmac at Tholthorpe at 8:15 p.m. along with twenty other Halifaxes from the two squadrons based there. They joined the bomber stream, over 700 strong, as it formed over southern England, climbing and heading East. They arrived over the aiming point in Essen at 10:15 at 22,000 feet and found that the Mosquito bombers of the Pathfinder Force had arrived just before them and had done their job well: the aiming point was well marked. The Coffey crew were in the final wave of bombers—their arrival (with their load of incendiaries) was timed to start massive fires in the chaos of shattered buildings, broken water mains and ruptured gas lines below them.

The March 26th attack on Essen was the last trip that Sergeant Wilfred Porter made with the Coffey crew. Like most RAF flight engineers, Sgt. Porter was an Englishman: Bob McWhirter's recollection was that he was from Liverpool. The details of why Porter left the crew are hazy. I have only a memory from my teenage years of a story told to me by my Dad, and what Bob McWhirter could recall of the incident, which wasn't much. He could remember the parting of ways, but not specifically what had caused the rift between my Dad and his flight engineer.

The story that Dad related to me when I was about sixteen hadn't stood out in my memory, as I had no context to put it into—it wasn't until thirty-five years later that I realized the anecdote was significant to the story I was researching. According to my Dad, he once (and I now know it was almost certainly sometime during the five-hour March 26th operation to Essen) gave his right-hand man, Sgt. Porter, a task to complete. The flight engineer left his post for a moment but was back in his seat so quickly that Dad didn't believe he had done the job properly and confronted him about it. An argument ensued, and since none of the other crew seem to have heard them, they must have been yelling at each other in the cockpit, not over the intercom. At some point, Dad lost his cool and pulled rank: "…look, you son of a bitch, you get back there and do it right, or you are going on report when we land!" The task was apparently completed to Dad's satisfaction at this point. Still, the vital bond of trust between pilot and flight engineer (perhaps already damaged by the accident on the tarmac at Thorpe Abbotts a week before) had finally broken. Dad saw his Commanding Officer later that day and requested the removal of Sgt. Porter from his crew. I remember Dad shaking his head ruefully when he told me the unhappy story and adding that "the fellow never flew with us again."

When I asked Bob McWhirter about the impact that Sgt. Porter's removal had on the crew, he told me that "your Dad wouldn't have made an issue about it with the rest of the crew." I took this to mean that as skipper of the crew, Dad's decision about the suitability of his flight engineer wouldn't have been up for discussion.

Sgt. Porter carried on with 420 Squadron with another crew and was seriously injured in November of 1944 when their Halifax clipped a tree and crash-landed upon return from an operation. I have attempted to find Porter's family over the years of my research, but every effort so far has led to a dead end. The fact that I could find nothing *does* tell me that he likely survived the war and that he did not rise to officer rank.

The remaining six members of the crew had two days off between ops, and during that time, were assigned a new flight engineer. This time the relationship formed would be a strong and effective one:

Sergeant Digby Willoughby would fly with the Coffey crew for the rest of their two tours. Whether my Dad and his crew knew it or not, they already had a connection with Willoughby, having acted as pallbearers at the funerals of most of his previous crew. The story of how Sgt. Willoughby himself avoided the same tragic fate is one of miraculous good luck.

Digby Hugh Callis Willoughby was born in the small town of Chapeltown, Jamaica in 1921, but grew up in the capitol city of Kingston. For some reason—even his children don't know why—he was known to everyone, all his life, as "Jimmy." His parents were originally from Nottingham, England, and the family were successful sugar and coffee plantation owners in Jamaica, with family connections to the English aristocracy.

After graduating from Cornwall College in Montego Bay, Jimmy decided to travel to England to join the RAF. A short article in the Jamaican Daily Gleaner noted that Jimmy was the first Cornwall alumni to join up and "do his bit for England," and that he had been a member of the Jamaica Reserve Regiment, the local militia.

As to his choice of joining the Royal Air Force as opposed to the Army, he may have been influenced by the life of his cousin, Percival-Nesbit Willoughby, a brilliant aviation pioneer who had recently been killed in England testing a flying-wing design.

Details about Jimmy Willoughby's voyage across the Atlantic, enlistment in the RAF and his life in England are sketchy, to say the least. His son Keith told me that his father "never spoke a word about the war," so his family know little about his life there. Like me (and, I am sure, many other children of veterans), Keith regrets that he didn't ask his father more questions while he had the opportunity.

At some point, likely in 1941, Jimmy enlisted in the RAF, but it seems there was a long wait before he started his training, as he served as a warden with Air Raid Protection (ARP) in the meantime. Sometime in 1942, Jimmy donned the uniform of a Leading Aircraftman 2 in the RAF (Voluntary Reserve) and began training as a flight engineer. He was probably among the first airmen to join this newly created trade, which removed the need for a co-pilot on Bomber Command aircraft. The RAF's new school for flight engineers was set up in Wales, at RAF St. Athan, and the curriculum had to be created from scratch.

The No. 4 School of Technical Training took up a good-sized portion of the sprawling base at St. Athan: dozens of hangers, workshops, stores and barracks were home to thousands of instructors, students and support staff.

During the months of training Jimmy went through, he would have become intimately acquainted with every square inch of aircraft in general, and the Handley-Page Halifax, in particular. Engines, airframes, electrical and hydraulic systems, equipment stowage, emergency exits, instruments, propellers, and fuel systems would have all been exhaustively covered. He would have spent a few weeks at the actual factory where the Halifax was built, and paid an extended visit to either the Bristol Hercules or Rolls-Royce Merlin factory to help build the engines that would be powering the aircraft he would be flying in.

A Bomber Command flight engineer was responsible for the proper functioning of all the parts and systems of the aircraft, a daunting task. The bombers Jimmy was assigned to were probably the most technically sophisticated aircraft flying at the time, filled front to back with complex, interconnecting technology.

His communication skills needed to be top-notch as well, for it was his job to be the primary interface between aircrew and ground crew, effectively communicating problems to their "Chiefie" and following up on them. The flight engineer inspected the aircraft before takeoff and, in the air, was responsible for a myriad of tasks, from monitoring fuel consumption to helping his pilot at take-off and landings. He had to try and repair anything that went wrong during a flight if he could, so keeping a cool head during an emergency was essential for problem solving and decisive action. His crewmate's lives might well depend on his abilities.

A host of drills on emergency procedures, operating the .303 Browning machine gun, basic navigation, and Morse code were all included in Jimmy's training. All-in-all, it was an exhaustively thorough curriculum, with one strangely missing component: there was no actual flying time. As odd as it might seem, Jimmy's training all took place on the ground. The system appears to have worked well, but the lack of flying time does seem an odd omission to me.

After completing his training, Jimmy Willoughby (now a Sergeant) proudly had his new one-wing FE brevet sewn onto his tunic, and in January of 1944, reported to the No. 1664 Heavy Conversion Unit at RAF Dishforth. He quickly became part of the crew skippered by Flight Sergeant Harry Skeet Hardy, a Canadian from Toronto, Ontario.

The Hardy crew had arrived at Dishforth at the same time as the Coffey crew, and they flew some of the same assignments, such as the two-day sea search at the end of January, and the February 3rd "bulls-eye" exercise.

At the end of conversion training, Jimmy received an assessment of 66% and a recommendation for a promotion—he obviously took to flying like a duck to water. He and the rest of the Hardy crew were assigned to 420 Squadron, and they arrived at Tholthorpe on February 8th, 1944, one day after the Coffey crew. Just like my Dad and crew had been, Flt. Sgt. Hardy and the rest of his crew were taken up on an orientation flight by Wing Commander McIntosh (and in the same Halifax, PT-B). For the next three weeks, the Hardy crew took part in the same training exercises that the Coffey crew did.

However, luck was not with them. On the night of February 29th, the crew and their Halifax met a tragic fate, one they shared with thousands of other Bomber Command crews-in-training, a fatal accident.

Four crews took off from Tholthorpe on the afternoon of February 29th (including Dad and crew), climbed to 20,000 feet in the clear skies and made their separate ways towards Wales. They were told to practice their corkscrew maneuvers during the three-hour exercise, and it was during their first attempt at the violent dive-and-climb maneuver that disaster struck the Hardy crew.

A post-accident investigation by Squadron Leader Epps of 426 Squadron concluded that the elevator control rods of Halifax PT-V likely broke as Flt. Sgt. Hardy pulled out of his first dive. The aircraft fell into an uncontrollable spin, but Hardy stayed in the pilot's seat, bravely trying to bring the stricken aircraft under control for at least long enough for his crew to bail out. The violence of the spin had smashed the crew's bomb aimer and navigator (Sgt. Cummings and Pilot Officer Hedrich) right through the clear Perspex nose of the Halifax, without their parachutes. The tail gunner (Sgt. Johnson) attempted to bail out with his chute, but the cords entangled in the spinning aircraft's tailplane and snapped—he, too, fell to his death.

Jimmy Willoughby had somehow managed to get his chute on, but in his fumbling to attach it, the ripcord had been snagged and released, and Jimmy watched in horror as white parachute silk billowed out inside the dark fuselage of the spinning Halifax. It was a mishap that should have meant his certain death.

Miraculously, the howling wind from the open emergency exit door caught the flapping silk of Jimmy's chute and sucked it out of the aircraft, dragging Jimmy with it! However, his incredible luck didn't end there. As he was yanked out of the Halifax, the spinning tailplane tried to kill him as it had Sgt. Johnson, but Jimmy only got a glancing blow, hard enough to knock him unconscious momentarily, but otherwise inflicting only some nasty cuts on his upper lip and nose.

Only one other crew member was able to escape, Flying Officer James (wireless operator), who was able to bail out at the last possible moment—any lower and his parachute would not have had time to open. Seconds later, the Halifax, still containing Flt. Sgt. Hardy and mid-upper gunner Sgt. Nixon, slammed into a farm near Aberystwyth and exploded.

The bodies of the five dead Canadians were transported to the cemetery in Chester and the two survivors to the hospital. Several days later, my Dad and his crew were sent to Chester to serve as pallbearers at the funerals of the Hardy crew, a sad duty that they had to repeat five times in succession.

One month later, having recovered from his injuries and my Dad in need of a new flight engineer, Jimmy Willoughby joined the Coffey crew.

Jimmy's logbook entry for the tragic night of February 29th is succinct and matter-of-fact, simply stating, "XCTY crashed. Bailed out. Lost 5 off crew." He elaborated a bit about the experience when he wrote home to his mother a few months later:

> Well, it was February 29th when it happened. We were doing a training flip at 21,000 feet when something went wrong, and that something I am not allowed to say, and we came down in a screaming dive: unfortunately with the terrific speed and force of gravity we were flung from post to pillar, and my chute was ripped open in the aircraft, but the wireless operator managed to open the escape hatch. By the greatest miracle I was thrown in that direction, and my chute caught the slipstream and dragged me out complete, and the wireless operator followed me, but the rest of the crew were unlucky. The wireless operator and myself got off with one or two cuts, but nothing to speak about. It has left me with a scar over my lip, but it is not bad now. Anyway, that seems to be all the bad luck I will have. So don't worry over me, I will be ok.

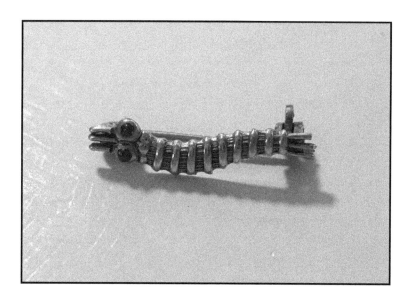

Jimmy Willoughby's Caterpillar Club pin. Photo courtesy of Willoughby family.

His survival via parachute automatically made him a member of the "caterpillar club," an unofficial group made up of those who had lived to fly again after bailing out, saved by their parachutes. The club had been started in 1922 by the Irvin company, makers of the parachutes. The company presented each new member with a very distinctive caterpillar (representing a silkworm) lapel pin: Jimmy's family still have his proudly on display.

Jimmy's family never heard the story of his remarkable escape directly from him—he never spoke about the war to his sons, and they only heard the story second-hand from an uncle.

Now, everyone has probably played the game that I learned as a kid (called "telephone," as I recall) in which a group of people sit in a large circle and relay a whispered anecdote into the ear of the person sitting next to them. The story is passed along, and by the time it reaches the last person in line, who tells it out loud, it has been so garbled from the original as to be laughable.

Something along these lines happened to Jimmy's story over the decades. When I managed to contact the Willoughby sons in 2015, I found that the story that had passed into family lore was that Jimmy's plane had crashed into a hayfield in France, that their Dad had jumped from the aircraft without a parachute. He had broken his leg and then was chased by a French farmer with a pitchfork, who thought Jimmy was a German.

The garbling of a story over the course of decades is, of course, perfectly understandable. A similar apocryphal story came up about my Dad supposedly flying a Lancaster back to England alone after all his crew had been killed. Malcolm Dingwall's grandson told me a childhood memory of a story his Grandfather had related about ground crew jamming bottle caps into the tires of the Lancasters to make for smoother landings! Such stories may be jumbled memories, or perhaps tall tales told to a child, but they certainly do make the job of a researcher interesting!

Jimmy didn't even get a training flight with his new crew (aside from the usual twenty-minute pre-operation air test) before being thrown into the breach on the night of March 30th, 1944, a night that would go down in history as the nadir of the war for Bomber Command. It was to be a night of "firsts" for Jimmy: as well as being his first trip as part of the Coffey crew, it was also his first flight after the tragic accident of February 29th, and his first-ever combat operation.

It was not to be a gentle introduction, as the March 30th raid on Nuremberg (Dad uses the German name "Nurnberg" in his logbook) went wrong in almost every way it could. Nearly a hundred "heavies" were lost, close to thirteen percent of the force sent. In human terms, some 545 young Allied airmen died that night, one more than Fighter Command's Spitfire and Hurricane squadrons lost during the entire Battle of Britain.[7] Over a hundred more airmen were captured after bailing out of stricken aircraft, some badly wounded.

Yet again, the combination of unpredictable weather and Bomber Harris's stubborn determination spelled disaster for the aircrews taking part in the raid.

A last-minute RAF Mosquito reconnaissance flight had warned that the cloud cover the weather forecasters had predicted had not materialized and that the route to Nuremberg might well be clear and

---

7   Obviously, I have no wish to downplay the fighter pilot's losses, only to highlight the fact that the sacrifice and courage of the "bomber boys" never received the same level of public recognition.

moonlit, a deadly combination for the night bombers. Conditions like that usually meant no deep penetration raids like the one planned for this night.

Harris decided to gamble on the weather: Nuremberg was a prime target, filled with factories as well as being the Nazi regime's spiritual centre, and it hadn't been visited by Bomber Command for a long time. It was too tempting a target to let a troublesome weather report interfere with the plans for its destruction. To be fair to Harris, many historians point out that if he had waited for perfect weather to mount a raid, the bomber campaign would never have happened. He had taken calculated risks many times before and had won, but the calculations were seriously awry on this night.

A commemorative postcard depicting combat during the Nuremberg raid. Author's collection.

At 10 p.m. that evening, Dad lifted his heavily laden Halifax (3,500 pounds of incendiaries nestled neatly in a dozen SBCs) off the runway and began to climb to their assigned height. All over England, bombers were already assembling, with 420 Squadron assigned a spot towards the rear of the bomber stream. The force crossed the English coast, leaving relative safety behind, and began to fly into a gauntlet of waiting night fighters.

Bomber Command used its full array of countermeasures to try to even up the odds for their crews. Spoof raids (complete with target indicators) were staged on several German cities, and Halifaxes on sea mining operations dropped *WINDOW* foil strips to try to appear on German radar screens as the main force. Top secret aircraft (code-named *ABC*) contained special equipment that could find and jam the night fighters' communications. RAF Intruder Mosquitos flew over Europe homing in on the night fighter's radar, attempting to turn the predators into the prey. But the German night fighter crews and their controllers were wise to many of the RAF's tricks, and the ruses didn't prevent the slaughter to come.

A relatively direct route to Nuremberg was chosen by the Bomber Command planners, a risky move that maximized bomb load (less fuel needed to be carried) but relied on cloud cover to help camouflage the attacking force. There would be no such helpful cloud on the route tonight. The clear, moonlit skies, devoid of the hoped-for cloud cover, left the bombers flying in conditions akin to daylight. To add to the danger, the frigid, clear air at their assigned height caused their engines to leave contrails, like a trail of breadcrumbs for the German night fighters to follow. What resulted was a massacre. There really is no other word for it.

A trail of burning Lancasters and Halifaxes was left strewn across Germany and France. In the clear night skies, Allied airmen watched in horror as their comrades engaged in mortal combat with the night fighters, falling in flames or erupting in massive explosions as the 20 mm cannon shells set off their bomb loads.

A remarkable photo taken by Ted Rutherglen sometime during the Nuremberg operation — the brightness of the sky that night is obvious. Carrying a camera on an operation, or even on the ground at the airbase, was strictly forbidden, but I am glad Teddy broke the rules, as his photos are now precious family heirlooms. Photo courtesy of the Dingwall family.

To prop up morale in the face of horrific losses, aircrews had been told by their intelligence officers that, in order to unnerve them, the Germans were sending up "scarecrow" shells or rockets. These were supposedly filled with oil and scrap metal to simulate a bomber exploding. In fact, there were no such shells—what the Bomber Command aircrews were seeing was the real thing. As late as 1995, a Lancaster pilot's autobiography repeats this persistent myth. It must have given some small comfort to uneasy airmen to believe it.

To add to the debacle, the attack on Nuremberg was a failure. In a maddening irony, crews who had fought their way across the continent in clear skies found the city covered by a 10,000 foot thick blanket of cloud. The Pathfinders had to resort to sky marking, their least effective method, and no Master Bomber was assigned to the attack, an inexplicable failure in planning.

About a third of the crews ended up bombing the wrong city altogether, dropping their loads on the nearby Schweinfurt.

After finding and bombing their aiming points as best they could, the badly mauled force began the long return trip to England, with combats and losses continuing right up to the English Channel.

The Coffey crew landed back at Tholthorpe at 6:00 a.m., after a brutal eight-hour and ten-minute flight. 420 Squadron was one of the only units taking part in the raid that could say that all of their crews returned safely.

Was there some factor (like training, high morale, or their placement in the bomber stream....?) that could account for the Canadian squadron's success? It's not likely, and I think the most plausible answer is one offered by one who was there, Bob McWhirter. Recalling that night and its losses, he commented simply, "I guess we were lucky."

After two months of training and combat operations, the Coffey crew was due for a break, and they were granted ten days leave. They likely spent it together, as a crew, in London.

The Coffey crew on the wing of Maisye, Tholthorpe, 1944.
L to R : McWhirter, Rutherglen, Coffey, Bayne, Hart and Willoughby.
Photo likely taken by Malcolm Dingwall. Photo courtesy of the Rutherglen family.

Bomber Command aircrews led a strange, almost schizophrenic existence in some ways. They would fly into an almost literal hell, night after night, enduring incredible stress and physical discomfort. They faced the possibility of a horrible death (can we even imagine falling without a parachute from 20,000 feet, to have one's body ripped apart by shrapnel, to be roasted alive while trapped in a burning aircraft or to be beaten to death by an angry mob of vigilantes?) at any point, in what could be a nine-hour long operation. And then, perhaps two or three nights in succession, operations would be "scrubbed" (cancelled), and they could take a bus into town and spend the evening dancing with young women, having a pint of beer at a pub, or going to the movies.

So, just twenty-four hours after returning from the horrific raid on Nuremberg, the Coffey crew found themselves "on vacation," as it were.

The most popular destination for aircrew on leave was London, where there were a wide variety of diversions and activities, and many different options for accommodation. Later that summer, when they had all (but for one) risen in rank and were relatively well-paid officers, they favoured the Strand Palace Hotel, a huge edifice that was built in 1909 and is still in operation today. However, for this visit in the spring of 1944, they likely sought less expensive digs, as all but one of the seven young men were still Sergeants.

Luckily for them (and for all the young Canadians stationed in England during the war), there was a wide range of services available to them, organized and staffed by dedicated professionals and volunteers. One of London's most popular destinations for Canadians was the five-storey, fifty-room Beaver House, a former London City Council building. It operated seven days a week and was always bustling with activity, which is unsurprising when one reads about the range of innovative services it offered to Canadian servicemen. There was a reading room, stocked with newspapers from some eighty towns and cities across Canada (albeit a few weeks out of date), and a post office where they could purchase writing materials and mail letters home. There was a bank where they could open an account, to which they could send part of their pay, saving up to have spending money while in London. There was a list of currently available accommodations, and not just for London: a "database" of sorts was maintained, which listed 500 homes across Great Britain where they could stay while on leave, should they wish to visit somewhere more rural.

One of the more innovative schemes Beaver House started was the Mother's Day flower system: servicemen could order and pay for flowers for their mothers back home in Canada, and Beaver House would arrange the cabling of funds and for delivery.

Dances and musical programs were staged, all at little or no cost to the airmen, soldiers and seamen who attended. Some of the activities offered were more cerebral, including lectures about political goings-on in Parliament, back in Ottawa. Educational tours were organized, taking young Canadians to places like the Tower of London and the House of Commons, accompanied by knowledgeable guides.

All-in-all, organizations like Beaver House and the YMCA did a stellar job of making sure young Canadian men, far from home and in unfamiliar surroundings, were made to feel welcome and looked after.

On another occasion later in the summer, the Coffey crew were the beneficiaries of the generosity of Lord Nuffield, head of Morris Motors, who was a noted philanthropist. He had started a program dubbed the Nuffield Aircrew Leave Scheme, which paid the tab for thousands of weary Bomber Command aircrew when they stayed (for up to a week) at any of some thirty hotels across the U.K. Taking advantage of Lord Nuffield's kind offer, our crew spent a memorable week at the grand Caledonian Hotel in Aberdeen sometime during the summer of 1944.

On another occasion, they travelled to Bournemouth, but this turned out to be less enjoyable: Bob McWhirter recalled that, in the lead-up to D-Day, the city "was literally taken over by American troops."

Upon their return from leave on April 10th, the Coffey crew took part in three training flights over the next week that, at first glance, seemed routine. However, when I really started looking at them some questions came up, and the stories behind two of these flights turned out to be far more interesting than I first thought.

YEAR 1944		AIRCRAFT		PILOT, OR 1ST PILOT	2ND PILOT, PUPIL OR PASSENGER	DUTY (INCLUDING RESULTS AND REMARKS)
MONTH	DATE	Type	No.			
—	—	—	—	—	—	— TOTALS BROUGHT FORWARD
		Summary for MARCH 1944		1 HALIFAX III		SUMMARY FOR MARCH
		Unit 420 SQDN Aircraft		2		
		Date MARCH 31 Types		3		GRAND TOTAL
		Signature JR Coffey		4		Lunden S/LDR.
						O.C. "A" FLT.
APRIL	11	HALIFAX III	"D"	SELF	CREW	CROSS COUNTRY
					LT. CHILD	
APRIL	13	HALIFAX III	"B"	SELF	CREW	C.H., S.B.A., LOCAL GEE
APRIL	15	HALIFAX III	"B"	SELF	CREW	
					F/S McADAM	FIGHTER AFFILIATION
					SGT. CAMPBELL	
					SGT. WHITE	
					SGT. POLLOCK	
APRIL	18	HALIFAX III	"B"	SELF	F/O BAYNE	"OPERATION" - PARIS (NOISY-LE-SEC)
					SGT. DINGWALL	H.E. - DEL. ACTION 72
					SGT. WILLOUGHBY	6 X 1000
					W/O RUTHERGLEN	9 X 500 1500 GALS
					SGT. HART	A/C ON - 178 TOTAL 1094
					SGT. McWHIRTER	A/C MISSING - 14

GRAND TOTAL [Cols. (1) to (10)]
543 H 25

TOTALS CARRIED FORWARD

The first, on April 11th, was a four and a half hour nighttime cross-country exercise that would be unremarkable but for the inclusion of the name of a passenger, a "Lt. Child."

Now, the rank of Lieutenant is not used in the RCAF or RAF, so I thought perhaps he might be an Army officer, but that immediately led to the question: why would an Army officer be flying with my Dad and his crew?

Lt. Child turned out to be Lieutenant J. H. Child of the No. 2 Canadian Infantry Reinforcement Unit, and his flight was part of the lead-up to D-Day. In a clear indication of how incredibly detailed the planning that went into Operation Overlord was, dozens of company officers in the Canadian Army were sent to RCAF stations throughout England as liaisons, to get a feel for Bomber Command's capabilities. Someone high-up must have had an inkling that Allied heavy bombers would be forced by necessity to take on an increased role in supporting ground troops after D-Day. The "strategic" bombing force would likely be finding themselves attacking targets that were perhaps only hundreds of yards away from friendly troops. It only made sense then, to have officers on the ground who had some idea of what the bomber boys were up against: what they could and couldn't do to help the Army.

There was a full moon this night, so Lt. Child would have been able to have a good look at the ground from 10,000 feet and was likely given an opportunity to view the moonlit terrain through Malcolm Dingwall's Mark XIV bombsight. I wonder if Child had ever been in an aircraft before? Did my Dad try and have some "fun" with the "brown job" (air force slang for any soldier) by practising a few corkscrews along the way...?

The No. 2 Canadian Infantry Reinforcement Unit was destined to be thrown into the fray in Normandy to replace losses suffered by the Canadian Army during the invasion. A search for Lt. Child in a list of Canadian war dead did not turn up his name, so I hope that means he made it home safely. If so, perhaps one of the stories he told his children years later was about the time he got to fly in a Halifax bomber and about how the pilot tried to make him airsick as a joke!

Two days later, on the 13th, the crew made a short fifty-five-minute flight, practising circuits and landings, Standard Beam Approach and navigation using the *GEE* system.

On April 15th, another short training flight is noted, a quick twenty-five-minute fighter affiliation exercise. Again, questions came up as I took a closer look at the entry: who were the four crew listed, and why wasn't the flight noted in either Ted Rutherglen's or Jimmy Willoughby's logbooks? The untangling of the story behind this entry in Dad's logbook took substantially longer than the original flight did!

One month earlier, Flight Sergeant William McAdam and his crew had taken off on their first combat operation on the night of March 15th, along with eleven other crews from Tholthorpe, including the Coffey crew. Their target was Stuttgart, and on the lead-in to their aiming point, McAdam's Halifax was hit by flak, destroying one engine and killing his navigator, Sergeant Briggs of Vancouver, B.C.

Sgt. McAdam, displaying the "press-on" spirit that Bomber Command was famous for, chose to continue to the aiming point, and to keep the fact he had been wounded in both legs from his crew. After completing their bomb run, the crew's bomb aimer, Sgt. Ranson, had to call upon the basic navigation training he had received in Canada at Air Observer School and take over as navigator. He gave his wounded skipper, Sgt. McAdam, a course back towards England, but with only three engines, the Halifax began to slowly lose precious altitude. At 5,000 feet, upon crossing the French coast, they were again pummelled by flak and another engine was put out of commission. Finally, at 3:10 a.m. McAdam put the badly mauled Halifax down on a grass emergency airstrip at RAF Friston in Sussex. Only when they were safely down did the crew discover that their skipper was wounded and faint from blood loss.

Four weeks later to the day, having recovered from his wounds, McAdam and three of his crew climbed aboard a Halifax for the short fighter affiliation exercise.

Although my Dad is listed as the pilot, I think, perhaps, he was there as "backup" in case McAdam was not up to the task, physically or mentally. In any case, it doesn't seem he was needed: Sgt. McAdam and crew completed the flight without issues and, displaying the courage and resilience so common in Bomber Command, went on to complete two tours and return safely to Canada.

After six operations in a row that had taken them deep into Germany, the Coffey crew (along with the other members of 420 Squadron) were once again directed back to Transportation Plan targets in France, tasked with hamstringing the Wehrmacht's mobility. The first raid, on April 18th, was against the massive railway marshalling yards at Noisy-le-Sec, a suburb of Paris.

Dad and crew took off from Tholthorpe just before 9 p.m. and joined almost two hundred other heavies making their way to Paris. The aiming point was carefully marked with red target indicators by Pathfinder Mosquitoes, and opposition was reported as moderate, with no night fighters encountered—just the usual flak and searchlights.

Malcolm Dingwall, the crew's bomb aimer, dropped his load of six 1,000-pound and nine 500-pound high explosive bombs (at precisely 2358.5 hours according to squadron records), all of which were equipped with 72-hour delayed action fuses.

These nasty devices were designed to explode three days after plunging into the ground, thus destroying any post-raid repair work that had been completed. In September of 2015, over 8,000 people were evacuated from the vicinity of Noisy-Le-Sec railway yards as munitions experts moved in to deal with three unexploded British bombs from this 1944 raid, which had remained buried for seventy-one years. Delayed action indeed!

Our crew arrived back at Tholthorpe just before 2 a.m. and were cleared to come in for a landing by the air traffic controller. On his final approach to the runway, Dad gave Jimmy Willoughby the go-ahead to lower Maisye's undercarriage, and that's when things went sideways. Despite repeated attempts, the wheels of the big bomber would not go down. My Dad, putting all that "overshoot" practice at the Operational Training Unit to good use, aborted the landing attempt, ordered full throttle from Jimmy and pulled the Halifax into a climb. This move gained them altitude and time to sort the problem out. Once they were clear of other aircraft, Jimmy engaged the emergency undercarriage system, which was powered by compressed air, and this time the wheels lowered and locked. The Tholthorpe control tower again cleared them to land, and they finally "pancaked" (touched down on the tarmac) at 2:15 a.m.

This equipment malfunction would be put on a "snag sheet" that Jimmy would give to their ground crew "Chiefie," and would follow up on later in the day to find out what had caused the problem and how they had remedied it.

The attack that night on Noisy-le-Sec was a success—the yards were so thoroughly wrecked they were not completely repaired until 1951. The bomber boys had proved that they could bomb with relative precision—despite their Master Bomber's radio transmissions being jammed by the Germans. Inevitably, however, some bombs did go astray, and many homes adjacent to the yards were destroyed, resulting in almost five hundred French civilian casualties.

Two days later, on the night of April 20th, it was the turn of the marshalling yards in Lens to receive the attention of Bomber Command. Over 1500 aircraft took part this night in attacks on Transportation Plan targets. One hundred and seventy-five of them, including the Coffey crew, attacked Lens, the rest bombing railway yards in Cologne, La Chappelle, Ottignies, and Chambry. The Luftwaffe defences were divided by these multiple attacks, and the RAF losses were light.

YEAR 19 4 4		AIRCRAFT		PILOT, OR 1ST PILOT	2ND PILOT, PUPIL OR PASSENGER	DUTY (INCLUDING RESULTS AND REMARKS)
MONTH	DATE	Type	No.			
—		—	—	—	—	—— TOTALS BROUGHT FORWARD
APRIL	20	HALIFAX III	"B"	SELF	F/O BAYNE	"OPERATION" - LENS MARSH. YARD
					SGT. DINGWALL	H.E - 9×1000
					W/O RUTHERGLEN	6 × 500 .
					SGT. WILLOUGHBY	1318 GALS.
					SGT. HART	A/C ON · 158
					SGT. McWHIRTER	A/C MISSING - 1 (TOTAL-14)
APRIL	23	HALIFAX III	"B"	SELF	CREW	PRACTISE BOMBING, HEIGHT AND AIR TEST.
APRIL	24	HALIFAX III	"B"	SELF	F/O BAYNE	"OPERATION" · KARLSRUHE
					SGT. DINGWALL	H.E. 1×2000
					W/O RUTHERGLEN	INC. 5×8×30
					SGT. WILLOUGHBY	5×90×4 2038 GALS.
					SGT. HART	A/C ON · 613 (TOTAL-908)
					SGT. McWHIRTER	A/C MISSING ·29
APRIL	26	HALIFAX III	"B"	SELF	F/O BAYNE	"OPERATION" · ESSEN (RUHR)
					SGT. DINGWALL	INC. 15×90×4
					W/O RUTHERGLEN	1808 GALS
					SGT. WILLOUGHBY	A/C ON · 219 (TOTAL 417)
					SGT. HART	A/C MISSING · 29
					SGT. McWHIRTER	

GRAND TOTAL [Cols. (1) to (10)]
561 Hrs. 55 Mins.   TOTALS CARRIED FORWARD

Dad and crew left Tholthorpe a little after 9 p.m. and dropped their load of 1,000-pound and 500-pound bombs just before midnight from 20,000 feet. It was another effective attack that destroyed railway lines, locomotive sheds, and repair shops. In their post-raid debriefing, the Coffey crew commented that the raid "appeared to be a good prang."[8]

It was their tenth operation, and they had now, statistically speaking, surpassed the average survival time for an operational Bomber Command aircrew. No longer a "sprog" crew, they were now approaching the realm of being considered "gen men:" experienced, competent and respected.

After a two-hour training/practice bombing flight on the afternoon of April 23rd, our crew were back on ops April 24th and 26th, returning to Germany both nights.

The April 24th attack on Karlsruhe, an important industrial city on the Rhine river, was essentially a failure. Bomber Command threw 637 heavies at the town, but a rookie Pathfinder squadron's inaccurate

8   A "prang" was RAF slang for any wreck, whether by accident or by design.

marking, combined with strong winds and thick cloud, resulted in bomb loads scattered far and wide, many falling in open country outside the city. Dad and crew, like all the other 420 Squadron crews reported in their post-op debriefing that they perceived the raid was a success:

> Attacked target at 0043 hours from 20,000 feet. Markers well concentrated with fires well centred in the Target Area. A good raid.

It wasn't unusual for aircrew returning from a raid to paint an overly rosy picture of effectiveness—really, it is just human nature to believe that one's efforts are successful (especially when you have risked your life to do so!). Bomber Command's leaders had realized this truth years ago and had put in place measures to get independent verification of raid results.

The first measure was a sophisticated photo reconnaissance program, using high-flying Mosquito bombers to take post-raid photos of the previous night's target. These photos were a very effective means of separating optimistic claims of success from reality.

Another measure was the cameras that the night bombers themselves carried. At the moment they dropped their bomb load, a photoflash flare was dropped as well, and the crew was required to fly straight and level for many long seconds until it went off, at which point their aircraft's camera would snap a photo of where their bombs had landed.

In 2019, a very kind researcher came across some of the Coffey crew's original 1944 target photos. I didn't even know these photos existed, so it was quite a surreal experience to open an email from the contact I had met only online and look at the grainy, black and white photos, each labelled with target, date, height, and my Dad's name.

Original target photo taken by the Coffey crew over Noisy Le Sec.
Courtesy of Richard Koval.

Several of the photos show ground detail, but most, like the one taken over Karlsruhe on the night of April 24th, offer nothing but cloud.

The raid on Karlsruhe may not have been very effective, but that didn't mean the costs were any less: twenty-nine crews failed to return that night, representing some two hundred young men. Fourteen Halifaxes had taken off from Tholthorpe, and two had been forced to turn back due to mechanical problems. Twelve bombed Karlsruhe, but only eleven returned safely to their base. One of 420 Squadron's crews was posted as "missing," and it wasn't until after the war that the fate of the Watterson crew was learned.

After bombing the target, Flying Officer Doug Watterson from Windsor, Ontario, was involved in a collision with another bomber, which had sheared off the nose of his Halifax. Somehow maintaining control over the damaged plane, Watterson turned it around and began to try to make it back to England. Luck was not with them however, and a German night fighter soon caught up with them and set them on fire. Watterson ordered all his crew to bail out, but only the two gunners made it out in time, all the others perishing when the burning plane exploded.

Five members of the Watterson crew were buried in a small Dutch cemetery, while rear gunner Mike Cassidy and mid-upper gunner Ray Tanner spent the rest of the war in a P.O.W. camp.

In 2005, Mr. Cassidy passed away in Canada, and his remains were taken to Holland, where he had received special permission to be buried beside his crewmates in the tiny Dutch town of Zuilichem. Mr. Cassidy was reunited with his comrades after sixty-five years, and his dying wish to be laid to rest with his crew brings home to us how tight the bond between Bomber Command aircrew could be.

After a one-day break, our crew were again lifting off the tarmac on April 26th, and once again heading for Essen, in the heart of Happy Valley, the Ruhr. They had almost five hundred other heavies with them, and the bomber stream was divided into four waves, timed to arrive in succession over Essen. Dad and crew were likely in one of the later waves, as Maisye was carrying a load of over 1,000 four-pound incendiaries.

Crews returning from Essen reported the city to be heavily defended, with smoke screens, decoy fires, light and heavy flak, and a massive display of searchlights, some clustered in groups of thirty to fifty. There was no more terrifying an experience for a bomber crew than to be "coned:" being picked out and becoming the focus of dozens of searchlights—and in short order, an equal number of flak guns. They would be like a moth caught in a flashlight beam, and the skipper of the unfortunate aircraft would sideslip, dive, and corkscrew to try and escape back into the darkness before the flak got them.

Prior to the raid on Essen, the Pathfinder crews had been urged to improve their marking after the poor results at Karlsruhe two nights before. They certainly rose to the challenge—the target markers placed on Essen were bang on the aiming point. After landing back in Tholthorpe, the Coffey crew reported their experience to the Intelligence Officer during their debriefing:

> Attacked target at 0136 from 21,000 feet. Heavy bomb bursts and fires were spread
> all around Target Indicators. A good job by Pathfinder Force and a good route.

A post-raid recon photo taken of the Krupp complex. Original WWII-era press photo.
Author's collection.

On the afternoon of April 27th, our crew found they were on again for that night, this time headed back to France to attack another Transportation Plan target. After two trips to the Ruhr in the past three nights, perhaps they were relieved, but in reality, there were no easy targets at this stage of the war: the German defences were formidable, and flak, searchlights, and night fighters would be waiting for them no matter where they went. The best that could be said about a French target was that at least the flight time was usually shorter than going to Germany.

The railway marshalling yards at Aulnoye, in northern France near the Belgian border, were a vital transportation hub for the Germans, and they were a prime Transportation Plan target.

YEAR 1944		AIRCRAFT		PILOT, OR 1ST PILOT	2ND PILOT, PUPIL OR PASSENGER	DUTY (INCLUDING RESULTS AND REMARKS)
MONTH	DATE	Type	No.			
—	—	—	—	—	—	— TOTALS BROUGHT FORWARD
APRIL	27	HALIFAX III	"B"	SELF	F/O BAYNE	"OPERATION" · AULNOY
					SGT. DINGWALL	MARSHALLING YARDS.
					W/O RUTHERGLEN	H.E. 7X1000
					SGT. WILLOUGHBY	8X500 1318 GALS.
					SGT. HART	A/C ON ·90 (TAR 1000)
					SGT. McWHIRTER	A/C MISSING· 36
APRIL	29	HALIFAX III	"W"	SELF	CREW	AIR TO AIR FIRING (P.N.G.
APRIL	30	HALIFAX III	"B"	SELF	F/O BAYNE	"OPERATION" - SOMAIN
					SGT. DINGWALL	MARSHALLING YARDS
					W/O RUTHERGLEN	H.E. 9X1000
					SGT. WILLOUGHBY	4X500 7200 GALS.
					SGT. HART	A/C ON - 294 HT.-5000'
					SGT. McWHIRTER	A/C MISSING -
Summary for ....APRIL........ 19 44				1 ..HALIFAX III..		SUMMARY FOR APRIL
Unit.....420 SQRN............		Aircraft		2..................		
Date.....APRIL 30/44........		Types		3..................		GRAND TOTAL
Signature....H/S Coffey L......				4..................		
						Deegan F/LT. O.C "A" FLIGHT.

GRAND TOTAL [Cols. (1) to (10)]

572 Hrs. 35 Mins.   TOTALS CARRIED FORWARD

Dad and crew left Tholthorpe a little before midnight and joined a force of some 225 headed for Aulnoye. In an impressive (and increasingly commonplace) show of force, Bomber Command mounted two other ops of equal size that night, one against the tank factories in the German city of Friedrichshafen and the other to attack the marshalling yards at Montzen, Belgium.

Maisye was loaded with 11,000 pounds of high explosives, and Malcolm Dingwall dropped his bomb load on the Pathfinder Force's well-placed target indicators just before 2 a.m. from the unusually low height of 5,000 feet. The bombing height put the force in range of the German light flak as well as the usual heavy flak—this tactic was essential to improve accuracy and minimize French civilian casualties.

Bomber Command had attacked the marshalling yards at Aulnoye twice before in recent months, but the results had not been decisive. Tonight's raid would finally leave the yards permanently out of commission: the post raid photos show an utter moonscape of craters and little else.

When I first began reading 420 Squadron's Operational Record Book for the period that Dad and crew were stationed there, I came across one terse entry that piqued my curiosity: on April 27th, a certain airman[9] was sent off to the innocent-sounding Aircrew Refresher Course in Sheffield ("for 3 weeks or more," according to the O.R.B.). What, I wondered, was this course, and what in the world would an experienced Bomber Command pilot need "refreshing" in, and why couldn't he receive the "refreshing" at his own squadron?

I decided to go off on one of the many sidetracks that I have mentioned before to find out a little about this so-called "Aircrew Refresher Course." The search led me down a disturbing rabbit hole into the system of bureaucratic cruelty and injustice known to all wartime aircrew simply as "L.M.F."

Upon investigation, the innocuous-sounding Aircrew Refresher Course turned out to be nothing less than a punishment camp, located at RAF Norton in Sheffield. The unfortunates sent there for weeks of route marches, drill, parades, and lectures were, in most cases, guilty of some minor disciplinary infraction (this was true for the airman in question, who returned to his squadron and crew, and completed a tour of operations), such as insubordination, pilfering, or being absent without leave, but many other "attendees" at A.R.C. were ordered there for a much more sinister reason.

L.M.F. stood for Lack of Moral Fibre, and the phrase stands high in the pantheon of cruel bureaucratic euphemisms, alongside the likes of "collateral damage" or "enhanced interrogation." In reality, L.M.F. meant "coward," and hundreds of brave young airmen, whose only real crime was reaching the limits of their endurance, were tarred with this slur during World War II.

Despite the fact that every Bomber Command airman was a volunteer, refusal to fly any longer was treated with deliberate, cruel condemnation. Even men who had flown dozens of operations could be labelled with the infamous L.M.F. designation, stripped of their badges and ranks and sent to the Aircrew Refresher Course, after which they would be inducted into the army as a private or sent to work in coal mines as labourers.

To add insult to injury, the L.M.F. system was haphazard, with individual Medical Officers and Commanding Officers able to show discretion or to manipulate the system depending on their opinion or attitude, or based on the airman's particular circumstances.

To play devil's advocate, the senior RAF officers who put in place and maintained this system truly felt it was essential: they well knew the strain aircrew were under and thought that if an "easy out" were available, many would take it. If this happened, Bomber Command would soon be left with nothing but inexperienced "sprog" aircrew, critically degrading the effectiveness of the campaign they were fighting.

It was a weak argument in at least two ways, the first being that it didn't take into consideration that were other viable alternatives to the black and white options of labelling an airman either a hero (if he carried on) or a loathsome coward (if he stated he couldn't).

The USAAF attempted to treat their airmen in a somewhat more enlightened fashion[10], giving some of those who needed it a rest break at a rural medical facility for a week or two before sending them back to their squadrons, an option that often proved to be successful in getting an airman back to his crew.

The second way the "easy out" argument was lacking validity was that it didn't give proper due to the amazing power of camaraderie among Bomber Command aircrews. Over and over again as I read aircrew autobiographies and other personal accounts during my research, I have been struck by the power of the bond that formed among the members of a heavy bomber crew. I believe this steadfastness is one of the

---

9   I will not name him out of respect.

10   Although they could be just as harsh and cruel to their airmen as the RAF - the American record on the issue is more haphazard. But at least they *tried* to have a compassionate option available.

main reasons the bomber campaign succeeded. If by some technological miracle a Bomber Command pilot like my Dad had been able to fly his operations by himself, I don't think he or anyone else would have lasted anywhere near as long as they did without psychologically crumbling. Even the fighter pilots in the Battle of Britain flew in teams, even if they were alone in the cockpits of their Spitfires and Hurricanes.

The bomber boys didn't want to let each other down, and *that* is the main reason I think only a tiny fraction of them refused to complete their tours, not the cruel threat of being labelled "L.M.F."

In his book *The Anatomy of Courage*, Lord Moran writes:

> Courage is a moral quality; it is not a chance gift of nature like an aptitude for games. It is a cold choice between two alternatives, the fixed resolve not to quit: an act of renunciation which must be made not once but many times by the power of the will. Courage is will power.

The men who implemented the L.M.F. system failed to see that this crucial willpower was fortified by high morale and a strong sense of camaraderie, not fear of punishment and shame.

As they carried on night after night after night, the young men of Bomber Command each had their own ways of dealing with the sometimes crushing stress of combat operations, some healthy, some not, with "overindulging" being one of the latter.

My Dad told me he was concerned about alcohol consumption among his crew, as he had seen "boozing" become a problem in some of the other crews at the station. He was determined that he and his six crew-mates were going home in one piece, and he felt strongly that staying focused was crucial if they were going to survive. On this, it seems all seven young members of the Coffey crew were in agreement—flying with a hangover (or worse) was not something any of them were going to tolerate. What they may have gotten up to while on leave is another matter!

The Coffey crew at Tholthorpe. L to R standing : Unknown, Unknown, Coffey, Bayne, Rutherglen, Unknown. L to R front row : McWhirter, Unknown, Willoughby, Unknown. Photo courtesy of the Rutherglen family.

Other methods of coping with the stress were more innocuous, such as superstitious pre-flight rituals like urinating on the tailwheel of the aircraft or the common practice of flying with good luck charms like a sweetheart's stocking or a teddy bear.

Dad's good luck charm. Author photo.

Around my neck, on a gold chain in place of the original parachute cord, I humbly wear my Dad's good luck charm. It is a piece of shrapnel (likely from a German 88 mm flak shell) which Dad told me had landed, glowing red, on the floor of his cockpit during an operation over Germany. Since the vicious little fragment of metal hadn't hit anything vital (neither metal nor flesh and blood) during its unwelcome forced entry into the Halifax, he considered it a bit of good luck. When Dad got back to Tholthorpe, he asked an "erk" to drill a hole in it so he could wear it around his neck on a cord. He flew with it for the rest of his two tours.

It is an object of "terrible beauty," burnished copper on one side, cold, ominous steel on the other, still bearing fabrication marks despite its violent final moments. It is surprisingly heavy for its size, and the thought of what it would do upon entering the human body when flying at speed is quite sickening to contemplate. After the war, it had been placed, along with other bits and bobs, into an old wristwatch case, and had stayed there for some thirty years.

I remember my Dad showing me the shard when I was a teenager; I thought it was "cool" and asked if I could wear it—I will never forget the way he looked me in the eye, hesitated, and then said, "yes." The hesitation seemed to say more than the spoken word, even to my immature ears, and I am glad to report the talisman immediately went back into safekeeping, where it stayed for another thirty-five or so years.

At the age of fifty, going through a bitter separation and divorce, I felt my own courage failing me, a thoroughly unfamiliar and quite surreal feeling of free fall into impotent anger and fear. On a whim, without giving much conscious thought as to why, I retrieved my Dad's lucky shrapnel from its box and put it around my neck for the first time—it has remained there since. To my Dad, it was a symbol of luck, but to me, it is also a symbol of something more—its weight on my neck is a constant reminder of the capacity we all possess for courage and resilience in the face of fear. Who couldn't use an occasional reminder of that in this life?

On April 29th, the crew took off at 3:15 p.m. on an overcast day for some air-to-air firing practice. This exercise should have involved meeting up with another aircraft over the Yorkshire Moors and firing at the fabric drogue that it would be towing on a long cable. The Moors were one of the sparsely populated areas assigned for these types of live-fire exercises, as the ammunition being shot at the drogue could fall to earth at surprisingly high velocity, with sometimes lethal results for civilians on the ground.

On this day, Dad's logbook notes "D.N.C.O." (for "duty not carried out") for the exercise, so for whatever reason, it seems the other aircraft was a no-show. The Coffey crew spent an hour and forty minutes "stooging about" (in RAF slang, to wander about, wasting time) and then returned to Tholthorpe.

The next night, April 30th, turned out to be their last operation with 420 Squadron, and the last time my Dad would ever fly a Halifax—I believe the Coffey crew likely knew that a big change was coming for them, but perhaps not exactly when.

They took off at just after 9:30 that evening along with 143 other bombers from around England and formed into a stream heading for northern France. Their target was the marshalling yards at Somain, and the force arrived there about two hours later.

The raid fell well short of success, ruined by an inaccurate target marking job by the first Pathfinder Mosquitoes to arrive. The Master Bomber ordered the main force to orbit the city and come in for another bombing run, giving the Pathfinders time to re-mark the aiming point. Unfortunately, not everyone heard the order, and many crews missed the aiming point by a wide mark. There seems to have been a lot of confusion that night in the skies over Somain, with various 420 Squadron crews reporting that the Master Bomber was "quite late," that he was "not heard," or that he was "quiet," that the marking was accurate, and that it was inaccurate. In the end, after everyone had dropped their loads of 500-pound and 1,000-pound bombs from a relatively low height of about 7,000 feet, the railway yards were damaged but far from destroyed. An embarrassingly large percentage of Bomber Command's ordnance that night ended up falling in rural pastures and fields.

One 420 Squadron Halifax failed to return from Somain that night, having crashed into the sea for reasons unknown, killing all aboard. Flt. Lt. Ed Northern and his crew were on their final operation before finishing their tour, and their wireless operator, Pilot Officer Alfred Ball, had in fact already finished his tour and had volunteered to go with the Northern crew to Somain, so they didn't have to fly with a replacement in his place. I suspect that Northern was a personal friend of Teddy Rutherglen, as Ted wrote the initials

"E.N." in his logbook next to the notation of one aircraft lost on the raid—there is something poignant about the stark simplicity of how Ted marked the loss of a friend.

Upon returning from Somain that night, I am sure there were many bitter comments made among the crews about the poor marking from the Pathfinder Force, a "cock-up" that had exposed them to significantly increased risks by having to orbit the target. I suspect that the Coffey crew stayed mum during the griping about the Pathfinders, as they were about to find out for themselves what was involved in marking the target for the main force. At the crew's request (after they had been scouted and recruited), they were being transferred to 405 Squadron, the only Canadian squadron in the Pathfinder Force.

The crew's move to the Pathfinders had been in the cards for a while. Recall that their assessment while at the No. 22 Operational Training Unit a few months previously had included a notation from the Commanding Officer, clearly stating he felt the Coffey crew were among the best in the course and recommending them for the Pathfinders. His assessment very likely made its way to the desk (or ears) of someone in the Pathfinder Force, who were always on the lookout for "up and coming" crews.

There were several pros and cons to joining the Force, the main con being the increased risk. The PFF tour was longer (forty-five ops instead of thirty), and a PFF aircrew (depending on the task assigned to them on a particular raid) often had to make two bomb runs over the target, once for dropping target indicators and another to drop their bomb load.

On the plus side, there was an immediate increase one level in rank, and the corresponding pay raise. And we must not forget the increase in prestige and status in wearing the elite gold eagle badge of the Pathfinders—a badge that aircrew carefully removed before each operation to avoid "special" treatment by the Germans should they be captured.

But there were two other considerations that I think were higher in their minds as our crew mulled over the idea of volunteering for the Pathfinders. When a regular crew finished their first tour of thirty operations, they were given a break of up to a year (as instructors or some other kind of non-combat duty) before re-forming with a new crew to complete the second required tour. The advantage of going to the Pathfinders was that they could get their whole two tours completed in one run and would be able to stick together as a crew for the entire time. I think this was a huge consideration—they were a tight, highly skilled (and lucky—no minor consideration!) crew, and they knew it. Best, they must have thought, to stick together and press on.

Another consideration that I think was forefront in my Dad's mind was that getting into the Pathfinders meant getting his time of service over with sooner and going home to my Mom and baby Gary. The possibility of getting back to them a year sooner was the motivator that made him decide to accept the increased risk of flying with the Pathfinders.

The final tipping point for Dad, a perk that would be the "icing on the cake" as it were, of joining the Pathfinders was that he would be able to realize (in the words of Bob McWhirter, who chuckled when he told me) "his big ambition."

He would be climbing into the pilot's seat and taking charge of the finest four-engine aircraft to take to the skies in World War II, the legendary Avro Lancaster.

The mighty Avro Lancaster. This particular example is one of two in the world still flying.
Photo taken by Dwight Coffey at an airshow in New Brunswick in the early 90's.

CHAPTER FIVE:
COOKIES, CANS, AND DOODLEBUGS

MAY 1944 — NOVEMBER 1944

On May 3rd, 1944 the boys reported to the Pathfinder Force's No. 1655 Navigation Training Unit (NTU) at RAF Warboys in Huntingdonshire, some 150 miles south of Tholthorpe.[11]

"Warboys" seems an entirely fitting (indeed, almost contrived) name for an RAF facility dedicated to taking the young men of Bomber Command to the next level of expertise in the bombing campaign against Germany. In reality, the name has a more prosaic origin, being a corruption of the old Anglo-Norman name for a woodsman or forester.

The NTU's job was to transition hand-picked aircrews from Main Force squadrons to the Pathfinder's specialized tactics and equipment. For Ken Hart and Bob McWhirter, the crew's air gunners, there would not be much of a change, but the transition would be substantial for the rest of the crew. Jimmy Willoughby, the crew's Jamaican flight engineer, would be cross-trained as a bomb aimer, freeing up Malcolm Dingwall to assist Bob Bayne as 2nd navigator. Bob would need the help—in addition to all his regular navigation paraphernalia, he would now also be operating a cutting edge, top secret ground mapping radar set code named *H2S*.

And as for their pilot—well, my Dad would be getting his hands on the pride of Bomber Command, an aircraft that Sir Arthur Harris referred to as their "shining sword," the mighty Lancaster.

The Avro Lancaster is a magnificent aircraft, elegant and majestic in flight, with clean, perfectly balanced lines even when sitting on the ground. To see one in person, as I was lucky enough to do at an airshow in England in 1983, takes one's breath away. The Battle of Britain Memorial Flight was performing that summer day, so I must have seen Spitfires and Hurricanes as well, but all I can remember is the Lanc. When she taxied to a stop near where I was standing, and I felt the prop wash and heard the musical growl from those four Rolls Royce Merlin engines, believe me, I knew I was in the presence of greatness!

By all accounts a joy to fly, it out-performed all other heavy bombers of the era, carrying more bombs farther and more efficiently, and was adored by her crews, especially her pilots. There is no doubt in my mind that the Lancaster was the finest four-engine bomber of the war.

---

11 Apparently, as we shall see, the crew got little notice of the exact date of their move to the Pathfinders, and left Tholthorpe in a mad rush...

The twist to the story of the Lancaster was that she rose like a phoenix from the ashes of a flop, the Avro Manchester, a twin-engine disaster. The Manchester's designer, the brilliant Roy Chadwick, took the sluggish, accident-prone Manchester, lengthened the wings, replaced the two engines with four of Rolls Royce's superlative Merlins, and to make a long story short, a star was born.

In passing, I must say that it seems to me that the Rolls-Royce Merlin engine was one of the unsung heroes of WW II—it powered some of the most successful combat aircraft of the era, including the Spitfire and the Mosquito. When the British first received shipments of the American P-51 Mustang fighter, they assessed it a disappointing under-performer, but then on a hunch, they replaced the American-supplied Alison engine with a Merlin. Almost overnight, the Mustang was transformed into the finest long-range escort fighter in the world. USAAF pilots put it to good use: while escorting huge formations of B-17s into Germany, they engaged and decimated attacking Luftwaffe fighters in massive daytime battles high over the Reich.

Flight Sergeant Coffey (Dad had been promoted from Sergeant while at the No. 22 OTU at the end of October) didn't know it yet, but he was now an officer and a gentleman, having been recommended for a commission while at Tholthorpe. The RAF made it official on April 30th, their final day with 420 Squadron. However, the wheels of notification moved slowly, and the logbooks of his crewmates don't reflect his new rank of Pilot Officer until around the end of May.

A man's rise to a commissioned rank was a big deal for the British military and for British society in general—it was not taken lightly. In the past, it was often only the "well-bred" and wealthy who could rise to officer rank, but the war had brought unwelcome (to some…) changes to the system, as it had to everything else. The arrival of tens of thousands of young "colonial" airmen in England had been hard enough for career RAF men to fathom. When these new arrivals quickly began to be promoted (often due to the staggering loss rates in Bomber Command) to officer rank, it was even tougher (again, for some) to come to terms with. Suddenly career RAF men had to share their officer's mess with twenty-something Canadians, Australians, and South Africans, and it inevitably led to occasional friction, frustration, and noses being put out of joint.

The Commonwealth airmen soon developed a (probably exaggerated) reputation for undisciplined behaviour and a casual attitude towards formalities, especially uniform dress codes. Although I have read many stories about the clashes that sometimes occurred between the RAF "establishment" and "colonial" airmen, without a doubt the funniest I have run across is told by Lancaster pilot J. Douglas Harvey, in his wonderful book *Boys, Bombs and Brussels Sprouts.*

The story involves one of his crewmates, who was particularly lax in his dedication to spit and polish:

> …Ken had little respect for the air force authority and his uniform was mostly of his own creation—usually a thick turtleneck sweater, no tie, and battledress with the blouse open. Rarely did he wear his hat, and often he wore brown leather loafers in lieu of the standard black oxfords.
>
> Late for a briefing one afternoon, he was running full tilt past the station headquarters when he was stopped by a roar coming from a ground floor window.

"You there, that man!" roared the voice. "Stop where you are!" (Ken) stopped. A form flung the window fully open and stepped through onto the grass. A Wing Commander staff officer, British, and very correct, marched up…

"Where is your tie, Sergeant?" he barked.

"I don't know, sir."

"Where is your shirt, Sergeant?"

"I don't know, sir."

"Where is your hat, Sergeant?"

"I don't know, sir."

Then, staring down at (Ken's) shoes, the Wing Commander bellowed, "By God, those are brown shoes you are wearing!"

(Ken) was tiring of the harangue. "Your eyes," he said, "are damn near good enough for aircrew."[12]

This friction between the Commonwealth airmen and the RAF establishment is an issue I have pondered often, and I think the quotation from my Dad—reproduced as the frontispiece of this book—gets at the heart of the matter:

Mine was not a war of bugle calls and roaring engines and magnificent defiance in
the clamour of battle;
Mine was a war of patience and endurance and stability;
of cunning and craft and stealth;
Of attention to details and giving my best to learn all there was to learn about the
job to be done.

The origin of the quote is a story in itself: sometime in the mid-eighties, on a visit to my parents' home in Williams Lake, I came across a sheet of paper in one of the books in my Dad's small library with this quote handwritten on it. Many of the words were crossed out and re-written, like Dad was trying to get it *just right*. I thought about asking him about the quote, but it seemed almost an invasion of his privacy, as obviously he had not meant for anyone else to read it. I settled on writing out my own copy of his words and saving them, which in retrospect was, I suppose, an even worse invasion of privacy! Be that as it may, I am very glad I did, as the piece of paper with the quote was gone when I went through his books after he died.

As is readily apparent from reading the quote, my Dad took his job seriously.

Rear gunner Bob McWhirter told me that he remembered my Dad as being a "very careful and conscientious pilot," and a story that my older brother Stuart told me reinforces this portrait.

---

12   From photos that I have from that period, it seems my Dad was one of those who toed the line a bit more, at least
     when it comes to dress and deportment—he looks smart and put together in all of them.

Stu recalls my Dad telling him that sometimes on days when he and his crew were not flying operations, he would rise early and watch the crews that had been on a night raid returning to the base. He would see the battle-battered Lancasters coming in for a landing with missing ailerons, holes in the wings, shattered canopies etcetera, and ask himself what *he* would have done if his plane had received such damage, visualizing himself in the other pilot's shoes. What actions would he have taken to bring the wounded plane home?

I don't believe my Dad was exceptional in this way—I think this kind of professionalism and dedication to doing the job right was the norm in Bomber Command, whether the crew was from Manchester, Perth, Auckland... or Czar. The young men of Bomber Command, in general, took the job they had been given seriously. No amount of preparation or training would guarantee a safe return, of course, but it surely must have helped increase the odds. And really, what more could a crew do in the face of the terrible losses incurred by Bomber Command? They may have engaged in some boisterous, beer-fueled antics on the ground, but really, was this behaviour any different from, or any more worthy of disapproval, than that engaged in by millions of young soldiers or seamen?

I remember reading a story in one of the better-known books on the subject of Bomber Command, about a Canadian bomber crew supposedly circling Berlin during a raid singing their skipper "Happy Birthday" over the intercom! I found myself feeling annoyed by the story, both because I was skeptical of its veracity (the author gave no source for the tale, so don't think I am out of line thinking it apocryphal), and also because the author seemed to relate the anecdote solely to reinforce this stereotype that Commonwealth flyers (specifically Canadians and Australians) were a wild, undisciplined bunch.

Dad commented once on this subject when I was about fifteen or so. I can't recall what prompted the conversation, but he told me that the men he flew with were not much on military decorum as far as proper uniform, haircuts, and "saluting everything that moved" went. He said their attitude was that they "were there to get a job done—everything else was B.S.," a sentiment he later expressed (a little more poetically!) on that piece of paper I copied.

I think the attitude Dad conveyed on these occasions is honest and to be expected—the vast majority of Bomber Command aircrew were not career military men after all. To automatically equate their occasionally indecorous attitude toward old school RAF sensibilities with reckless, unprofessional behaviour in the air seems grossly unfair to me.

Now, lest anyone get the impression that my Dad was a young man without a sense of fun, I hasten to add that Bob McWhirter's characterization of his skipper as "careful and conscientious" preceded a story that portrayed another side altogether:

> "... on occasion, for our benefit, I think, we did some *very* low flying... I can still remember these Land Army[13] girls" (and here he paused to laugh delightedly at the memory) "of course I had a good view, being in the tail turret! We came up over a rise, and here I could see these Land Army girls, all lying flat on the ground... scared the pants off them, I guess!" (pause for more laughter). "That sort of thing didn't happen very often, but I think he did it for our benefit, to break the monotony (of long training flights)."

I am sure my Dad loved the thrill of low flying, but I wonder if it wasn't part of his careful preparation for operational flying as well. Many a bomber crew made it safely home, evading flak and fighters by flying

---

13   The Women's Land Army was created to organize women into service in the agricultural sector, freeing up men to serve in the military.

at tree-top level when necessary, and it took great skill. My Dad probably didn't mind showing off his flying prowess to his crew either—nothing wrong with them having confidence in his abilities! And besides, we must remember, low flying was one of the things good old Sergeant Glass had exhorted him to "practice!" back at Elementary Flying Training School in 1942!

Upon receiving notice of their commission, each new officer was given a sum of money (£85.00 is a figure I have read) and sent to London to get outfitted in the uniform of an officer and gentleman. Bob McWhirter, the little tail gunner from Saskatchewan, kept the receipt he got for his new kit and kindly made a copy for me in 2016. On the receipt (dated June 2, 1944 from Horne Brothers Limited, Oxford Street—they had branch stores across Britain) is recorded Bob's purchase of everything an officer required. The list includes tunic and slacks, greatcoat, shoes, socks, RAF caps, shirts, socks, pyjamas, gloves, a tie, and a steel trunk to keep it all in. The fact Bob kept this simple piece of paper his whole life gives, I think, an indication of the pride the humble farm boy from rural Saskatchewan felt at becoming an Officer in His Majesty's forces.

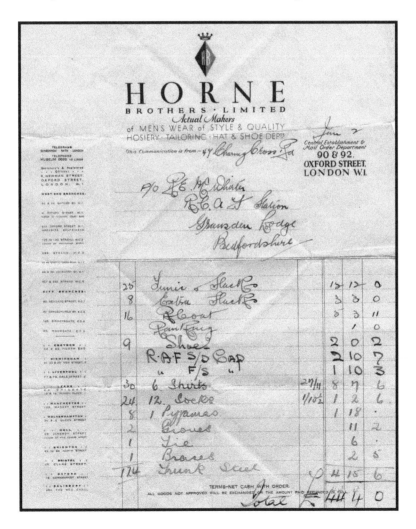

An Officer and a Gentleman. Horne Bros. receipt courtesy of Bob McWhirter.

Along with the new promotion (the stint as Pilot Officer short-lived in Dad's case, as he would be promoted again within a month, this time to Flying Officer) came a raise in pay and a handsome scroll to commemorate the occasion. The RCAF sent my Dad's scroll to my Mom back in Provost, Alberta—she received it in November of 1944, just after Dad had finished his tour of operations and was preparing to return home to Canada.

The language used in the scroll is delightfully formal and elegant and I find it quite fun to read aloud:

> George the Sixth, by the Grace of God, of Great Britain, Ireland and the British
> Dominions beyond the Seas, King, defender of the faith, Emperor of India etc.
> To Our Trusty and well beloved Jesse Ray Coffey Greetings. We, reposing especial
> Trust and Confidence in your Loyalty, Courage and good Conduct, do by these
> Presents Constitute and Appoint you to be an Officer in Our Royal Canadian Air
> Force of Our Dominion of Canada from the Thirteenth day of April 1944. You
> are therefore carefully and diligently to discharge your Duty as such in the Rank
> of Pilot Officer or in such other Rank as We may from time to time hereafter
> be pleased to promote or appoint you to… and you are in such manner and on
> such occasions as may be prescribed by Us to exercise and well discipline, both the
> inferior Officers, and other ranks serving under you and use your best endeavours
> to keep them in good Order and Discipline. And We do hereby Command them
> to Obey you as their superior Officer, and you to observe and follow such Orders
> and Directions as from time to time you shall receive from Us, or any your superior
> Officer, in pursuance of the Trust hereby reposed in you.

It's too bad the scroll didn't arrive while Dad was still Overseas—I am sure it would have had more of an impact on him than it did when, likely burned out and war-weary, he first got to see it in January of 1945. I have a feeling the mellifluous words may have rung a bit hollow for him at that point.

The Pathfinder Force was set up as their own Group (8 Group) within Bomber Command in 1942 as part of a program to improve bombing accuracy, which for the first years of the war was embarrassingly imprecise. Despite the courage and perseverance of the aircrews, they often simply couldn't find their aiming points, and tons of bombs, hundreds of aircraft, and thousands of young men were being lost with precious little to show for it. Ineffective tactics and obsolete technology were a combination that threatened to bring the bomber campaign to an end before it could prove its true worth.

It was felt that a specialized force (specifically trained and manned by the most proficient crews recruited from throughout Bomber Command) was needed, one that would be sent in to the target area first to find the aiming point and light it up for the Main Force, who would be following minutes behind. There was some resistance to the plan, especially from "Bomber" Harris, who disliked the idea of any part of his command being labelled "elite"—he worried it would lower morale in the rest of the force. His objections were overruled (one of the few times, I think), and the Pathfinders began operations in 1942, with steadily increasing success. By the time the Coffey crew volunteered for Pathfinder training in 1944, the Pathfinder Force had proved its worth and was an integral part of Bomber Command.

YEAR 1944		AIRCRAFT		PILOT, OR 1ST PILOT	2ND PILOT, PUPIL OR PASSENGER	DUTY (INCLUDING RESULTS AND REMARKS)
MONTH	DATE	Type	No.			
—	—	—	—	—	—	— TOTALS BROUGHT FORWARD
					P.F.F. N.T.U. — WARBOYS —	
MAY	9	LINK	—	SGT. JONES	SELF	BEAM APROACH, FIG. 8
MAY	11	LANC. III	"S"	F/LT. JONES	SELF + CREW	CROSS COUNTRY - No. 14
MAY	13	LANC. III	"R"	F/LT. BERRIDGE	SELF	DUAL CIRCUITS - CONVERSION
					F/O WHEATE	
					SGT. KENSEL	
					W/O RUTHERGLEN	
					SGT. WILLOUGHBY	
MAY	13	LANC. III	"R"	SELF	DITTO	SOLO CIRCUITS
MAY	13	LANC. III	"T"	SELF	CREW	SOLO CROSS COUNTRY - No.14
MAY	14	LANC. III	"T"	SELF	CREW	SOLO CROSS COUNTRY - No.24
					F/LT LYNNA	
MAY	14	LANC. III	"R"	F/LT BERRIDGE	SELF + CREW	NIGHT CIRCUITS
MAY	14	LANC. III	"R"	SELF	CREW	SOLO NIGHT CIRCUITS

SUMMARY FOR N.T.U. - WARBOYS 19. H.T.   1. LANCASTER III   SUMMARY FOR N.T.U.
UNIT .... AIRCRAFT .... 2. ....
DATE MAY 15.44 TYPES .... 3. ....   GRAND TOTAL
SIGNATURE .... Coffey .... 4. ....

D.H. Bean W/C
O.C. Flying N.T.U.

GRAND TOTAL [Cols. (1) to (10)]
585 Hrs. 10 Mins.   TOTALS CARRIED FORWARD

The first week of training at RAF Warboys seems to have been classroom-based, as the Coffey crew did not take to the air until May 11th. It must have been torture for Dad to be in and around all those beautiful Lancasters and not able to take one for a spin! However, the Pathfinder Force had a wide range of cutting-edge techniques, tactics, and equipment that needed to be learned before anyone was trusted taking off in a PFF aircraft.

As I noted earlier, Jimmy Willoughby would be getting cross-training as a bomb aimer so he could relieve Malcolm Dingwall, who in turn, would take up duties as second navigator, assisting Bob Bayne. The new *H2S* ground mapping radar was a wonder, giving an image of the ground on a cathode ray tube display at the navigator's station—it could see through cloud and haze and darkness, making the dream of accurate "blind bombing" a reality. Best of all, the equipment was self-contained in the Lancaster—it couldn't be jammed by the Germans.[14] But the set was notoriously difficult to read and operate, and Bob still had to maintain all his regular navigation duties, plotting their course on charts as he always had. The tiny picture that *H2S* gave him of the terrain directly below was of little help with general navigation.

I laughed when I read Dad's very first entry for his time at the Navigation Training Unit—itching to fly a Lancaster, he instead found himself back inside the claustrophobic confines of a Link trainer on May 9th.

Their first flight in the Lancaster was on May 11th, when Flt. Lt. Jones took Dad and crew up for a three hour, forty-minute cross-country flight. Ted Rutherglen called this a "mock op" in his logbook. Jimmy Willoughby's logbook adds that they engaged in some "practice bombing" as well. I am sure Dad was at the controls for much of the flight, under the watchful eye of Flt. Lt. Jones, but he may have handed the control yoke over to Jones for takeoff and landing.

May 13th was a busy one for our crew. The first flight of the day for Dad was thirty minutes of circuits and landings with Flt. Lt. Berridge providing instruction.

When the Lancaster landed, the instructors hopped out, and Dad and crew were deemed fit to fly on their own—the Coffey crew took ownership of Lancaster QS-R for a thirty minute flight of circuits and landings. Neither Malcolm Dingwall (bomb aimer) or Ken Hart (mid-upper gunner) list these two flights in their logbooks, so perhaps they were busy with some classroom instruction. Their spots, it appears, were taken by Flying Officer Wheate and Sergeant Kensel. An hour after landing from this second flight, they climbed into another Lancaster, this one coded QS-T, and took off at 1:35 p.m. for a three hour, ten minute "mock operation," a pre-set, cross-country flight coded "No. 14" in Dad's logbook, the same route they had taken with Flt. Lt. Jones on May 11th. Jimmy Willoughby, the trainee-bomb aimer, noted in his logbook that at some point on the flight, they did some practice bombing, and he achieved a "200 yard error" from "10,000 ft." It was probably not up to Pathfinder standards yet, but not bad for a flight engineer on only his second ever bomb run!

The 14th of May was another busy day for the crew, and their final one at Warboys. At 11:45 that morning, they took off to complete a cross-country exercise ("No. 24") that lasted almost four hours. Accompanying them was Flt. Lt. H. Lymna, who was an experienced navigator and bomb aimer who had already completed a tour of operations with 35 Squadron and was at Warboys as an instructor. I am betting that it was Lymna's job to assess the crew and give the ultimate thumbs up or thumbs down as to whether they were ready for the move to the Pathfinder Force.

The exercise was another "mock op" with "practice bombing" according to at least two of the crew's logbooks, and this was their final flight at the Navigation Training Unit. It must have gone well, as the next day they were told to pack their belongings and were then transported the twenty or so miles to their new home, RAF Gransden Lodge, where they joined the only Canadian squadron in the Pathfinder Force, 405 "Vancouver" Squadron.

---

14 Although the Germans could find the H2S signal and follow it to its source. Bomber Command learned the hard way not to allow crews to use the H2S continuously, lest a night fighter home in on the Lancaster using it.

In the summer of 1983, I pedalled my Raleigh ten-speed bicycle into Little Gransden, Cambridgeshire, and headed for the heart of any English village, the local pub. I was seven months into an amazing year-long cycling tour of Ireland and the U.K., but today was one I was especially looking forward to—I was going to visit the airfield where Dad and crew had been stationed.

The Chequers Pub didn't appear to be a popular tourist destination, as I seemed to stand out like a sore thumb—the kindly gentleman behind the bar asked me what had brought me to "the big city" as he poured me a pint of Whitbread bitter. When I told him (and the other locals who seemed to be intently listening in) I was here to visit the old airfield where my Dad and crew had spent eight months in 1944, I was treated like an old friend. While I enjoyed my pint and ploughman's lunch, I was told many stories about the war years that, I am sorry to say, I neglected to write down and they are now lost. I do recall meeting one older man who said he had driven a tractor on the base, towing the heavily laden bomb trolleys to the waiting Lancasters.

After lunch, following the careful instructions of my new friends, I made my way to the disused airfield. It wasn't far away—I arrived shortly after leaving the pub and surveyed a view that I imagined must have been similar in some ways to the one Dad, Bob, Malcolm, Jimmy, Teddy, Ken, and Bob must have taken in thirty-nine years previously. However, in other ways, the bucolic, peaceful view that greeted me must have been very different indeed from the busy bomber station that our crew found when they arrived on May 15th, 1944.

I arrived on a beautiful, sunny summer day and wandered about in the knee-high fields of oats and wildflowers, alone but for the songbirds and insects. I made my way to the derelict two-storey control tower, which looked forlorn but somehow dignified, like an elderly veteran on Remembrance Day, a bit dishevelled perhaps, but still standing proudly.

The control tower at Gransden Lodge, summer 1983. Photo by author.

I explored the ground floor of the tower and on one wall, I found a faded sign, originally painted in bold white letters on the brick:

Signals Traffic Room. All Signals and Telegrams To Be Handed in At Window

Access to the upper floor of the tower was thoroughly (and sensibly) blocked off, but I was twenty-one and stupid—I propped my bicycle against the outside wall of the building and tried to reach the area by standing on the seat in an attempt to scramble onto the catwalk that partially encircled the outside of the upper floor. No luck, and just as well, as who knows what kind of condition the floor up there was in after so many years of neglect? I am sure the ugly irony would not have been lost on my Dad if I had broken my neck at Gransden Lodge forty years after he managed to make it home safely! I did find a souvenir to take home, however—lying on the ground was a small triangular piece of wire-reinforced glass, no doubt from one of the smashed, boarded-up ground floor windows.

Some of the runways and perimeter tracks at Gransden Lodge remained, although the asphalt and concrete were showing their age badly, as I recall. As I walked up and down the faded and cracked grey tarmac where, four decades earlier my Dad had no doubt taxied his Lancaster many times, I tried to imagine this peaceful setting as it once was, home of one of Bomber Command's bustling airbases.

Facilities-wise, it wouldn't have differed much from Tholthorpe—cinderblock buildings and Nissen huts on a flat landscape. Gransden Lodge was a bit smaller, though, as it housed only one squadron rather than the two that lived at Tholthorpe. The commanding officer was Squadron Leader Reg Lane, whose C.V. as an operational Bomber Command pilot was extensive and impressive, to say the least: Lane was no desk-bound administrator.

It didn't take long for 405 Squadron to put the Coffey crew to work—no "familiarization" flights or "dual circuits and landings" at Gransden Lodge; it was straight to business. Just four days after their arrival, they took off in Lancaster D for Dog with nine other aircraft from 405 Squadron to join a force of forty-four attacking an obscure hill in France named Mont de Couple.[15]

The attacking force was made up entirely of Pathfinder Force Lancasters and Mosquitoes, which I think shows the importance Bomber Command placed on destroying the radar jamming facility the Germans had built on this otherwise unremarkable French hill in the Calais area. The installation, code named *Nachtfalter* (moth) by the Germans, was one of many built in 1940 after the fall of France. It was used to jam British *Oboe* radio transmissions, disrupting navigation and communication. The facility had played a key role in a daring German operation often referred to as the "Channel Dash," during which three German battleships made a successful run from the French port they were trapped in, up the English Channel right under the noses of the British, and back safely to their German home ports. The Mount Couple installation was obviously a dangerously effective tool for the Germans: Allied commanders planning the invasion of France ordered it put out of commission before D-Day.

---

15 Almost universally written as "Mount Couple" in Bomber Command documents, Dad calls the target "R.D.F. (for radio direction finding – a wartime name for radar) Hut" in his logbook.

YEAR 1944	AIRCRAFT		PILOT, OR 1ST PILOT	2ND PILOT, PUPIL OR PASSENGER	DUTY (INCLUDING RESULTS AND REMARKS)
MONTH	DATE	Type	No.			
—	—	—	—	—	—	— TOTALS BROUGHT FORWARD
				ATTACHED	No.405 P.F.F. SQUADRON
May 19	Lancaster	"D"	SELF	F/O BAYNE	OPERATION - MOUNT COUPLE
				F/S DINGWALL	R.D.F. HUT
				SGT. WILLOUGHBY	18 x 500 G.P.
				W/O RUTHERGLEN	1400 GALS.
				SGT. HART	
				SGT. McWHIRTER	
May 21	LANC III	"D"	SELF	F/O BAYNE	OPERATION · DUISBERG
				F/S DINGWALL	
				SGT. WILLOUGHBY	14 x 8x30 INC.
				W/O RUTHERGLEN	1 x 4000 H.E. 1400 GALS.
				SGT. HART	A/C ON - 507
				SGT. McWHIRTER	A/C MISSING - 30
May 22	LANC. III	"D"	SELF	F/O BAYNE	OPERATION - DORTMUND
				F/S DINGWALL	
				SGT. WILLOUGHBY	6 x 2000 H.E. 1400 GALS.
				W/O RUTHERGLEN	A/C ON - 345
				SGT. HART	A/C MISSING - 27
				SGT. McWHIRTER	- ONE FLAK HOLE IN NOSE

GRAND TOTAL [Cols. (1) to (10)]
594 Hrs. 35 Mins.
TOTALS CARRIED FORWARD

As the small force approached the target, the *Oboe* signal guiding the target marking Mosquitoes failed (it seems it was a technical problem at one of the broadcasting towers, not jamming by the Germans). Since the "Mossies" couldn't mark the target with their brightly coloured Target Indicators, the raid continued with the Lancasters using an old-school timed run from the coastline, which they could see on their very new-school *H2S* ground mapping radar.

Unfortunately, the cathode ray tube *H2S* display was notoriously difficult to read, and it took a lot of practice to interpret it—three crews from Gransden Lodge were stumped. With the target markers missing, they simply couldn't find the Mount Couple installation, although some of them reported seeing explosions in the distance. Following the instructions given at the pre-operation briefing, the Stronach, Smith, and

Coffey crews headed out to sea and jettisoned part of their bomb loads into the ocean[16] before heading back to their base.

Not an auspicious start to their careers as Pathfinders perhaps, but luckily the rest of the force they had been part of were more successful, and the Mount Couple facility, with its ninety transmitting arrays, was destroyed. French police reported the raid had inadvertently killed one local civilian, seventeen horses, and twenty-two cows as well.

A trio of ops deep into Germany was to follow this quick trip to France for the Coffey crew. The three operations were to be the last "Bomber" Harris could stage against Germany proper before he was ordered to divert his forces almost exclusively to pre-invasion targets in France.

The first of these three ops was on May 21st, against the German industrial city of Duisberg, a target they would revisit later in their tour. Like its next-door neighbour Essen, Duisberg was filled with factories and railway yards, and was also home to a huge inland port on the banks of the Rhine river.

This would be our crew's first trip to Germany in their new Lancaster and their first time delivering one of the famous 4,000-pound "cookie" bombs. The cookie was a somewhat crude but deadly effective weapon, which looked almost like two oil drums welded end to end—but much bigger. It had a thin metal skin to maximize the amount of high explosive that could be stuffed into the casing—it was also known as the "blockbuster," as its blast could apparently level a city block. It had to be dropped from at least 6,000 feet, lest the explosion destroy the aircraft dropping it. They were dropped in the thousands during the bomber campaign, and as late as 2017, unexploded cookies were being found during construction work in the Ruhr, each time necessitating the evacuation of tens of thousands of people while bomb disposal experts disarmed them.

The standard load of high explosive and Small Bomb Containers that their Lancaster carried this night was referred to by air and ground crew alike as "cookies and cans."

One of the many tactical innovations that the Pathfinder Force implemented during the Bomber Campaign was assigning "roles" to all their crews, based on their skill sets. New crews would start as Supporters, carrying standard high explosive bombs only, no target indicators or marker flares. Their job was simply to "support" their Pathfinder comrades who were marking the target by helping take the heat off them, drawing fire from the defences and keeping heads down by causing chaos with their bomb loads. As crews gained experience and skill, they would be given increasingly more demanding responsibilities in marking the target, either "visually" (if they could see the aiming point) or "blind" (if cloud covered the target).

Dad and crew were part of a force of 532 aircraft that night and were designated as "Supporters" during this raid, as they would be for the next dozen or so operations. They carried a load of one 4,000-pound cookie and over a hundred thirty-pound incendiaries. Twenty-two *Oboe*-guided Pathfinder Mosquitoes were the first arrivals over the cloud-covered city. They marked the aiming point with *Wanganui* flares, which had to be replaced repeatedly as they drifted away on their parachutes. The Coffey crewed bombed at 1:10 a.m. on a "triangle" of red *Wanganui* flares, and by this time, the glow of the white phosphorous target indicators was reported to be visible even through the thick cloud.

The operation was judged a success, and all five Lancasters from 405 Squadron returned safely to Gransden Lodge—twenty-nine other Bomber Command crews were not so lucky, most falling victim to night fighter attacks. Dad and crew landed back at Gransden at about 2:30 in the morning, but their "day" wasn't over yet. After taxiing their Lancaster to its designated pad and handing it off to their waiting ground crew, they then had to turn in their flying gear. Then came a lengthy debriefing with

---

16   To lighten their weight for a safer landing.

the squadron's intelligence officer, who would want to know everything about the raid from their perspective. Finally, they could eat a hasty breakfast before at last crawling into their cots for a few hours of exhausted sleep before it was time to rise at noon on May 22nd to begin the process of pre-operation briefings and preparations again.

Perhaps just sixteen hours after collapsing into sleep in their Nissen hut that morning after returning from Duisberg, they were taking off again, headed to another German industrial city in the Ruhr, this time Dortmund.

Dortmund was overdue to be hit, as it had been a year since it had last endured a major Bomber Command attack.

Bomber Command sent a total force of 361 Lancasters and sixteen Mosquitoes to Dortmund that night, and crews reported clear skies over the city, making for easy and accurate target marking by the Pathfinder Mosquitoes. A little before 1 a.m., Malcolm Dingwall called out "bombs gone!" over the intercom to his crew as the load of six 2,000-pound high explosive bombs fell away from their Lancaster's bomb bay.

We can see a notation in Dad's logbook, "one flak hole in nose," and the fact that it rated a special mention seems significant, as Bob McWhirter told me in 2016 that their plane often came home "peppered" with small flak shrapnel holes. This one must have been big, and since it likely occurred over Dortmund, I am wondering if Malcolm Dingwall might have had a close call that night, as he would have been lying prone in the nose of the Lancaster at the time, looking down at the burning city through his bombsight.

By 1944, Germany had turned anti-aircraft defence into a science. Millions of Germans were involved in producing, manning, and supplying the flak guns, searchlights, radar installations, and night fighters that protected the Reich.

One of the most effective tools in the German arsenal was the infamous "88," an 88 mm cannon that was arguably the finest piece of artillery used by any side in World War II—it could lob a twenty-pound shell up to 24,000 feet, and a battery of four guns could put up eighty shells a minute. As well as being used in an anti-aircraft role, it was also an outstanding anti-tank weapon. I think perhaps there are more than a few Allied tank crews who owe their lives to the fact that most of Germany's "88" production was pressed into service to defend against the RAF and USAAF, rather than sent to the Eastern Front or to Normandy.

May 24th was a training day, and the crew took part in an exercise, the details of which are a bit "disputed." According to some of the Coffey crew's logbooks, it was an "air-to-air firing" exercise, but at least one other notes that it was "fighter affiliation and air-to-sea firing." Perhaps it was all three...?

YEAR 1944		AIRCRAFT		PILOT, OR 1ST PILOT	2ND PILOT, PUPIL OR PASSENGER	DUTY (INCLUDING RESULTS AND REMARKS)
MONTH	DATE	Type	No.			
—	—	—	—	—	—	— TOTALS BROUGHT FORWARD
MAY	24	LANC. III	"D"	SELF	CREW	AIR TO AIR FIRING
MAY	25	LANC. III	"H"	SELF	F/O BAYNE	OPERATION - AACHEN
					SGT. WILLOUGHBY	
					F/S DINGWALL	1 X 4000 H.E.
					W/O RUTHERGLEN	16 X 500 G.P. 1400 GALS
					SGT. HART	A/C ON - 200
					SGT. McWHIRTER	A/C MISSING -
MAY	26	LANC. III	"M"	SELF	CREW	CROSS COUNTRY - "Y" RUNS
MAY	26	LANC. III	"D"	SELF	CREW	CROSS COUNTRY, "Y" RUNS, S.B.A.
MAY	27	LANC. III	"V"	SELF	F/O BAYNE	OPERATION - RENNES A/F.
					SGT. WILLOUGHBY	18 X 500 H.E. 1400 GALS.
					F/S. DINGWALL	HT. - 12,000'
					P/O RUTHERGLEN	
					SGT. HART	
					P/O McWHIRTER	
MAY	28	LANC. III	"V"	SELF	F/O BAYNE	OPERATION - COASTAL GUN
					SGT. WILLOUGHBY	BATTERY - NEAR DUNKIRK
					F/S DINGWALL	
					P/O RUTHERGLEN	18 X 500 H.E. 1160 GALS.
					SGT. HART	HT. 12,000'
					P/O McWHIRTER	
		GRAND TOTAL [Cols. (1) to (10)]				
		608 Hrs. 50 Mins.				TOTALS CARRIED FORWARD

The next night, May 25th, the crew took off just after midnight and, along with six other crews from Gransden Lodge, joined a total force of about 450 headed to Aachen, a vital railway hub on the German-Belgian border. The two marshalling yards in the city would be critical to the Germans for the movement of troops and supplies, so Bomber Command was ordered to destroy them as part of the Transportation Plan that was preparing the way for D-Day.

The size of the force sent to Aachen that night was larger than was usually sent against a railway target—I think it is safe to assume that Bomber Command was less concerned about "collateral damage" because it was in Germany rather than in France.

The Coffey crew were again given the role of Supporters this night, carrying a 14,000-pound load of high explosives, and were assigned to the western of the two aiming points in Aachen. This night over Aachen marks Jimmy Willoughby's first time as the crew's designated bomb aimer. As they approached the target, Malcolm Dingwall would be working the *H2S* radar set, and Jimmy would take his spot, lying prone in the nose of the Lancaster. It was Jimmy who would guide my Dad to the aiming point and "press the tit" to send their bomb load cascading down onto the target markers 18,000 feet below.

The attack was deadly accurate and the railyards of Aachen were badly damaged. Another smaller raid two nights later finished the job. The broken remains of Aachen would become the scene of some bloody fighting five months later as American forces made it the first German city to be captured in World War II.

Up to this point in his logbook, my Dad had scrupulously noted the numbers of aircraft taking part in an operation, and the numbers missing. The trip to Aachen marks the last time he would do so, and even this time, it was only a partial effort, leaving blank the number of crews who failed to return.

Why the change, I wondered? He continued to carefully keep track of each of his crewman's names, bomb load, fuel on board and so on, but he never again made a note of how many crews went missing. I can only speculate about the reasons—had the tremendous losses become disheartening? Had he lost too many comrades? Was his confidence slipping in the face of the grim statistics? They had just completed their eighteenth operation and were well past the average survival time for a Bomber Command crew. Did he begin to wonder if recording the deaths of so many other aircrews night after night was perhaps bad luck for his own? And let us bear in mind: the cruel reality was that, as far as surviving two tours of operations in Bomber Command went, luck was pretty much all they had going for them.

The Pathfinder Force placed a major emphasis on regular training, no matter how experienced a crew was. I don't think the Coffey crew's two *H2S* training flights on May 26th were directly related to their failure to find the aiming point at Mount Couple the prior week; it was just part of the regimen.

The flights were referred to in their logbooks as "Y runs," code for training flights using the top-secret *H2S* ground mapping radar—the use of code words wasn't just for logbooks, as even in squadron documents, the *H2S* sets were cryptically referred to as "special equipment."

One flight that day took them north to King's Lynn, Norfolk, and then back to Gransden Lodge. After landing and assessing the success and accuracy of Bob Bayne and Malcolm Dingwall, they took off again and headed west to Northampton. On each run, the two navigators would use the fuzzy image of the *H2S* display to guide my Dad through the assigned route.

The airport at Rennes-Saint-Jacques, France is a busy (albeit small) international airport that has seen a lot of history since it was built in the 1930s. Seized by the Germans for use by the Luftwaffe after the fall of France in 1940, it became home to Messerschmitt and Junkers fighter-bombers. By 1944, it was a busy Luftwaffe base well-stocked with Germany's formidable Focke-Wulf FW190 fighters. These were a clear and present danger to the Allied forces who would be landing on the beaches of Normandy in a week's time.

Fifteen Lancs from 405 Squadron took off around midnight, May 27th, and headed for Normandy, part of a smallish force of about eighty-five in total. It wasn't the first (or last) time Rennes-Saint-Jacques was attacked, but airfields are notoriously easy to repair, as the Luftwaffe learned when they tried to ground the Spitfires and Hurricanes of the RAF by taking out their bases during the Battle of Britain.

The weather this night was clear, visibility good: many crews reported they could clearly see the runways and hangers in the light of the target marking flares and target indicators being put down by the Pathfinders.

The Coffey crew carried a load of eighteen 500-pound bombs and dropped them on the bright green target markers from a height of 12,000 feet. I wonder if the crew felt any special sense of satisfaction when Jimmy called out "bombs gone!" over the intercom, knowing their bombs were dropping on Luftwaffe fighters?

Official records of the raid indicate that the attack was very successful, reporting "much damage to the airfield installation and there was a large explosion, probably the bomb dump."

The next night, May 28th, they took off again during the busy lead up to D-Day, this time to attack a coastal gun emplacement at Fort Mardyck, near Pas-de-Calais, an area that the Germans became convinced would be the landing site of any invasion. Allied intelligence services worked hard to keep them labouring under this misconception. One of the myriad ruses they organized was the staging of Bomber Command attacks in the Calais area—the guns of Mardyck posed no threat to the actual invasion fleet, which would be heading to Normandy.

The artillery at Mardyck consisted of six 15.5-centimetre French cannons that the Germans had captured during the fall of France and had pressed into service as part of Hitler's Atlantic Wall.

The Pathfinders' aiming point was not far off the beach, and many Gransden Lodge crews reported seeing clusters of bombs exploding in the shallow water opposite the gun emplacements. However, many more did find their mark on the well-placed target indicators—there were reports of a "prolonged explosion" during the raid, which was likely the ammunition dump going up.

On May 30th, the crew took off at 10:40 in the morning on a fine spring day for what was supposed to be a routine fighter affiliation flight, but which unexpectedly ended up involving laundry and a "rocket"...!

As I mentioned before, the crew had left 420 Squadron in Tholthorpe in a rush: it appears they received little or no advance notice of their transfer to RAF Warboys. In their haste to leave, some of the crew had left behind clothing that was out for laundering, and on the sunny afternoon of May 30th, after playing "tag" with a Spitfire for a while, someone on Lancaster O for Oboe came up with the bright idea of flying to Tholthorpe to pick up the missing items.

YEAR 1944		AIRCRAFT		PILOT, OR 1ST PILOT	2ND PILOT, PUPIL OR PASSENGER	DUTY (INCLUDING RESULTS AND REMARKS)
MONTH	DATE	Type	No.			
—		—	—	—	—	— TOTALS BROUGHT FORWARD
MAY	30	LANC. III	"O"	SELF	CREW	CROSS COUNTRY - FIGHTER AFFIL.
						LANDED THOLTHORPE
MAY	30	LANC. III	"O"	SELF	CREW	THOLTHORPE - BASE
JUNE	11	LANC. III	"M"	SELF	F/O BAYNE	OPERATION - TOURS
					F/S DINGWALL	MARSHALLING YARD
					SGT WILLOUGHBY	18 X 500 G.P.
					SGT HART	1700 GALS
					P/O McWHIRTER	1200 FT.
					P/O RUTHERGLEN	
JUNE	13	LANC III	"U"	SELF	CREW	XCTY., 4 "Y" RUNS, 4 BOMBS
					P/O MILNE	
					P/O JOHNSTON	
JUNE	14	LANC III	"M"	SELF	CREW	XCTY, 8 "Y" RUNS 4 BOMBS
JUNE	14	LANC III	"M"	SELF	CREW	XCTY, 5 "Y" RUNS, 4 BOMBS
JUNE	15	LANC III	"M"	SELF	CREW	XCTY, 8 "Y" RUNS, 4 BOMBS
JUNE	15	LANC III	"M"	SELF	F/O BAYNE	OPERATION - LENS MARSH.Y
					F/S DINGWALL	18 X 500 G.P.
					SGT WILLOUGHBY	1700 GALS
					P/O RUTHERGLEN	7000 FT.
					SGT HART	
					P/O McWHIRTER	

GRAND TOTAL [Cols. (1) to (10)]

630 Hrs. 35 Mins.

I am no expert on RAF protocols, but I think it is safe to assume that the use of one of Bomber Command's precious and expensive Lancasters to run domestic errands would have been frowned upon by the "higher-ups." My Dad seems to have made two bad decisions that spring day over Yorkshire: the first was not quashing the idea as soon as it was brought up, as was his right as skipper (assuming it wasn't Dad himself who came up with it!). The second mistake is even more inexplicable—on approaching Tholthorpe, my normally level-headed father decided to have some fun by "beating up" the airfield, making several low passes to show off his spiffy new Lancaster to the poor slobs below who were still flying Halifaxes. I can picture the scene in my mind clearly: the Lancaster racing over RAF Tholthorpe, waggling its wings jauntily, all four Merlins roaring, and the Coffey crew inside laughing and joking.

The fun ended when they landed.

While one of the crew went to pick up the missing laundry, Dad was ordered to report to 420 Squadron's Commanding Officer. Upon arriving, he was given a dressing down (a "rocket" in RAF parlance), likely by Wing Commander G. McKenna, who undoubtedly made it crystal clear he didn't appreciate unscheduled visits and unnecessary low passes over his airfield by cocky young Pilot Officers from other squadrons. He may also have reminded my Dad that he was an officer and the skipper of his crew and should be setting a better example. Furthermore, using one of His Majesty's Avro Lancasters to attend to a personal errand was a waste of precious aviation fuel. Oh, to have been a fly on the wall!

Shortly thereafter, Lancaster O for Oboe lifted off the tarmac at Tholtherope and made the fifty-minute flight back to Gransden Lodge, my Dad at the controls feeling somewhat chastened, no doubt, but at least in possession of clean laundry.

June 6th 1944 is a date that quite rightly has gone down in history—D-Day and the beginning of the liberation of Nazi-occupied Europe.

Surely the Coffey crew would have been busy on the big day....? Actually, no—they were on leave in London for ten days. At first, the fact they had been granted leave seemed inexplicable; I couldn't fathom why Bomber Command would not insist on "all hands on deck" at such a critical time. However, after researching the various deceptions and ruses that the Allies had put in place to try to fool the Germans about the time and place of Operation Overlord, things made more sense. What tongues would have been set wagging had the regular leave granted all Bomber Command crews had suddenly been cancelled?

So it was that our crew learned about the action around D-Day in the same manner as everyone else in London, via the BBC, newspapers, and newsreels. Sometime during their ten-day stay in London, the crew went to the cinema together. Bob McWhirter recalled that, in an amazing coincidence, the newsreel showing in the theatre that evening included a closeup of Lancaster M for Mother at Gransden Lodge, preparing for an operation on D-Day (attacking a vital crossroads in Normandy, as it happens). This particular Lanc was one they had flown in only once, but were soon to become very familiar with.

Upon return to Gransden Lodge from their leave, my Dad reported to the base hospital, complaining of "night sweats and loss of weight." He was examined and given a routine X-ray to rule out tuberculosis. In the end, all the tests came back negative, and he was given no treatment—perhaps a kindly Medical Officer suggested the symptoms were not unusual considering the tremendous stress he was under and recommended exercise or other distractions.

It was good advice, and there was certainly no shortage of sports to take part in—the squadron records show that activities as diverse as baseball and boxing were organized and encouraged. And let's not forget basketball! Bob Bayne, the crew's "standout basketball operative" (in the words of a sports columnist for the Ottawa Citizen), continued to organize games, and at some point arranged for a group USAAF airmen from a nearby B-17 base to visit Gransden Lodge.

"Individually, they appeared no better than we did," recalled Bayne, "It was the manner in which they played together, their teamwork, which beat us. There was a fellow with the Yanks who must have been six-foot-six and how that fellow could rap 'em in!"

On the evening of June 11th, the Coffey crew took off in Lancaster M for Mother (the same aircraft they had seen on the big screen just a few days previously), which was now assigned as their "personal" aircraft, and was proudly bearing their signature "Maisye" nose art.

When the Coffey crew were first assigned M for Mother as "their" aircraft, they all noticed that the ground crew team that came with the Lancaster were decidedly standoffish with them. It took a few ops for them to understand the reason for the initial cold shoulder. It seems M for Mother had a reputation as an "unlucky" airplane, one whose crews often didn't come back. The ground crew were trying not to get attached to a new crew that might not be around long.

An unknown airman gives a "thumbs up" from the cockpit of Maisye.
Photographer unknown, photo courtesy of the Rutherglen family.

Bomber Command's target on the night of June 11th was the marshalling yards in Tours, a vital transportation hub for the Wehrmacht, who were desperately rushing troops and equipment to the Normandy area.

Maisye was one of fifteen Lancasters from 405 Squadron, part of a total force of 320+ that Bomber Command had dispatched against four separate railway targets in France.

The stereotypical Bomber Command attack was made from 10,000 feet or above, and this is what most of us picture when we think of a bombing raid—hundreds of bombers, miles above an enemy city. But the young men of Bomber Command repeatedly proved that they were capable of low-level bombing runs when the situation required it, and this night over Tours was one of those times.

When the attackers arrived over Tours and attempted their bomb run, they found the target covered in a thick blanket of solid 10/10ths cloud. There was a Master Bomber assigned to the raid, and he told the force to descend below the cloud cover, which brought them down to a height of just 1500 feet.

They made another run, but the yards were still obscured and a third run was ordered, this time at only 1200 feet. This whole time the attackers were being shot at by light flak and machine guns from the ground defences—in wireless operator Ted Rutherglen's logbook, he notes that they got "a very hot reception, flak came up like rain. No damage, but unbelievable." This third bombing run was successful—the Master Bomber instructed the attackers to aim for the yellow target indicators now visible on the railway tracks. The Coffey crew reported they could see trains as they released their 9,000 pounds of high explosives. Their post-raid report states that they could see "many craters and the end of one train blown away. Good attack." Ted Rutherglen summed up the raid in his logbook with the RAF slang term "Good Prang."

On June 16th, the Coffey crew flew an operation to France that was, whether they knew it or not, part of the opening blow of a campaign dubbed Operation Crossbow, the battle to defeat Hitler's V-1 flying bombs and V-2 rockets, what he called his "Vengeance" weapons.

The V-1 was a somewhat crude weapon—basically, a 2,000-pound bomb kitted out with stubby wings and a pulse jet engine, a form of propulsion that gave the weapon its distinctive rapid "putt-putt" sound. It flew across the English Channel at about 3,000 feet and then dived to earth when an internal mileage counter cut off the fuel supply to its engine. It only had a range of about 150 miles, so the launching sites were all on the coast of France, concentrated in the Pas-de-Calais area.

Crude, perhaps, but it could fly in any weather at speeds a bit faster than any fighter could manage, and it needed no pilot. The second of these Vengeance weapons was the V-2, and it was a true rocket, capable of supersonic speeds and equipped with a proper guidance system. There was no possible defence against the V-2 other than trying to destroy its launch sites.

Three days previously, on the 13th, the first of the V-1 flying bombs had hit England, and the threat of a full-scale assault by these fearsome weapons had Allied leaders on the verge of panic.

The Allies knew that Hitler planned to build launching facilities for both weapons that would allow his forces to launch up to 6,000 each *day* against England. This would be the equivalent of a major Bomber Command attack every day—attacks that could not be defended against, and that would proceed regardless of the weather.

The "robot bomb" is really an aerial torpedo. The engine (*upper right*) works merely by exploding with a spark a mixture of gasoline and air, the jet issuing out at the rear. Rudder is set before launching for direction and drift and is controlled by a cheap gyro. Mass-produced, it might cost $1,000, a little more than its explosive equivalent of a one-ton bomb.

"ROBOT BOMB"
It is ineffective now but may be the way the next war will begin

"That thing," called variously the "robot bomb," "doodlebug," "buzzbomb," "whizbang" and "Hitler's secret weapon," is examined on these pages. It was first heard in England coming out of the night, June 15, "like a giant washing machine," a pinpoint of light growing into a trail of fire, moving at 350 mph. When its engine stopped, it dove and exploded on contact with the ground. It seemed to the English threatening at first, then ghostly, then a damned nuisance. It was totally inaccurate and it came over from France in small numbers. Once again the Germans had used their weapon too little and too soon.

The aerial torpedo, as it is in fact, can however be enormously improved by modern science. Manufactured secretly, it could be launched in peacetime on a dark and rainy night so that a sleeping capital would be hit with 100,000 tons of explosive in a night.

The V-1 flying bomb depicted in a wartime Picture Post article.
Original from author's collection.

Allied commanders had become aware of the Vengeance weapons early in the war, since a high flying Mosquito photo-reconnaissance plane had brought back photos of strange goings-on at an obscure research facility in Peenemünde, on Germany's Baltic coast. Between the pictures, other gathered intelligence, and Nazi officials themselves bragging about the new "secret" weapons about to be unleashed, the Allies knew a great deal about the threat. A large Bomber Command attack was organized—it was the first precision night attack the force had attempted in the war, and required weeks of special training for the crews involved. The operation took place on August 17, 1943—at the time, Dad was going through his training at the Advanced Flying Unit in Shropshire.

The operation badly damaged the facility and killed a number of important scientists, but in the end, it only delayed the deployment of the V-1s and V-2s. However, this months-long delay may well have been crucial, as it meant the new weapons were not ready to be launched during the time the Allies were building up their invasion forces in the channel ports of England in the spring of 1944. It doesn't take a flight of fancy to imagine the effect thousands of flying bombs and rockets could have had on the densely-packed D-Day staging areas—the Peenemünde raid may well have changed the course of the war.

So it was that in mid-June, Operation Crossbow was begun. A frustrated "Bomber" Harris was directed to divert much of his power against the flying bomb and rocket sites—once again, he felt it was a mistake to give the Germans any reprieve from pounding their industrial base in the Ruhr and elsewhere.

The Crossbow sites themselves were, in Harris' words, "extremely unrewarding targets"—the V-2 bunkers were yards thick with reinforced concrete, impervious to standard high explosive bombs. The V-1 "ski" sites (named for their shape when seen from the air) were small, well hidden in orchards and forests, and easily repaired.

Despite the difficulties, the "bomber boys" managed to drop about 120,000 pounds of high explosives on the dozens of sites from June to September; some they destroyed outright, many others required repeat visits. By chipping away at them repeatedly, they accomplished what we might call today a "denial of service"—damaging them, interrupting launch schedules, slowing repair work, and making access to the sites difficult, if not impossible. Indeed, Harris notes almost gleefully in his book that "…by ploughing up the ground all round them with moderate-sized bombs… even a goat would have found it difficult to get to the site, and trucks and railroads never had a hope."

In the end, the V-1 and V-2 programs were a pale shadow of what Hitler had envisioned. To paraphrase Harris, Hitler created the most powerful weapon of the future, but had failed to protect it from the most powerful weapon of the present, the heavy bomber. On the home front, effective defences were hurriedly developed (at least against the V-1), including a belt of anti-aircraft batteries and barrage balloons along the south coast and specially-modified RAF fighters that could keep up with the V-1s just long enough to blow them up before they reached their intended targets.

Even so, the damage and death inflicted on the British was immense, with over 2400 V-1s hitting England causing thousands of deaths. The V-2 caused similar havoc when it finally came into service in September 1944. One can only imagine the devastation that would have occurred had the numbers of V weapons launched been in the order of sixty times more, as Hitler had planned.

Well over a hundred Allied bombers were lost and hundreds of aircrew killed taking part in Operation Crossbow.

Our crew even had close encounters of the personal kind with the "doodlebugs" or "buzz bombs," as they were popularly dubbed. Dad told me that while the crew were on leave at some point during the summer of '44, he was literally blown out of his hotel bed and onto the floor by the force of a V-1 blast in London.

Bob McWhirter had a second close call that same summer when he was cycling home to Gransden Lodge at night, returning from a visit with a family in Potten, which was about six miles from the airfield. He was on a dark, lonely country lane when he heard the unique staccato buzzing sound of the V-1 pulse jet engine approaching.

"It came closer, casting an eerie glow in the overcast sky," he recalled, and then the engine cut out overhead, signalling that it would shortly be crashing to earth and exploding. Bob dived off his bike and into the ditch on the side of the lane and waited tensely for the detonation of the V-1's 2,000-pound warhead—luckily, when it did come, it was far enough away that he was unharmed.

It was against this threat that, on June 16th, Maisye lifted off the tarmac at Gransden Lodge carrying a bellyful of 500-pound bombs, and joined a force of 450 aircraft attacking four different flying bomb launch and storage sites.

YEAR 1944		AIRCRAFT		PILOT, OR 1ST PILOT	2ND PILOT, PUPIL OR PASSENGER	DUTY (INCLUDING RESULTS AND REMARKS)
MONTH	DATE	Type	No.			
—	—	—	—	—	—	— TOTALS BROUGHT FORWARD
JUNE	16	LANC. III	"M"	SELF	F/O BAYNE	OPERATION - NOBALL
					F/S DINGWALL	P-PLANE FACTORY
					S/ WILLOUGHBY	18 X 500 G.P.
					P/O RUTHERGLEN	1700 GALS
					S/ HART	H.T. - 11 000'
					P/O McWHIRTER	
JUNE	18	LANC. III	"X"	SELF	CREW	XCTY, 8 "Y" RUNS, 4 BOMBS
JUNE	19	LANC. III	"M"	SELF	CREW	XCTY, 8 "Y" RUNS, 4 BOMBS
JUNE	20	LANC. III	"M"	SELF	CREW	XCTY 8 "Y" RUNS, 4 BOMBS, F/A.
JUNE	21	OXFORD	"S"	F/LT. GARDINER	SELF	OVAL, ORBIT & S.B.A.
JUNE	22	LANC. III	"M"	SELF	CREW AK HANSEN	XCTY, 8 "Y" RUNS, 4 BOMBS, F/A, SBA
JUNE	23	LANC. III	"M"	SELF	F/O BAYNE	OPERATION - ST. OMER AREA
					F/S/. DINGWALL	P-PLANE FACTORY
					S/. WILLOUGHBY	12 X 1000 HE
					P/O RUTHERGLEN	2 X 500 G.P.
					P/O McWHIRTER	1150 GALS.
					S/. HART	11000 ft.
JUNE	24	LANC. III	"M"	SELF	F/O BAYNE	OPERATION - ST. OMER AREA
					F/S DINGWALL	P-PLANE FACTORY
					SGT. WILLOUGHBY ST. HART	18 X 500 G.P.
					P/O RUTHERGLEN	1500 GALS
					P/O McWHIRTER	13000 FT.

GRAND TOTAL [Cols. (1) to (10)]
645 Hrs. 40 Mins.

TOTALS CARRIED FORWARD

When I first started looking at the June 16th entry in Dad's logbook ("Operation Noball"), I was mystified, as a quick Google search revealed no location in France with such an odd name. A little further digging clarified things a bit; Bomber Command's overall campaign against the V weapons was dubbed Operation Crossbow, but the individual targets were coded "*Noball*" sites. Where the term *Noball* comes from is still a mystery—some have speculated that it was because the pulse jet/rocket engines of the V weapons had no ball bearings, but this seems a stretch to me. My personal pet theory is that the code name was inspired by a ribald song popular at the time, sung to the tune of the Col. Bogey March:

Hitler has only got one ball,

Goering has two, but they're too small,

Himmler gives something similar,

And poor old Goebbels has NO BALLS at all!

A few minutes before midnight, the attacking force made its bombing run on the V-1 facility, which was camouflaged in pastures around Renescure, a tiny village outside St. Omer. The facility is listed as a "P-Plane factory" (P-Plane stood for "pilotless plane," another wartime slang for the flying bomb) in Dad's logbook, but the installation at Renescure was a storage/staging facility, not a "factory." It consisted of dozens of pre-fab concrete buildings and had space to store about 160 V-1 flying bombs. It was equipped with a railway spur to the main line to facilitate their delivery and then dispersal to launching sites.

The target was obscured by cloud this night, but the Pathfinders had placed bright red target indicators on the aiming point, and their glow was visible through the cloud—the bombing was reported to be accurate and effective.

After the war, the remnants of the solidly constructed concrete buildings at Renescure were pressed into the service of local farmers, and many are still in use today as garages and cowsheds.

For the next five days, the crew took part in intensive navigation training. Air Vice-Marshall Don Bennett, head of the Pathfinder Force, was passionate about a maintaining a high standard of training for his Force, especially in the area of navigation, a skill that he was personally an expert at—indeed, one of the world's foremost.

Although his crews came to him already rated as among the most highly skilled in Bomber Command, he wouldn't let them rest on their laurels—the maintenance and the refining of skills would be constant.

No surprise then that on June 18th, 19th, 20th, and 22nd, the Coffey crew took part each day in multiple "Y runs", lasting from an hour and half to almost three hours each. Each involved flying to predetermined "targets" in England and dropping "bombs," based entirely on direction from navigator Bob Bayne and second navigator Malcolm Dingwall, who would operate the *H2S* set in their curtained off cubicle. The exercises were focused on navigation, but my Dad and air gunners Ken Hart and Bob McWhirter would get a workout as well, as on two of the days, mock attacks were staged by determined but friendly RAF fighters. Bob recalled that my Dad "got very proficient at throwing that big aircraft all over the sky." I am sure Bob Bayne and Malcolm Dingwall got very proficient as well... at hanging on to their maps and navigation tools!

On the fourth day, most of the crew got a break, but Dad had a training flight in his old friend the Airspeed Oxford—for about an hour, he practiced Standard Beam Approach landings with a Flt. Lt. Gardiner, who may have been an RAF instructor from a Beam Approach Training (B.A.T.) flight, at Gransden to give pilots some follow up training. If he ever needed to land in dense fog, Dad's skill in the S.B.A. technique could well save his life and those of his crew.

On the last day, June 22nd, there were more Y runs, mock bombing, fighter affiliation, and S.B.A., and this time the crew had a passenger, Aircraftman Hansen. His presence during the flight is a bit of a mystery: perhaps he was a new member of ground crew, being taken along for the experience? I'm sure the bond of trust and respect between airmen and the ground crew who kept them flying would only be strengthened by doing this. It was a fine English summer day, and I am sure A/C Hansen got some wonderful views of the English countryside from 10,000 feet.

Over the course of the next four nights, the crew made three more trips to France, all against the V-1 "ski" launching sites. The first was near St. Omer (Coubronne), the next only a few kilometres away at Middel-Straete and the last near Abbeville at Oisement/Neuville-au-Bois. All were reported to be bombed accurately, but the last site would require a return visit after repair work was completed by the Germans.

| YEAR 1944 | | AIRCRAFT | | PILOT, OR | 2ND PILOT, PUPIL | DUTY |
MONTH	DATE	Type	No.	1ST PILOT	OR PASSENGER	(INCLUDING RESULTS AND REMARKS)
						TOTALS BROUGHT FORWARD
JUNE	27	LANC. III	"M"	SELF	F/O BAYNE	OPERATION - ABBEVILLE AREA
					F/S DINGWALL	P PLANE BASE
					Sgt. WILLOUGHBY	18 X 500 G.P.
					P/O RUTHERGLEN	1700 GALS
					Sgt. HART	11000 P.T.
					P/O McWHIRTER	
JUNE	28	LANC. III	"M"	SELF	F/O BAYNE	OPERATION - METZ MAR. YD
					F/S DINGWALL	7 X 1000 H.E.
					Sgt. WILLOUGHBY	6 BDLS FLARES (4X85)
					P/O RUTHERGLEN	1600 GALS
					Sgt. HART	12000 P.T.
					P/O McWHIRTER	
JUNE	30	LANC. III	"Y"	SELF	CREW	X-CTY, 5 "Y" RUNS
JUNE	30	LANC. III	"M"	SELF	F/O BAYNE	OPERATION - VILLERS-BOCAGE
					F/S DINGWALL	18 X 500 GP. 2ND FRONT
					Sgt. WILLOUGHBY	1150 GALS
					P/O RUTHERGLEN	10000 P.T.
					Sgt. HART	
					P/O McWHIRTER	
SUMMARY FOR: 405 SQDN				1. LANCASTER III		JUNE TOTALS.
DATE - June 30/44		TYPES		2. OXFORD		
SIGNATURE - J.R. Coffey P/O				3.		
				4.		S/LDR OA "B" FLT.
GRAND TOTAL [Cols. (1) to (10)] 652 Hrs. 10 Mins.						TOTALS CARRIED FORWARD

On the night of June 28th, the crew took off on their 29th operation, this time against a railway marshalling yard in Metz, France, near the border with Germany. For the first time the Coffey crew were designated Illuminators, a step up from the role of Supporters. As well as their load of seven 1,000-pound bombs, they also had six bundles of hooded flares, in case they were called on by the Master Bomber to illuminate the area to facilitate target marking. At the start of the attack, the force was called off by the Master Bomber and told to do a "dummy run," as he felt the aiming point was not marked or lit up well enough for accurate bombing. The Master Bomber (or Master of Ceremonies as he was sometimes called) this night was also from Gransden Lodge. Flt. Lt. L. L. MacKinnon was an Alberta boy like my Dad, and a seasoned veteran with an unusual background, having spent five years in the Royal Canadian Artillery before transferring to the RCAF in 1941.

The second run was successful, as the target was reported as "well lit up" by this time. The Coffey crew's services as Illuminators was not required this time, and after they dropped their high explosive load on the tracks and trains below, they, like several other crews, returned to England with their flares still in their cans.

The operation was a success—after the Pathfinders had finished marking, illuminating, and beginning the destructive process, the main force of one hundred Halifaxes arrived and dropped a further three hundred tons of bombs on the Metz railyards.

The June 30th attack on the crossroads near the tiny French village of Villers-Bocage was precisely the type of operation Bomber Command *didn't* want to do: a tactical target requiring pinpoint accuracy, with friendly troops dug in near the aiming point. Many felt that the bomber boys were neither trained nor equipped to carry out this type of mission. Even "Bomber" Harris himself had grave reservations—the possibility of even a single stray load of bombs slamming into Allied positions was very real. However, necessity required that chances be taken—the Allied armies were stalled in Normandy in the face of fanatical resistance by the German defenders, who were taking every advantage of the perfect cover offered by the thick hedgerows that lined every field and lane in that part of France.

Hitler had ordered that every foot of French soil be defended to the death, and as a result, the British and Canadian armies' advance from the beachheads was bogging down. Their commanders were dreading the prospect of another World War I-style war of trenches and attrition, with its consequent bloodbath.

Elements of two SS Panzer divisions and their supplies were positioned near Villers-Bocage, and Allied intelligence warned that more were on the way, preparing for an assault on the British and Canadian troops nearby, using the vital crossroads near the village. Bomber Command was tasked with destroying the Panzers and the crossroads. The attack was organized in great haste—the Coffey crew were on a training flight that day, doing *H2S* "Y" runs, something they would not likely have been doing had they known that they were "on" that evening. When they landed, Maisye was hastily refueled and bombed up, and the crew were equally hastily briefed on the operation.

The timing was critical, so the route to the target was pretty much a straight line—no doglegs or feints to throw off the German night fighter controllers on this trip, as HQ wanted the target smashed before darkness fell. The Coffey crew were not to be trusted yet with the critical job of marking the aiming point, especially one like this where the stakes were so high. They would be bombing with the initial Pathfinder Force, but carrying a simple load of high explosives.

Takeoff time was about 6:30 p.m., with the time on target being 8 p.m., and for the first time, there is green ink in my Dad's logbook, denoting a daylight raid. This must have been quite an experience for our crew, who would for the first time be able to see their fellow Lancasters and get a real sense of the power and size of the force they were part of. The other new (and likely *very* pleasant) sensation was to know that for the first time ever, they had an escort—dozens of Spitfires were flying thousands of feet above the Lancasters—ready to pounce on any German fighters that attempted to molest them. Two hundred and fifty-six heavies took part in the raid, and 1100 tons of bombs dropped.

Original wartime press photo of the attack on Villers-Bocage.
Note the "stick" of bombs falling away at the top of the photo. Author's collection.

What an exhilarating and heartening sight it must have been for the Canadian and British troops dug in nearby! Hundreds of Lancasters on their bomb runs, unflinching in the face of the light and heavy flak bursting around them—I can picture the cheers from the soldiers as they watched the 500-pound bombs cascading down on their nemeses, the SS Panzer divisions. After the initial Pathfinder Force opened the attack, the Master Bomber ordered the remainder of the force to descend to 4,000 feet due to the smoke and dust obscuring the aiming point.

Dad's post raid report stated that the crew saw a massive explosion twenty-five seconds after Jimmy Willoughby had loosed their 9,000-pound load of high explosives. Another Gransden Lodge crew, skippered by Flying Officer Townsend, saw the same explosion, describing it as "a sheet of dull red flame lasting five or six seconds, turning smoke brown and then black." Perhaps one of the Coffey crew's bombs had found a Panzer ammunition dump?

Reports from the Army stated that a cloud of fine dust had enveloped the area for hours after the raid, and many of the Panzers and the crossroads were effectively destroyed.

Things went well for Bomber Command on this raid in support of the Army, but only a matter of weeks later, on August 14th, over a dozen Canadian soldiers near Caen were killed by Pathfinder bombs when the soldiers set off yellow smoke canisters to mark their positions. The smoke was mistaken for target markers by some of the Pathfinder crews. It was a tragic comedy of errors, but "Bomber" Harris accepted responsibility for it. He disciplined several Pathfinder crews for not following the orders given at the pre-raid briefing. I am relieved to report our crew was not involved in this sad debacle.

The Villers-Bocage operation was my Dad's 30th "op"—had he remained at 420 Squadron, he would now be "screened," having finished a tour. He would likely have been sent to an Operational Training Unit to serve as an instructor for a year before being called upon to return to a front line squadron and complete a second tour with a new crew.

For better or worse, the Coffey crew had decided to stick together—to roll the dice and try and complete both of their tours in one go with the Pathfinders. They were now a close-knit "Band of Brothers." Indeed, ahem, one might even go so far as to say they were "thick as thieves"...

Sometime in the summer of 1944, an unknown Cambridgeshire farmer lost part of his crop to a band of nefarious RCAF bandits.

The Great Corn Robbery is a story I am lucky enough to have heard from both my Dad and from Bob McWhirter, albeit on different occasions some thirty years apart.

Like most aircrews, the Coffey crew stuck together for the most part, even when they weren't flying. And as at every other Bomber Command station in the U.K., there was no shortage of bicycles at Gransden Lodge, so exploring the Cambridgeshire countryside by bicycle was a regular pastime on their non-flying days.

On one such ride, likely on a sunny summer day, they passed a lush field of corn. To a native of the British Isles, the sight would not likely have inspired much in the way of hunger pangs, but to the Canadian boys, what immediately came to mind was a traditional Canadian treat, hot corn on the cob smothered in salty melted butter.

One can only speculate what Jamaica native Jimmy Willoughby made of their excitement—he must have been mystified, but perhaps got caught up in their enthusiasm.

At any rate, a plan was hatched. The boys decided that it was too risky to take the corn in broad daylight (too risky...! let's bear in mind what these young men did for a living!), so the conspirators returned to the field at night, armed with gunnysacks and flashlights borrowed from their ground crew.

"We couldn't wait to treat all the guys in the billet to a huge feed of delicious corn on the cob, something we hadn't tasted over there," according to Bob McWhirter. The bandits made off with their loot and returned to Gransden Lodge, where they proceeded to put the cobs into a pot of boiling water.

Alas, sweet corn was apparently an unknown quantity in the England of 1944, and the corn they had pilfered (a variety known as "dent" or "field" corn) "tasted awful, fit only for animals." In fact, that is exactly who the corn was intended for—the boys had risked all for what amounted to cow fodder.

Disappointing as their ill-gotten gains were, I am sure the harmless adventure was a welcome distraction from the crushing stress and cold sweat of their combat operations. Another welcome distraction was no doubt letters and parcels from loved ones at home—they must have meant a very great deal to all those serving overseas.

I know one of the very first "war stories" my Dad ever told me was about these precious parcels. He recalled that my Mom, some 4,000 miles away in Alberta with baby Gary, would send him packages filled with small gifts, ranging from hand knit socks to chocolate bars, gum, and Canadian cigarettes. What made my Dad chuckle every time he told the story was that each of these small items was individually gift wrapped, complete with ribbon. I can easily picture my Dad's delight in receiving such a package in the circumstances he was in—it must have made his week.

Two of the photos I received from the Rutherglen family in 2016 show my Dad reading what looks like a card from home, decorated with what I think is my brother Gary's baby handprint. The photos were clearly taken moments apart, and the faraway look in my Dad's eyes is evocative of a young father and husband far from home, longing to be back where he belonged: with his family.

Both photos courtesy of the Rutherglen family.

Jimmy Willoughby was also the recipient of packages from his parents back in Jamaica—his sometimes consisted of a stale, hollowed-out loaf of bread, inside which a bottle of island rum would be carefully ensconced!

July of 1944 was one of, if not *the* busiest month in the history of Bomber Command.

Allied forces had a firm grip on their beachheads and a good sized chunk of the territory around them, but the progress was stalled, and the final outcome was in no way decided. The young airmen of Bomber Command were called upon to assist their comrades on the ground (as well as continue to try and stop the V weapon attacks); the Coffey crew and thousands of other crews were to fly operations into France on an almost daily basis during July of 1944.

We can see the month's hectic pace is clearly reflected in Dad's logbook; for the first time, his usually meticulously-kept records look rushed, scribbled even. No more careful notations of each crew member on board and of the bomb and fuel load, just a hastily jotted line consisting of the date and, surprisingly, an often vague target ("Paris area," for example).

Their first operation in July was on the 2nd—it was a return trip to the V-1 launch site at Oisement, which had been repaired since their last visit on June 16th. They arrived over the site at 2:03 p.m. that day and bombed using *H2S*, still referred to in the squadron records as "special equipment." Fourteen crews from Gransden Lodge took part in the attack (one of three that Bomber Command made that day against V-1 sites in France), and one reported damage from "predicted flak."

YEAR 1944		AIRCRAFT		PILOT, OR 1ST PILOT	2ND PILOT, PUPIL OR PASSENGER	DUTY (INCLUDING RESULTS AND REMARKS)
MONTH	DATE	Type	No.			
—	—	—	—	—	—	TOTALS BROUGHT FORWARD
July	2	LANC III	"M"	SELF	P/O BAYNE	OPERATION - OUISEMONT
					P/S DINGWALL	PPLANE
					F/ WILLOUGHBY	11X1000
					P/O RUTHERGLEN	4 X 500
					SGT HART	1100 GALS
					P/O McWHIRTER	11000
JULY	4	LANC III	"M"	SELF	CREW	F/A , 4 BOMBS
JULY	5	LANC III	"M"	SELF	P/O BAYNE	OPERATION - WATTON
					P/S DINGWALL	P/PLANE
					F/ WILLOUGHBY	11 X 1000 H.E. Fighter attack
					P/O RUTHERGLEN	4X500 G.P. FLAK HITS
					SGT HART	1100 GALS 142 holes
					P/O McWHIRTER	12000 PT.
JULY	6	LANC III	"M"	SELF	CREW	OPERATION - ABBEVILLE
JULY	7	LANC III	"M"	SELF	CREW	OPERATION - CAEN
JULY	9	LANC III	"M"	SELF	CREW	OPERATION - DUNKIRK area
JULY	10	LANC III	"M"	SELF	CREW	OPERATION - PARIS area
JULY	11	LANC III	"M"	SELF	CREW	5 "Y" RUNS, 3 BOMBS
JULY	11	LANC IV	M	SELF	CREW	AIR TO AIR FIRING
JULY	12	LANC III	M	SELF	CREW	OPERATION - VARIES
						PARIS - HOW VC
JULY	15	LANC III	M	SELF	CREW	TACTICAL A NUCERT N.W. PARIS
July	19	LANC III	M	SELF	CREW	TACTICAL A ROLLEZ ISLE DE ADO

GRAND TOTAL [Cols. (1) to (10)]
685 Hrs. 20 Mins.

TOTALS CARRIED FORWARD

German anti-aircraft defences were extremely sophisticated by this stage of the war, and "predicted flak" was especially feared by bomber crews. Some batteries of 88 mm flak guns were equipped with radar that could "predict" the exact position of an approaching aircraft at any given moment, calculating the aircraft's speed, direction and height in order to send a volley of shells to meet it. The 88 mm shells travelled at about 1,000 vertical feet a second, so the calculations were exacting. The shells were fused so that they exploded in a box pattern around the target aircraft—even if they didn't score a direct hit, the unlucky airplane would be showered with deadly shrapnel.

The Gransden Lodge crew was lucky this day, only being slightly damaged, and all fourteen Lancasters from 405 Squadron returned home safely.

Late in the morning of July 4th the crew took off on another training flight, this one involving four mock bombing runs and then some fighter affiliation, playing a game of "I got you!" with a friendly Spitfire, to keep everyone on their toes. Looking back from seventy-five years on, the timing of this particular exercise seems very fortuitous, for it turns out that the next night the skills and training of the whole crew would be put to the ultimate test. They would be fighting for their collective lives against an adversary who was most assuredly *not* playing games.

It wasn't unheard of for a Bomber Command crew to complete an entire tour without their air gunners firing a shot in anger. Or for a crew to have to contend with multiple night fighter attacks on one operation—like their very survival, it was sometimes just a matter of luck.

On the night of July 5th, the Coffey crew's luck ran out… or luck was with them, I suppose, depending on how you look at it!

The attack they were taking part in that night was one of their shortest, just two hours, and was directed against a V-2 rocket (again, Dad uses the code name "p-plane" in his logbook) base in France. The name of the target is listed in Dad's logbook as Watten, and I didn't have any reason to question this until I began to read the 405 Squadron's records closely.

There were indeed two Lancasters from Gransden Lodge attacking the Watten V-2 site that night, but the Coffey crew was not one of them—they were, in fact, part of a force of ten from 405 Squadron that was sent to attack Wizernes, another major V-2 site some ten miles from Watten. I put down my Dad's logbook error to a bit of sloppy inattention to what, to him, was likely a minor detail in geography. After all, his job was to fly the plane; Bob Bayne would tell him where to go and how to get there.

The giant bunker complex at Wizernes was built into the side of a chalk quarry and was one of several Hitler ordered built in Belgium and France to launch the new V-2 rockets at England. Inside the complex were to be facilities for producing the liquid oxygen the V-2 used for fuel, railway lines in tunnels, launching pads and lodging for hundreds of workers and soldiers. One hundred and twenty thousand cubic meters of concrete was used in the construction, including a domed, five-meter thick reinforced concrete roof.

The Allies were aware of the construction and were determined to prevent the base from becoming operational—they began bombing the site in March of 1944. In all, almost two dozen attacks were made against Wizernes, including dropping over twenty of the massive 12,000-pound Tallboy bombs that only the Lancaster was capable of carrying.

The July 5th raid was aimed to disrupt the construction and repair work being undertaken by the Germans, and Maisye was carrying a load of 14,000 pounds of high explosives.

Dad and crew took off at about 11:30 that night and approached Wizernes, along with a hundred or so other RAF bombers, just an hour later. The site was well defended, and the 88 mm flak scored hits on several aircraft, including Maisye, although the damage was not severe. The real trouble started soon after they had dropped their bomb load on the red target indicators the Pathfinder Mosquitoes had placed near the concrete dome—they hadn't realized it yet, but they were being stalked.

The Junkers Ju 88 was one of the Luftwaffe's premier warplanes, a twin-engine heavy fighter equipped with radar to find its prey in the pitch dark. It was armed with machine guns and four deadly 20 mm cannons, which were effective from a much longer range than the .303 Brownings the Lancaster's air gunners were using. Many were also equipped with a devastatingly effective weapon that the Germans code-named *Schräge Musik*, a pair of 20 mm cannons facing upwards out of the top of the fuselage. With this weapon, the night fighter could approach a bomber from below, completely unseen, and fire upwards into the belly or wings of his target. The unfortunate Lancaster or Halifax would be on fire and doomed before the crew even knew what hit them.

There is no doubt that luck played a huge role in whether a Bomber Command crew survived their tours or not, but on this night, it was a battle of skills that took place, not luck.

The business-end of a Messerschmitt Bf 110 night fighter. Note the upwards-firing cannons poking out of the fuselage behind the cockpit, and the radar array on the nose used to find it's prey in the dark. Photo by author, RAF Museum, Hendon. Circa 1983.

The Coffey crew were on the ball, with every member focused on doing their job. Wireless operator Ted Rutherglen was standing in the back of the cockpit area, keeping watch through the Perspex astrodome, standard procedure when he wasn't busy with his radio equipment. Bob McWhirter and Ken Hart, the crew's gunners, were scanning the night skies, constantly rotating their hydraulically powered turrets in slow arcs as they peered into the darkness in every direction, looking for any telltale movement.

It was Bob McWhirter in the tail turret who spotted the Ju 88 first, "sneaking up on us from behind and below," in his words. Bob called out a warning over the intercom, and my Dad began evasive maneuvers, likely putting Maisye into a corkscrew—but this Luftwaffe pilot was no rookie, it seems. With his much superior airspeed, he was able to get into attack position before Dad could affect an escape, and the Lancaster was slashed with cannon and machine-gun fire from end to end. The plane's canopy was shattered, and Ted Rutherglen fell to the cockpit floor, his face cut badly by flying shards of Perspex. The cannon shells and machine gun fire tore through the Lancaster's fuselage and took out Maisye's hydraulic and electrical systems, leaving Ken Hart and Bob without their electric gunsights. Nevertheless, they both kept up a steady stream of .303 machine gun fire at the attacking Junkers—Bob recalled that without a gunsight, he had to gauge his fire using the track of his tracer shells and ended up spraying gunfire "like a garden hose."

They held the Junkers at bay, and Ken Hart told his brother after the war that the fighter had "followed them for quite some distance, but didn't attack again."

Artist Piotr Forkasiewicz's amazing depiction of the Coffey crew
under attack after leaving the V-2 complex at Wizernes.
Artwork copyright 2018 Piotr Forkasiewicz, used with permission.

Was the German hoping his initial attack would result in the "Lanki" (Luftwaffe slang for the Lancaster) showing some sign of a mortal wound? Was he running short of fuel or ammunition? I think that in all likelihood, the pilot of the Junkers was looking for some kind of opening against the obviously skilled gunners and decided that attacking this particular Lancaster again was too risky. There were easier targets about, ones whose gunners weren't so alert.

For whatever reason, the Nachtjager eventually broke off his pursuit and disappeared, leaving Maisye to limp home to Gransden Lodge.

It was likely Malcolm Dingwall who tended to the wounded wireless operator, using bandages from the first aid kit to staunch the flow of blood from Ted Rutherglen's facial lacerations. Luckily, it was a quick trip back to Gransden Lodge, where they were met by the hospital "blood wagon" after they had landed and taxied to their dispersal pad. Ted was loaded into the ambulance "covered in blood," according to Bob, and taken to the airbase hospital, where a surgeon treated his cuts and removed as many of the fragments of shattered astrodome as he could. In his logbook, Ted simply noted that he had "received face full of perspex."

Poor Maisye, Avro Lancaster ND412, did not get off lightly from her encounter with the night fighter—she got her crew safely home, but the next day the ground crew counted 142 separate holes in her, and with the electrical and hydraulic systems destroyed, the damage was too severe for the Squadron to fix. She was shipped off to a repair depot and, after extensive work, she eventually returned to battle with 630 Squadron, surviving the war, and finally, like thousands of other Lancasters who had done their bit, sent to be scrapped in 1947.

The V-2 rocket base at Wizernes was never completed, and Hitler's plan to launch forty to fifty rockets a day at London from it was never realized—British and Canadian troops captured the facility in early September.

When I ponder the Coffey crew's encounter with the German night fighter, I often wonder how it affected them—they had had close shaves before, but I think this one-on-one battle must have been different. The incident must have made a profound psychological impact on Teddy Rutherglen, for one—the cannon shells that had shattered the astrodome he had been standing under must have come within inches of his head. In addition to the tiny Perspex fragments he carried embedded in his face for the next thirty years, the close brush with violent death must have left a lasting mental burden as well, and it's a subject we will revisit.

My Dad, Jimmy Willoughby, Malcolm Dingwall, and Bob Bayne would all have been in the path of the cannon and machine-gun fire as it slashed into the fuselage and cockpit canopy—they must all have had close calls. Dad was the lucky owner of the only piece of armour plating in the Avro Lancaster: the back of the pilot's seat. The protective plate covered his body from the back of his head down, and I wonder whether it came back from Wizernes scarred and dented from the impact of the night fighter's gunfire. If so, it wouldn't be the last time that summer that a member of the Coffey crew would be saved by the back of his seat, as we shall see...

The Coffey crew at work, unknown date. Centre and right (likely), Coffey and Willoughby. Photographer likely Teddy Rutherglen. Photo courtesy of the Rutherglen family.

Ken Hart, too, I think, must have been deeply affected by the Ju 88 attack, but perhaps in a more positive way. Recall that Ken had been part of a tragic accident two years prior and had been court-martialed; at the Heavy Conversion Unit he had told his new crewmates that he would tell them about the incident that led to his grounding when they finished their tour.

For Ken, the attack over Wizernes was likely a vindication—he, like Bob McWhirter in the tail turret, had remained calm and effective under fire, protecting his crewmates and helping to drive off the attacker. Here was proof that the faith he had shown in himself by volunteering for aircrew duties again after having been grounded was well justified.

Ken Hart at work in his office, the mid-upper turret. Photo taken from the cockpit astrodome, looking backwards. Photo courtesy of the Rutherglen family.

Mentally, I think it must have been a more self-confident and focused Ken Hart that climbed into the harness of his mid-upper gun turret on their next operation on the night of July 6th. Ken brought home a physical souvenir from the Junkers encounter as well—upon removing his flying gear after they landed, he found a cannon shell fragment lodged in the thick leather of his flying jacket. His family still have the memento.

The crew's dramatic encounter certainly didn't earn them a respite, as they were back to work that very evening, just sixteen hours after landing from their operation to Wizernes.

I was surprised by two facts about their July 6th operation to a V-1 site in France: one, the Lancaster they took off in was another LQ-M, this one helpfully labelled "M-2" in Ted Rutherglen's logbook. It turns out that each squadron had a reserve of planes available, and the Coffey crew simply took over M-2 (serial number JB707) as their own—no time for sentimentality—"the king is dead, long live the king," I suppose.

The other surprising fact was that Teddy Rutherglen flew with them after being patched up at the base's hospital. But perhaps I shouldn't have been surprised—aircrews were tight-knit. Teddy likely wouldn't have been happy with the idea of his crew having to fly with a replacement "spare bod." Not only because it was considered bad luck, but also because he would have to make up any missed operations with another crew sometime in the future. Best, he likely thought, to grin (painfully…) and bear it, and press on.

The crew lifted off the tarmac in the early evening of July 6th and made their way to the Abbeville area, amid a hundred or so other Lancasters, to attack a flying bomb launch site at Richemont Coquereaux, one of five V-1 sites Bomber Command attacked that night. The ruins of the installation at Coquereaux are still visible today, the smashed concrete covered in undergrowth in a prosaic French woodland field.

The relentless pressure on Bomber Command continued; the next day, the crew took off for another attack in support of Allied ground forces, who were bogged down outside the strategically critical French city of Caen.

The British Second and Canadian First Armies were unable to break the fierce resistance of the German armour (including the infamous Waffen SS Panzers commanded by Colonel Kurt Meyer) and infantry who were facing them in Caen. Bomber Command was called upon to try and break the stalemate—but they would be bombing close to Allied troops, so accuracy was paramount.

The planners of the operation decided that the German and Allied lines were far too close together to gamble with an aiming point right on the German positions: it was just too risky. The aiming point was placed as close to the enemy as the planners dared, with the hope the attack would soften up German resistance and boost morale in the Allied ranks.

The Coffey crew was part of a force of 450 heavies that dropped over 2,000 tons of high explosives in the course of a forty-five minute attack. Accuracy was bang on, but the effectiveness of the operation depends on who you ask.

Colonel Meyer of the SS was interrogated by the Allies after the war. He minimized Bomber Command's contribution—but perhaps his opinion is not surprising considering he was a senior officer in an organization (the Waffen SS) known for its vainglorious arrogance, and the commander of a unit (12th Panzer Division Hitler Jugend) that had, one month previously, murdered dozens of unarmed Canadian P.O.W.s in Normandy. I think it unlikely such a man would give any credit for his retreat to Allied bomber crews.

It is true the attack actually killed few German troops, but the bottom line is that Allied armour and infantry was able to advance the next morning (and there was consternation in some quarters that they hadn't attacked as soon as the Lancasters left), whereas before they been stalled. The raid had at least softened up resistance, and I am not surprised in the least. I imagine being on the receiving end of a Bomber Command attack must have been a life-altering experience, assuming one survived: there were reports of enemy soldiers wandering about like zombies after a Bomber Command attack, deafened and in shock.

For the British and Canadian soldiers, the display of their side's massive airpower must have been a shot in the arm. The Canadian Army certainly had no reservations about the effectiveness of the raid and cabled Bomber Command H.Q. a message that was soon posted at every squadron in the force:

> Heavy attack just taken place. A wonderfully impressive show and enormously appreciated by the Army. The Army would like their appreciation and thanks sent to all crews.

I am sure it must have been a real morale booster for Dad and crew to read this and to know that, at least for now, they were attacking the German military directly and making a very visible and direct contribution to Allied victory. I have little doubt there was some bragging done by bomber crews as well, mostly to do with coming to the aid of the "brown jobs" in the Army!

History wouldn't be history without some controversy, and the raid on Caen that day attracted more than its fair share after the war. Much as in the case of the 1945 attack on Dresden, the postwar criticisms levelled at the Caen operation by some (often self-serving, in my opinion) commentators and historians are almost a microcosm of the judgment they pass on Bomber Command in general.

The controversy surrounds the unfortunate deaths of hundreds of French civilians killed in the northern suburbs of Caen that day. It is challenging from our modern perspective to address the issue of civilian deaths without sounding cold and lacking compassion—we have all heard too often the uncaring, bureaucratic phrases like "collateral damage." However, there is no getting around the fact that Bomber Command's explosives killed, and that thousands of French civilians were their unintended victims during the German occupation.

To keep things in perspective though, it bears repeating that Normandy was a battleground in the summer of 1944—whole armies were fighting to the death, and battleships were lobbing 16" shells onto French soil, including Caen. Artillery and tank battles raged daily, as did savage village-to-village, house-to-house infantry combat. British anti-aircraft crews based in Normandy, with little or no Luftwaffe to battle, were using their 40 mm Bofors guns to blast French farmhouses and even churches to clear them of German infantry. This ferocious warfare had been going on for a month before the July 7th Bomber Command raid on Caen, which had been in answer to a plea from the Army to help them break the stalemate.

British planes dropped leaflets on Caen the day before, warning civilians of the danger looming. The Germans themselves had ordered the French residents to leave, but like many of us would be, many people were loath to leave their homes, and they stayed put, hoping for the best.

The operation was as accurate as the technology of 1944 allowed, but there is no doubt the people who remained in Caen that day suffered terribly.

The French people, in general, paid a heavy price for their Liberation, and singling out Bomber Command for any special responsibility for that suffering seems to me to be horribly unfair. But it is an attitude I have come across in my research repeatedly: the Bomber Campaign, some claim, was cruel, ineffective, and immoral.

The pundits may use weasel words, praising the individual bravery of Bomber Command's airmen, but they basically accuse them of participating in war crimes.

In the 1990s, an atrocious, taxpayer-funded, film entitled *Death by Moonlight* was put out by the National Film Board of Canada. It portrayed the volunteers of Bomber Command as dupes of the evil Arthur Harris and his lust for the blood of German civilians.

I only had the stomach to watch the film all the way to the end many years after it was produced, and was shocked when I watched one scene in which the very same Yorkshire farmer who had kindly shown me around Tholthorpe in 1982 was shown doing the same for two Canadian ex-aircrew some ten years later. I don't know whether Geoff ever saw the finished film, but I think he would have been hurt to see men he so obviously revered being portrayed in such a poor light.

More recently, the otherwise excellent National Geographic television series *Last War Heroes* left a bad taste in my mouth as well, after I watched the episode that touched on the July 7th Bomber Command attack on the German defences at Caen.

Referring to it as "carpet bombing," and numbering the Lancasters involved as "over 2,000" (in reality less than 500), it includes an interview with a British infantryman who recalls the bombs that day falling on them by mistake, killing sixty of his comrades and *600* Canadians.

In reality, there are no reports of *any* Allied casualties from that day's raid, and I think it's quite likely the old soldier's comments were either edited out of context or that he was (and I mean no criticism—all our memories are fallible) simply misremembering, and his statement wasn't fact-checked. In either case, the short segment seems typical to me of some of the sloppy and misleading post-war portrayals of Bomber Command's work.

I suppose it is simpler and easier to throw out a line like "carpet bombing" rather than to try and explain the complexities of *OBOE*, *H2S* and Master Bombers, or to try and elaborate on the incredible efforts Bomber Command went to in trying to perfect navigation and target marking techniques and technologies during the course of the war. Or to remind us that the Bomber Campaign was just one component of the five years of savage global warfare required to bring down Hitler's monstrous Nazi empire. Simpler and easier perhaps, but in the course of doing so, the reputations of some 100,000 brave young airmen are maligned.

During the Bomber Campaign, there was a phenomenon noted of an occasional aircrew, in the face of heavy flak and blinding searchlights, losing their nerve as they made their final approach to the aiming point and dropping their bomb load early, on the edge of the target. These crews were scathingly referred to by their leaders (and peers) as "fringe merchants." I think it is an apt label for some post-war pundits and historians: "fringe merchants" who, out of a deliberate desire for controversy or sheer lack of diligence, lose their nerve and hit only the edges of the truth.

All sixteen Lancasters from Gransden Lodge returned safely from Caen to their base at about 11 p.m., but, in a sad and ironic example of the vagaries of war, Flying Officer R. A. Pearson (a navigator on the Weicker crew) died soon after debriefing when he crashed his personal motorcycle while returning to his quarters.

Bob McWhirter remembered Pearson and told me that he was the "only American" in the squadron, so he must have been one of the thousands of Yanks who crossed the border to join the RCAF in the years before America entered the war.

The next day, July 9th, the crew was off again, returning to France to try and take out the V-1 launching site hidden among the trees in the tiny hamlet of L'Hey, near Noordpeene.

Visibility was good when the attacking force arrived at about 2 p.m., with the target markers well placed, and the Coffey crew dropped their load of 1,000-pound and 500-pound bombs from 12,500 feet. The Master Bomber overseeing the raid seemed pleased with the attack, encouraging all the crews with calls of "Keep it up! Wizard bombing!" over the radio.

L'Hey was one of six V-1 sites hit by Bomber Command that day. I note that in Dad's logbook entry for July 9th, he again plays fast and loose with geography, describing their destination as being in the "Dieppe area." He likely got his target mixed up with another of the sites being attacked that day by 405 Squadron, Mont Candon, which is indeed close to Dieppe. Interestingly, the other five Coffey crew logbooks that I have copies of note their destination as "Dunkirk area," which is still pretty vague, but far closer to reality than my Dad's! Bob McWhirter told me that the logbooks of the pilot and navigator were expected to be kept scrupulously up-to-date and that sometimes he and other crew members would borrow them to copy out information if they had gotten behind in their entries. This practice would account for the occasional identical misspellings I have run across in multiple logbooks ("beachead" on August 7th, for example).

The following morning, July 10th, they were off again to France, this time to the V-1 storage site at Nucourt, about sixty kilometres outside Paris. It was a dawn raid, and they were over the target just after 6 a.m., but the thick cloud hampered the raid's accuracy—the Master Bomber gave the coded order "*square mile*" over the radio, which meant crews were to use whatever method (*H2S*, visual sighting of the aiming point, or bombing on target indicators) that worked best for them.

The Nucourt facility was cleverly located inside some natural limestone caverns, but French resistance had gotten word to England of the German's work, and a number of attacks were mounted against the site. The USAAF had hit it just the week before, and the July 10th Bomber Command raid would be followed up with others until the cavern roof finally collapsed, entombing hundreds of V-1s inside.

On July 11th, Gransden Lodge was stood down from operations, but it certainly wouldn't be a day of leisure for the base: ground crew would be doing repairs and maintenance, trying to catch up after the hectic schedule of the last ten days, and Dad and crew were training, flying *H2S* runs, mock "bombing," and some air-to-air firing thrown in for good measure. I wonder if Ken and Bob were especially keen to blast away at the drogue (being towed on the end of a long cable by another aircraft) after their close encounter of the Junkers kind on July 5th?

It was back to work on July 12th, Maisye lifting off the runway (along with eleven other Lancasters from 405 Squadron) a little past six in the evening to make the short trip to the railway marshalling yards at Varies, outside Paris.

In an example of the care taken by Bomber Command to try and minimize French civilian casualties, the Master Bomber gave the coded order "*Marmalade*" to the 150 or so attackers as they were approaching the target, aborting the attack. The cloud cover was too thick, preventing almost all the crews from seeing the yellow target indicators—one crew managed to spot them through a break in the cloud and drop its load, but all the others turned around and headed back to England.

On the way back over the English Channel, they all jettisoned a small portion of their bombs to make for a safer landing. They all made a point of noting in their post-op debriefing that they had aborted "over enemy territory," to make sure they got credit for the trip as part of their tour.

The Coffey crew's next op was a return visit, on July 15th, to the V-1 storage facility at Nucourt, and a new technique was being tried during this daylight raid, a tactic code named *Heavy Oboe*. The lead Lancaster in the formation was guided to the aiming point with *OBOE*, the two-beam navigation system, and when it dropped its bomb load, all the other Lancs followed suit. It turned out to be a very effective system, but it did rely on all the Lancasters being able to see each other, and on this day, the heavy cloud spoiled things somewhat. Some of the attacking force could see their leader and bombed, but many (including the Coffey crew) could not; they followed their orders, returning to base with their bomb load.

Three days of downtime followed for the crew, and then on July 19th, they flew their last operation of a hectic month.

Their target was yet another V-1 launch site, this one at Rollez, near Calais. This time the weather cooperated, and with clear skies prevailing, the force of about fifty followed the lead Mosquitoes to the aiming point at about 2:00 in the afternoon. The "Mossies" dropped their load, and everyone else following them waited for a second or two and then dropped theirs—it was reported to be a devastating raid, and Rollez didn't require a return visit.

Our crew had flown nine combat operations and three training flights in eighteen days, a punishing schedule. They were granted some well-deserved leave, and like many tight-knit Bomber Command crews, likely spent it together in London.

Teddy Rutherglen and Bob McWhirter in Service Dress uniform, perhaps heading off on leave. Date and photographer unknown. Photo courtesy Rutherglen family.

The crew returned from leave at the beginning of August and flew their first op of the month on the 3rd, a daylight raid against another Noballs V-1 target in France. The site at L'Isle-Adam is located in a picturesque forested area just north of Paris and is usually described simply as a V-1 storage facility—the full story is a bit more interesting.

The Germans built the secret installation in 1943, and it was specifically designed to try to hide it from the RAF's photo-recon aircraft. The buildings were constructed low to the ground and spread out, with berms of earth sloping up the sides, which helped them avoid casting telltale shadows in photographs taken from above.

YEAR 1944		AIRCRAFT		PILOT, OR 1ST PILOT	2ND PILOT, PUPIL OR PASSENGER	DUTY (INCLUDING RESULTS AND REMARKS)
MONTH	DATE	Type	No.			
—		—	—	—	—	TOTALS BROUGHT FORWARD
AUG	3	LANC III	M	SELF	CREW	OPS - ISLE DE ADAM (N.W PARIS
AUG	4	LANC III	M	SELF	CREW	OPS - TROSSY ST. MAXIMIN (N. PARIS
AUG	5	LANC III	M	SELF	CREW	OPS - NOVELLE (NR. ABBEVILLE)
AUG	6	LANC III	J	SELF	AC. TIPPER CREW	CROSS COUNTRY
AUG	6	LANC III	M	SELF	CREW	CROSS COUNTRY
AUG	7	LANC III	M	SELF	CREW	OPS - BEACHEAD S.W. CAEN Δ NO. 5
AUG	8	LANC III	M	SELF	CREW	OPS - FORÊT DE LUCHEUX (ILL)
AUG	9	LANC III	M	SELF	CREW	AIR TO AIR, 4 BOMBS.
AUG	12	LANC III	M	SELF	CREW	8 BOMBS, F/A.
AUG	12	LANC III	M	SELF	F/O BAYNE	OPERATION - RUSSELSHEIM
					SGT WILLOUGHBY	8 X 1000 H.E (ILL)
					P/S DINGWALL	6 X 4 X 85 FLARES.
					P/O RUTHERGLEN	1500 GALS
					SGT HART	17000 FT.
					P/O MCWHIRTER	
AUG	14	LANC III	H	SELF	CREW	4 BOMBS, XCT NO. 7
					P/O JOWSETT	
AUG	16	LANC III	M	SELF	F/O BAYNE	OPERATION - KIEL
					SGT WILLOUGHBY	1 X 4000 HE, 6 X 1000 4/A.
					P/S DINGWALL	WANGANUI FLARES
					P/O RUTHERGLEN	1500 GALS, 17000 FT.
					SGT HART	
					P/O MCWHIRTER	(EMERGENCY 'SKY MARKERS)

GRAND TOTAL [Cols. (1) to (10)]
717 Hrs 30 Mins.
TOTALS CARRIED FORWARD

A narrow-gauge railway line was built into the forest, and French locals were forbidden to enter the area. Whatever the Germans were hiding there must have been important, and the French resistance soon got word to London of the facility.

There is little doubt some elements of the V-1 program were stored there, like handling equipment and disassembled launch ramps, perhaps even the flying bombs themselves, but also likely weapons and ammunition destined for use by the Wehrmacht or Waffen SS.

The Bomber Command attack this day was the fourth of five in total—the BBC wireless service broadcast coded messages meant for the local Resistance, warning them of the impending attack, but for some reason, they were missed.

The weather cooperated for a change—visibility was good when the force arrived over the aiming point at just after 2 p.m., and dropped their load of 1,000-pound and 500-pound high explosive bombs on the red target indicators.

The attackers were met with heavy flak over L'Isle-Adam, and the 405 Squadron's Herbert crew was hit as they approached the target, setting one of their Lancaster's engines on fire. Flying Officer Herbert extinguished the fire by diving down to 13,000 feet, and the crew carried on to bomb the aiming point and then limp home to Gransden Lodge.

The Germans were livid that their carefully hidden facility was being targeted so accurately, and they had no doubts as to who to blame, grabbing two young men from the local village and executing them in cruel, random retaliation. The long-suffering civilians had to endure the inevitable unintended results of heavy bombing as well: dozens were killed and injured by stray bombs over the course of the five raids required to put the German facility out of commission.

The fifth raid, the coup de grâce, came the very next day when Bomber Command returned, and the Master Bomber reported a "large explosion with impressive mushroom of smoke from the centre of the target area."

Dad and crew were also over France this day (August 4th) but on their way to a different target altogether: the V-1 storage dump at Trossy St. Maximin, north of Paris. The facility was dug into a disused limestone quarry and was a tough nut to crack. It had been attacked on each of the previous two days—this was the third attack in a row.

The flak was intense over the site, and one of Gransden Lodge's Lancasters, C for Charlie (the O'Conner crew), was badly hit as they approached the aiming point. The crew's flight engineer, lying in the nose in the bomb aimer's position, was struck in the knee by shrapnel, and their Lancaster's hydraulics were damaged. They managed to bomb nonetheless, and made it safely home.

On August 5th, our crew were again on their way to France to yet another V-1 launch site. This one was at Noyelle en Chaussée (labelled "Novelle" in Dad's logbook), a tiny village near Abbeville.

The Coffey crew were one of four crews from 405 Squadron taking part in the attack, which again utilized an *Oboe*-guided lead aircraft (in this case, a Mosquito) to lead a small formation of Lancasters into the aiming point. Unfortunately, the weather again foiled the plan. The attackers ran into a solid wall of cumulus nimbus cloud as they were closing in on Noyelle en Chaussée, which caused severe icing on their wings—this could be a deadly problem, as the buildup of ice effectively changed the shape of the wing, leading to a loss of control.

Three of Gransden's Lancasters turned back to escape the icing, and also because they could no longer see the Mosquito they were supposed to be following in to the aiming point. Dad reported that he was in the process of doing the same when he suddenly spotted the Pathfinder Mosquito in a break in the cloud, "swung back in line," and was able to spot the "puff of smoke" from the Mosquito's bombs on the aiming point. They lined up on the target, and the Coffey crew succeeded in dropping their load of high explosives on the site.

The raid this day was scattered, but eventually the site was destroyed, and its remains are still there today, with the remnants of the launch ramp still facing northwest, towards London.

The "Novelle" operation was to be the crew's last daylight raid for a very long time—they would not be seeing the reassuring sight of an escort of friendly Spitfires and Mustangs again until their very final operation.

On August 6th, the crew were stood down from operations, but that didn't mean a day of rest—they flew two cross-country training flights, each about an hour and a half long. Interestingly, on the first flight they had a passenger, Aircraftman Tipper, who was likely a new member of their ground crew, along for the ride on what the squadron records say was a beautiful summer day.

On August 7th, Bomber Command was again pressed into service in aid of the Army, this time to support *Operation Totalise*, an armoured thrust toward Falaise.

There was a road leading out of Caen towards Falaise, and 1,000 heavies were assigned five aiming points on either side of it. The Allied troops on the ground would use tracer fire and searchlights to create a "lane" of sorts down the road's length, and Bomber Command would bomb the flanks of this "lane." The tons of bombs cascading down would destroy some of the German defenders, and force the rest to keep their heads down and their eyes off their gunsights while the Allied tanks made their move.

Dad and his crew were flying one of twelve Lancasters from Gransden Lodge assigned to aiming point five. Approaching the aiming point at only 8,000 feet, it must have been a remarkable (and unique) sight, with horizontal tracer fire and searchlights creating a sort of flarepath leading them to the aiming point, which was marked with red target indicators by the first Pathfinders. By most accounts, the raid was a success, with British and Canadian armour beginning their rapid advance the moment the Lancasters left.

Our crew's "Summer in France," so to speak, came to an end the next night—after August 8th, all their future operations would take them into the heartland of Germany.

The target on the night of August 8th was labelled "Forêt De Lucheux," but it was not the forest they were attacking; it was the fuel storage dump hidden within it. Under camouflaged canvas tarps were thousands of 200 litre drums and 20 litre Jerrycans of gasoline destined for the endlessly thirsty Panzers of the Waffen SS.

The small force of Lancasters and Mosquitoes approached the aiming point just before midnight, and the attack commenced. The Master Bomber had to tweak the aiming point once or twice, but very shortly, bombs connected with gasoline and massive fires and explosions were seen by all.

Dad and crew were assigned the role of Illuminators for this attack, a step up in the Pathfinder hierarchy, carrying flares as well as bombs, placing them where and when the Master Bomber ordered. In this case they were not needed, and they were brought back to Gransden.

On August 9th and 11th, there were training flights involving air-to-air firing, mock bombing runs, and fighter affiliation (Dad lists the second flight as being on the 12th, but all the other crew members' logbooks note it as the 11th).

After the relatively short (and mostly daylight) operations they had been involved in for the previous six weeks, the four-hour and thirty minute flight on August 12th to attack Russelsheim, in the heart of Germany, must have been an unpleasant adjustment. Flying in the dark the whole trip with no fighter escort and facing the Reich's massive night fighter and flak defences must have left the crew thinking nostalgically of French destinations like Mardyck and Oisemont!

The crew were part of a force of 297 heavies sent that night to Rüsselsheim, their main goal being to destroy the Opel Motor Works. Opel had built cars before the war, and was actually owned and operated by the Ford Motor Company before being nationalized by the Nazis, who switched the huge plant to making fighter planes and Junkers Jumo aircraft engines.

On this night, the Coffey crew were again assigned the role of Illuminators, and in addition to their load of eleven 1,000-pound bombs, Maisye was also packing six Small Bomb Containers, each filled with four seven-inch hooded flares.

These ingenious devices were used to light up the target area, helping the assigned Pathfinders to see ground detail and accurately place their target markers.

When the flares fell out of their Small Bomb Containers, a parachute deployed, and the flare ignited, emitting a blinding white light for two or three minutes as it descended to earth. An asbestos shroud deployed as well, directing the light downwards, protecting aircrew from the intense glare (as it would ruin their night vision.) Despite the best efforts of the Master Bomber, some of the brightly coloured target indicators went astray to the south, and the Opel factory got away with light damage, with many bombs falling on the misplaced markers.

During their post-raid briefing, the Coffey crew reported very poor visibility due to thick cloud and industrial haze. They couldn't see ground detail or markers, and to make matters worse, the often-finicky *H2S* set stopped functioning, leaving Bob Bayne, Malcolm Dingwall, and Jimmy Willoughby to estimate the aiming point as best they could.

On August 14th, the Coffey crew were off on another daylight training flight, dropping four imaginary "bombs" on the nearby village of Babraham during an almost two-our exercise. Along for the ride was a Pilot Officer Jowsett, whose identity has defied my research skills. His name doesn't appear among any 405 Squadron aircrew rosters, so my best guess is that he was a newly arrived administration officer (a meteorologist perhaps, or an intelligence officer).

On August the 16th, the crew took off at dusk to make the long trip to Kiel, on Germany's Baltic coast. The route took them out over the North Sea, across Nazi-occupied Denmark and then directly south to their target. Kiel was a major German seaport and shipbuilding centre, a hub of U-boat activity, and an essential part of the supply line delivering arms and supplies to the Eastern Front. It was a frequent target of Bomber Command, and the Coffey crew would come to know it well, this being the first of three trips they would make there.

The crew were designated as Emergency Sky Markers on this trip, and in addition to their 10,000-pound load of high explosive, they also packed a dozen *Wanganui* flares. These high-tech (for 1944) pyrotechnics were designed to cascade down, forming a bright cone of lights in the sky that would serve as an aerial aiming point on cloudy nights. The Germans referred to them as "Christmas trees," as that is what they resembled as they fell to earth—their code name comes from the hometown of one of the Pathfinder commander's aides, who happened to be from New Zealand.

Things went pretty well on this operation, and our crew's two navigators reported that they had gotten a good view of the Kiel canal and the coastline on their *H2S* set. Visibility was good enough that the crew reported they could see their single 4,000-pound bomb and eight 1,000-pound bombs exploding on the western edge of the harbour—with a bit of luck, they may have hit a U-boat in dry dock or some other naval vessel. The docks, shipyards, and surrounding area were reportedly heavily damaged. The crew's *Wanganui* flares were not called for this night, and they returned with them.

August 18th was a hectic day for the crew, starting with an almost three-hour training flight involving fighter affiliation and once again "bombing" the unlucky village of Babraham. They had another mystery passenger on this flight, a Pilot Officer Wilson—it's possible this may have been G. E. Wilson, a bomb aimer with the 405 Squadron's Kettlewell crew, but if so, I don't know why he would have been along for the exercise.

YEAR 1944		AIRCRAFT		PILOT, OR 1ST PILOT	2ND PILOT, PUPIL OR PASSENGER	DUTY (INCLUDING RESULTS AND REMARKS)
MONTH	DATE	Type	No.	—	—	—
—	—	—	—	—	—	TOTALS BROUGHT FORWARD
AUG.	18	LANC. III	O	SELF	CREW	F/A, 8 BOMBS, XCTY
					F/O WILSON	
AUG.	18	LANC. III	M	SELF	F/O BAYNE	OPERATION - BREMEN
					SGT. WILLOUGHBY	11 X 1000 H.E.
					F/S DINGWALL	WANGANUI FLARES
					P/O RUTHERGLEN	1500 GALS, 15000 Ft.
					SGT. HART	S.O. HIT BY FLAK - O.K TO BASE
					P/O McWHIRTER	(EMERGENCY SKY MARKERS)
AUG	25	LANC. III	M	SELF	F/O BAYNE	OPERATION - RÜSSELSHEIM
					SGT. WILLOUGHBY	1 X 4000 H.E
					F/S DINGWALL	8 X 500 H.E.; WANGANUI FLAR
					P/O RUTHERGLEN	1970 GALS, 14,000 Ft.
					SGT. HART	
					P/O McWHIRTER	(EMERGENCY SKY MARKERS)
AUG.	26	LANC. III	M	SELF	F/O BAYNE	OPERATION - KIEL
					SGT. WILLOUGHBY	1 X 4000 H.E.
					F/S DINGWALL	15 X 90 X 4 INC.
					P/O RUTHERGLEN	1500 GALS, 17,000 Ft
					SGT. HART	WANGANUI FLARES
					P/O McWHIRTER	(EMERGENCY SKY MARKERS)

GRAND TOTAL [Cols. (1) to (10)]

797 Hrs. 40 Mins.

TOTALS CARRIED FORWARD

Late that evening, the crew climbed into Maisye and began their pre-takeoff routines—the Lancaster was loaded with 1500 gallons of high octane aviation fuel and 11,000 pounds of high explosives, ready to make the trip to Bremen, another vital German seaport.

Fighters and flak were waiting for them, but in reality, they had already stepped into the breach the moment they jumped off the Motor Transport truck at their dispersal pad and approached Maisye.

Every soldier, seaman, and flyer who went into combat in WW II had their own unique set of challenges and dangers that had to be faced, but it seems to me that the heavy bomber crews really had things stacked against them more than most.

From the moment they climbed aboard the aircraft, their well-being, their very lives, were forfeit at any moment, whether from enemy action, accidents, equipment failures, or from the very nature of the environment in which they operated. It was a unique way of fighting a war, separated from their comrades (both inside and outside their aircraft) and in the pitch dark. At least a soldier could feel grounded (literally), with his comrades beside him and the location of the enemy known—the bomber crews were not allowed even that small comfort in their kind of war.

Their aircraft was literally a flying bomb, filled with high explosives, incendiaries and gasoline. As it picked up speed for takeoff, the lives of its crew were in the hands of the men and women who had built and serviced their aircraft, especially its engines. The Lancaster could easily cruise on three engines, but it certainly couldn't take off, fully loaded (heavier than any peacetime rules would allow), on any less than four. If there was any malfunction, even a loss of power in just one engine, a fiery crash was almost inevitable.

As they climbed into the night skies to join the perhaps 1,000-strong bomber stream, the risk of mid-air collision began, and the threat never ended until they were back safely on their dispersal pad hours later.

Once they got above 8,000 feet or so, they were reliant on bottled oxygen to breathe—unconsciousness quickly overcame any crew member whose oxygen supply was compromised by a malfunction.

One night over France, on their way to Germany, my Dad announced over the intercom that he was switching on the oxygen supply and that everyone should don their masks. Apparently, Dad did regular check-ins with the crew during their flight, and when he called out to Bob McWhirter in the rear turret at some point, the reply he got was slurred and incoherent. Dad asked Malcolm Dingwall to grab one of the small portable oxygen tanks the Lancaster was equipped with and check on Bob.

A moody portrait of Malcolm Dingwall, taken by Teddy Rutherglen.
Date unknown. Photo courtesy of the Rutherglen family.

Malcolm made his way back through the Lancaster's fuselage (no easy task in full flying suit—the Lancaster's interior was notoriously cramped) and luckily found the turret facing to the rear, so he could access the doors: when he got them apart, he found Bob near unconsciousness. Malcolm quickly found the problem, a loose connection on the oxygen line, and reattached Bob's supply. Bob laughed when he told me about the incident: "…I guess your Dad had the oxygen turned up pretty high, cause boy, when it hit me…!"

The temperature at 20,000 feet was another obstacle for the bomber crews—it could easily reach -40 centigrade, and the unpressurized Lancaster, with its millimetre-thick aluminum skin, offered little protection from the cold. The only heating in the aircraft blew hot air into the wireless operator's station—Ted Rutherglen roasted while all the other crew froze.

I remember asking my Dad one time about the cold and commenting that it must have been miserably uncomfortable. He replied that the temperature wasn't the worst of it, that what he hated most was the cold, tension-induced sweat that he was bathed in most of the trip.

The air gunners were equipped with electrically heated flying suits, but they too suffered from the occasional malfunctions. Bob recalled one operation when the electrical wires of his suit shorted out and began burning the heel of one foot—he had no choice but to unplug the whole suit and told me he "darn near froze!" for the remainder of the trip. It was more than an uncomfortable inconvenience: a rear gunner who was numb with cold was a gunner who was distracted and slower to react, and this could be fatal for his crew.

Should the crew need to abandon the aircraft for any reason, the odds were again stacked against them. Getting out of the Lancaster wearing a parachute was no easy task: there were only two small emergency exits, and trying to get to them in the dark in a spinning, smoke-filled aircraft would have been far from straightforward. Even if one did make it out successfully and see that blessed canopy of silk open up above you, the danger was nowhere near over. No one knows the true number of Allied airmen who managed to parachute to earth, only to face a beating or worse at the hands of the Gestapo or an angry mob of German civilians. The official stance of the Nazi regime was that the young men of Bomber Command were terrorists ("terrorflieger" or "luftgangsters"). Their lives were forfeit—lucky indeed was a downed Allied airman to be taken into custody by Luftwaffe personnel, who generally had a reputation for reasonably honourable behaviour when it came to Allied P.O.W.s.

If the aircraft had to ditch in the North Sea or English Channel, the crew would somehow have to scramble out of the sinking Lancaster (assuming the pilot managed to bring it for some kind of safe "landing" on the often rough seas) and board the small dingy that would automatically deploy (and then inflate) from its cubby hole in the wing. From there, survival via one of the RAF's air-sea rescue launches was a possibility, but far from certain.

Honestly, when I look back on the myriad dangers Bomber Command aircrew faced nightly, from atrocious weather to equipment failures, from hypothermia to hypoxia to mid-air collisions, I often feel that it would only be a slight exaggeration to say night fighters were the least of their worries.

Having mentioned parachutes and dinghies, I think it is worth another quick detour from the crew's next operation to talk about their training on these two lifesaving pieces of equipment.

Towards the end of Dad's logbook, there is a summary page of all the parachute and dingy drills he and his crew took part in.

"Dry dingy" practice took place at the airfield—on dry ground unsurprisingly. It was a drill for abandoning the aircraft in the correct sequence—assuming their crash positions, exiting the aircraft in a set order, who grabs the dingy, who enters dingy first, and so on—the whole routine was choreographed and timed.

"Wet dingy" was more challenging and took place at a pond or indoor pool (Ripon, York, and Cambridge are mentioned in Dad's logbook). In full flying gear, the crew had to jump in the water, get to the upside-down dingy, right it, and then all scramble aboard.

Dry dingy practice. Original wartime press photograph from author's collection.

Bomber Command aircrews never actually made a parachute jump as part of their training—all their practice took place on the ground. The parachute drills focused on donning the parachute quickly and then getting out of the aircraft: if you could get those two things right, the rest (pulling the ripcord) was relatively easy!

In passing, I must mention that when I interviewed Bob McWhirter in 2015, I briefly touched on the subject of parachutes, and I got the distinct impression he dreaded the prospect of bailing out more than flak or night fighters!

Like the dry dingy drill, parachute practice was carried out at their airfield. A stack of old mattresses was placed under the emergency exit in the aircraft's nose, and they practiced over and over again against the stopwatch.

"Bail out!" called my Dad over the intercom, and everyone would strap on a parachute and head for one of the two exits, those jumping out of the nose hatch landing on the mattresses.

The strength that Bomber Command now possessed is evident when we look at the statistics for the night of August 18ᵗʰ—more than 1,000 aircraft were dispatched, spread out over no fewer than five different targets.

Dad and crew were part of a force of 288 (Gransden Lodge contributed twelve Lancasters) sent to attack the German port city of Bremen, which was bustling with industrial activity, from dockyards to shipbuilding, to steel mills, as well as massive railway yards, U-boat pens, truck factories, and a Focke-Wulfe aircraft factory.

It was one of those nights when everything seemed to go right for Bomber Command—the weather cooperated with clear skies over the target, and the Pathfinders had accurately marked the aiming point. Bob Bayne and Malcolm Dingwall reported they could see the bridge over Bremen's Weser River on their *H2S* screen, confirming they were right on target. Jimmy Willoughby dropped their load of eleven 1,000-pound bombs into the centre of three target markers they could see burning on the ground.

It was a devastating attack, described as one of the most effective of the whole war, destroying dockyards, factories, and residential areas, and sinking almost a hundred ships.

One small component of the August 18ᵗʰ raid on Bremen that fascinated me was the role played by a diabolically clever ruse that had been carried out the night before. While the Coffey crew and their comrades were bombing Kiel on the night of August 16ᵗʰ, another small group of Bomber Command squadrons were planning a devious little operation that would lay the track for Dad and crew's *next* trip to Germany.

Bomber Command's 100 Group was a secret, and perhaps that is why their remarkable work is so little known—I had certainly never heard of it before I began researching my Dad's time in the RCAF.

The squadrons in 100 Group flew an odd assortment of aircraft, from elderly Flying Fortresses to Short Stirlings. Still, each of these seemingly unremarkable aircraft was jam-packed with bleeding-edge electronic goodies designed to frustrate German defences. They could jam radar, drown out the night fighters' radio communications, make ten aircraft appear as 1000 on German radar screens, and generally create havoc.

On the night of August 17th, 100 Group faked an attack on Kiel, approaching across the sea along a specific route, behind a screen of radar jamming techniques (code-named *Mandrel*) that made it impossible for the German radar operators to tell what was behind it. At some point, they deliberately dropped a portion of the screen, feigning a malfunction—suddenly, the German defence controllers could see the blips of dozens of aircraft before the "malfunction" was "repaired," and the screen went back up. The Germans were convinced it was a real attack and scrambled twelve Nachtjager squadrons, who then flew in vain for hours, burning precious aviation fuel in search of the sizable attacking force that didn't exist.

In reality, the blips they had seen when the jamming screen went down were dozens of Wellingtons, crewed by students from Operational Training Units, flying behind 100 Group's radar jamming B-24 Liberators. The hoaxers turned around and beat it back to England when the German night fighters scrambled to intercept them.

The finale of the August 17ᵗʰ faux attack happened the next night. As the Coffey crew and hundreds of other crews approached Bremen, they followed the same route as the previous night's spoof and behind the same type of screen. This time the Germans decided it was another fake-out, and by the time they realized it was the real thing, it was too late to take effective action. As the old saying goes, *"Fool me once, shame on you; fool me twice, shame on me."*

Although the night fighters had been hoodwinked, the flak was another story: it was heavy and accurate. At some point over Bremen, Maisye took a serious hit from flak shrapnel in the starboard outer engine, and it was badly damaged. Jimmy Willoughby, his job of bomb aimer now complete, was back at his post as flight engineer and likely "feathered" the engine, shutting it down to prevent it overheating and erupting in flames. The magnificent Lancaster would have no problem getting them home on three engines, albeit at a slightly reduced speed.

For the next six days or so, the weather closed in on England, bringing thick cloud, heavy rain, and strong winds. Several small raids were put on by other Bomber Command squadrons, but Gransden Lodge had a bit of a respite for the duration of the atrocious weather.

The Coffey crew's next operation was on August 25th, a return trip to Russelsheim and another crack at the Opel factory. This time the planners laid out a much different route to the target than the previous trip—the fourteen Lancasters from Gransden Lodge would be spending a gruelling seven hours plus in the air this time, compared to four and a half the last time.

Dad and crew were again designated Emergency Sky Markers, and Maisye carried a load of *Wanganui* flares in addition to the 8,000 pounds of high explosives.

They took off at just after 11 p.m. and started the long, southerly route to Russelsheim that Bomber Command H.Q. had plotted to try and disguise the true target—they crossed the coast over Normandy as if heading into France or southern Germany.

The Coffey crew, along with over four hundred other Lancasters and Mosquitos, approached the aiming point in Russelsheim at about 1 a.m. However, on the final approach, Jimmy Willoughby found that his bombsight was malfunctioning, which was, of course, a severe impediment to accurate bombing.

The British Mark XIV bombsight was a remarkable piece of high technology, ideally suited to the type of bombing that Bomber Command was engaged in: night bombing from medium heights.

Its mechanisms made complex calculations to allow for wind drift, type of bomb being dropped, and the like, as well as making calculations to allow for accurate bombing even if the aircraft was in a shallow dive or climb. Stuck without this essential tool of the trade, Jimmy (perhaps with Malcolm Dingwall's help) resorted to using his Emergency Sighting Angle, doing all the necessary calculations on a circular slide rule and dialing in the adjustments on the bombsight by hand. While he was doing all this and giving course adjustments to my Dad, they were being shot at by flak and hunted by night fighters, whose numbers over Russelsheim were reported as being "considerable."

The target was well marked by the Pathfinders, and the Coffey crew bombed successfully and made their way back to Gransden Lodge without further problems. Another 405 Squadron crew was not so lucky.

The Weicker crew (in Lancaster O for Orange) were attacked without warning by a night fighter as they approached Russelsheim, and their aircraft was set on fire and badly damaged. Flt. Lt. Weicker put the Lanc into a steep dive to escape, and when he levelled off thousands of feet below, found that he had indeed thrown the night fighter off (and put out the fire), but in the process had lost three of his crew! His flight engineer, mid-upper gunner, and wireless operator had all bailed out, *without orders*, which he emphasized in his post-raid report.

By this, he was referring to standard bomber crew procedure: all members of the crew would be notified (via intercom, or if that wasn't working, a small red light at their post that could be illuminated from the cockpit by their pilot) when their skipper wanted them to prepare to bail out, and then a final order to either stand down or to jump.

I can't find it in my heart to be critical of what the three did—they were in a burning, smoke-filled aircraft, diving seemingly out of control, likely thinking they were only seconds from plowing into the ground. For all they knew, their pilot was dead and unable to give the appropriate orders. In those chaotic seconds, the three young airmen made a choice, one they obviously thought was the right one to survive.

With a wounded rear gunner and missing half his crew, Weicker flew the damaged Lanc home to Gransden Lodge, where the "blood wagon" met them and took his one remaining gunner to hospital for treatment of a bullet wound in his ankle.

Three replacement airmen arrived at Gransden Lodge a few days later, and after a month of training flights, Flt. Lt. Weicker led his re-formed crew back on operations. After completing his second tour and returning home to Canada, I am sorry to relate that he met a tragic end, perishing along with twenty other pilots when the Dakota transport plane ferrying them crashed in Estevan, Saskatchewan, in 1946.

When I first came across the story of the Weicker crew in the 405 Squadron's records, I became curious about what ended up happening to the three missing crewmen: I wondered if they had managed to escape and evade back to England, or had ended up in a P.O.W. camp for the rest of the war? Did they ever learn that their skipper had actually flown what they thought was a doomed aircraft back to England?

The first two out of the plane were the flight engineer (Sgt. Abbs) and the wireless operator (Flt. Lt. Brown)—both of whom were captured soon after hitting the ground, and they spent nearly a year in a German P.O.W. camp before being liberated and returned home to Canada.

Brown filled out a questionnaire during his repatriation and could not offer any insight into what happened to Flt. Sgt. Nairn, the third crew member. Brown said he saw Nairn behind him as he left what he thought was a fatally stricken Lancaster, but he couldn't state for certain that Nairn had actually bailed out.

Two weeks after Lancaster O for Orange returned to Gransden Lodge missing three of its crew, the Squadron reported to its H.Q. (with a copy to Ottawa) that the "fate" of the three airmen "cannot be determined at this particular time." Several months later, word must have come via the Red Cross that Brown and Abbs were in custody at a P.O.W. camp, but there remained no information as to the fate of Flt. Sgt. Nairn.

It wasn't until September of 1945, some three months after Allied soldiers had liberated his two comrades from a German P.O.W. camp, that Ross Bell Nairn was finally found.

The war was over by then, and the area around Homburg, near Saarbrucken, was under the control of Allied occupation forces. One day a German forester named Herr Senf approached American authorities with a troubling story. While searching for a convenient spot nearby his tree farm to dump green waste, he crossed a forest trail and came across an old crater on the former grounds of Schloss Karlsburg, a ruined 18th-century castle. As he was dumping his load of branches and foliage, he noticed something odd at the bottom of the crater and investigated—what he found was a parachute harness and the badly decomposed remains of a man.

To Herr Senf's credit, he did the right thing and immediately contacted American Occupation authorities, who assigned a U.S. Army Quartermaster Corps Captain named Frederick T. Shroyer to investigate. Captain Shroyer made two trips to the remote location, which is in a mountainous, forested area several miles outside Homburg, and later made a detailed map of the route.

Captain Shroyer found the spot and confirmed that a body was at the bottom, badly decomposed and covered only in some leaves. There was no I.D. on the corpse: the airman's dog tags were conspicuously absent. Shroyer must have wondered how Flt. Sgt. Nairn had ended up in the crater. Had he broken his neck upon landing in the thickly treed forest? But the body was described as "lying neatly arranged," so if he had died upon impact, who had put the body in the crater, and why had they apparently removed his dog tags? Or had Flt. Sgt. Nairn been badly hurt during his landing, crawled into the crater in hopes of evading capture, and then died from his injuries or exposure?

Captain Shroyer (who I think displayed admirable diligence: he was, after all, a Quartermaster, not an investigator) decided to make a second trip to the site with a Medical Officer in tow. When they arrived, the doctor quickly determined what had likely happened to Ross Nairn.

Upon examining the skull, he found a neat hole, unmistakably made by a 9 mm bullet, just behind Flight Sergeant Nairn's ear: the young Canadian had been executed.

I have at various times over the years I have been researching this book experienced emotions ranging from mirth to anger to frustration, but never before had I sat at my desk and cried, as I admit I did when I read the terse line in the seventy-five-year-old report stating the doctor's findings that day.

The vindictive cruelty of the act, so callous and unnecessary—and most of all the damned unfairness of it—it all struck me like a slap in the face. I suppose that in the big picture of all the millions of murders, all the death, all the cruelty and unfairness that is an integral part of the story of WW II, the cold-blooded execution of Ross Nairn might seem an unremarkable crime, but for some reason, the story hit me on a very personal level.

Captain Shroyer determined the victim was likely RAF and reported his findings to the War Crimes investigators. The bureaucratic wheels turned slowly, but eventually an RAF team made its way up the forest trail five miles outside Homburg, where they found… *nothing*.

Someone had removed Flt. Sgt. Nairn's remains from the crater. The RAF team dug through the dead leaves and detritus until they reach solid ground, but nothing remained of the airman or his parachute harness.

It is all conjecture, but some conclusions do seem self-evident. Ross Nairn was not killed in a fit of rage by an angry vigilante group—the 9 mm bullet hole was made by a Luger or Walther pistol, the weapon of an officer or Nazi official and not something a local citizen would likely be allowed to possess. Nairn must have been captured (or given himself up) somewhere nearby and then marched a short distance down the forest path to the convenient crater and executed. The man with the pistol may have committed the murder, but there were almost certainly others there who were complicit.

Someone had obviously noted the arrival of Captain Shroyer and his team, and word got back to the murderer, who arranged to have Flt. Sgt. Nairn's pitiful remains moved to thwart any further investigation into the crime.

Inquiries were made with the locals, but unsurprisingly no information was forthcoming, and Ross Nairn was officially designated as having "no known grave." He is commemorated with a plaque at Runnymeade, a special memorial in England for the over 20,000 airmen who, like Flt. Sgt. Nairn went missing without a trace.

I have made attempts to track down Ross Nairn's descendants, but so far, no luck—he was unmarried, and his siblings have all passed on.

In my records, I keep a copy of Captain Schroyer's map, and if I ever visit Germany, I will make a point of going to the small town of Homburg. On my personal bucket list has been added a goal to someday walk a trail in that forest near the ruins of the castle and to place a bouquet of flowers in a spot that I can only hope will be somewhere near wherever Ross Nairn rests.

On August 26th, after a few hours of fitful sleep, the Coffey crew were roused to begin preparing for another night's work, this time a return trip to the German Baltic port of Kiel.

Visibility was good when they arrived over the port city at about 11 p.m. along with almost four hundred other Lancasters—the Germans had lit a long line of fires to create a smokescreen across the city, but this tactic was no longer as effective as it had been in the past, as the Pathfinders were equipped with *H2S* radar, which could see through smoke, darkness, or cloud.

Jimmy Willoughby dropped Maisye's load of incendiaries and a 4,000-pound cookie, and the crew returned to their base without incident.

YEAR 1944		AIRCRAFT		PILOT, OR 1ST PILOT	2ND PILOT, PUPIL OR PASSENGER	DUTY (INCLUDING RESULTS AND REMARKS)
MONTH	DATE	Type	No.			
—	—	—	—	—	—	TOTALS BROUGHT FORWARD
AUG	29	LANC. III	M	SELF	P/O BAYNE	OPERATION - STETTIN
					P/O DINGWALL	3 X 1000 H.E.
					Sgt. WILLOUGHBY	10 CANS FLARES
					P/O RUTHERGLEN	2100 GALS, 17,500 Ft.
					Sgt. HART	
					P/O McWHIRTER	(BLIND ILLUMINATORS)
AUG.	31	LANC. III	Y	SELF	CREW	Y-RUNS, AIR TO AIR FIRING.
AUG	30	OXFORD	S	P/O McGEAGH	SELF	S.B.A.
		SUMMARY FOR 405 SQDN.			1. LANCASTER III	AUGUST. TOTALS:
		DATE: August 31/44			TYPES 2. OXFORD	
		SIGNATURE: JK Coffey F/O			3.	
					4.	C.W. Perry ..... S/LDR. OC. "B" FLIGHT.
SEPT.	15	LANC. III	M	SELF	P/O BAYNE	OPERATION - KIEL
					W/O DINGWALL	4 X 1000 H.E.
					P/O WILLOUGHBY	10 CANS FLARES
					Sgt. HART	1650 GALS, 17000 Ft.
					P/O RUTHERGLEN	
					P/O McWHIRTER	(BLIND ILLUMINATORS)
SEPT.	17	LANC. III	M	SELF	CREW	AIR TO AIR, F/A, S.B.A.
SEPT.	18	LANC. III	M	SELF	CREW	XCTY No. 7, F/A, S.B.A.
SEPT.	25	LANC. III	M	SELF	CREW	XCTY.

GRAND TOTAL [Cols. (1) to (10)]
269 Hrs. 35 Mins.   TOTALS CARRIED FORWARD

My Dad's 49th operation was a trip to another major Baltic seaport and industrial centre, Stettin, which is today named Szczecin and is part of Poland. The trip turned out to be the crew's second-longest, a gruelling eight and a half hours, the route taking them across the North Sea, then over the northern part of Nazi-occupied Denmark, and south over Sweden before the final leg to Stettin.

It was a violation of Sweden's official neutrality to fly over its territory, but it was done regularly by Bomber Command, and the Swedes made a show of firing their anti-aircraft guns at the bombers. However, often the shells were conveniently fused to explode thousands of feet below the Allied planes. They were basically harmless fireworks that put on a good show for any Nazi diplomats in Stockholm who might be watching.

Maisye carried a load of three 1,000-pound bombs and ten Small Bomb Containers packed with hooded flares. Visibility was good over Stettin, and the force of four hundred had no trouble finding the aiming point, despite some clever decoy target indicators the Germans had placed outside the city. Damage to the city was heavy, with dozens of factories, hundreds of homes, and thousands of tons of shipping destroyed.

The long trip to Stettin was the Coffey crew's final operation for August, the final two days of August made up of training flights, one for the crew as a whole, the last just for Dad, as he practiced Standard Beam Approach landings in his old friend the Airspeed Oxford.

The month of September 1944 was a relatively quiet one for our crew, with only one operation. For the first two weeks of the month, they were on leave, likely in London, and they must have been an impressive sight as they strolled down Piccadilly Circus together. They were seasoned veterans now (and all except Ken Hart were officers), their uniforms proudly displaying not only the gold eagle wings of the Pathfinder Force, but also the much-coveted winged "O" that signified they had completed a tour of operations.

Coffey, Bayne and Dingwall sometime in the late summer of 1944.
Damaged original photo from author's collection.

Statistically, they all should have been killed long ago, and they must all have been aware of this, although like all youth, they probably felt they were exceptional and that death was a fate that awaited other crews, not them.

It must have been after the war that my Dad began to ponder death and how (and why) he had dodged a fate that had befallen about seven out of ten of his comrades. I think he (and likely the other aircrew who came home as well) no doubt suffered some degree of survivor's guilt, something that had never occurred to me until I went through my Dad's possessions after he died.

Dad had well-stocked bookshelves all his life, and I credit my love of reading to his influence, but he didn't own many books about the Second World War. Most of his modest library consisted of novels by writers like Neville Shute (his favourite by far) and Louis L'Amour, interspersed with books on woodworking, his favourite pastime. There were just two Bomber Command memoirs on his shelves, one of which was entitled *Lancaster to Berlin*, and written by a former RCAF skipper named Walter Thompson (a fine book, by the way).

Dad's cheap, paperback copy of Thompson's memoir was dogeared and well-thumbed, but when I picked it up for the first time, I was surprised to see that Dad had also highlighted numerous passages, something I never saw in any of his other books. The subject matter in the passages he chose to highlight dealt, almost exclusively, with loss rates and death meted out by flak and night fighters.

When I think of my Dad, the image that often comes to my mind is what I think of as his signature pose, standing by the living room window early in the morning, looking out onto Okanagan Lake with a Peter Stuyvesant cigarette in one hand and a cup of instant black coffee in the other, deep in thought.

At the time, I didn't give much thought to what was going through his mind: perhaps I just assumed he was making plans for his day. It is only now, after years of research into what he must have gone through during those nine months of combat in 1944, and with the bit of wisdom and perspective that age has granted me, that I can look back and ponder what more likely may have been going through his mind.

I know my Dad was a very restless sleeper; Mom told me that was the reason they had to switch to twin beds, but until recently, I had never given any thought as to why he slept poorly. What thoughts were going through my Dad's mind that prevented him from sleeping peacefully?

My older brother Stuart recalls that in the mid-1970s, he and my Dad were watching the television news, a story about returning Vietnam vets and a new phenomenon being called "Post Traumatic Stress Disorder." My Dad blurted out, half to himself, "maybe that's what I have…" but he wouldn't elaborate when questioned by his son. Like so many of his generation, he kept his inner turmoil and troubles to himself; that's what a man did. It is only by looking back from the vantage point of a grown man pushing sixty, that I begin to have even an inkling of the mental burden my Dad (and millions like him) must have carried with him every day. It truly grieves me to realize that memories of flak and dead friends may have haunted my Dad.

A portrait of Dad, likely taken at Tholthorpe in the spring of 1944 by Teddy Rutherglen.
Photo courtesy of the Rutherglen family.

The Coffey crew's first (and only) operation in September 1944 was a third and final trip to the seaport of
Kiel. They (and almost five hundred other heavies) raced across the North Sea at 2,000 feet to avoid the
German radar and then climbed to their attack height of 17,000 feet as they approached the aiming point
just after 1 a.m. They carried a load of 1,000-pound bombs and hundreds of illumination flares, which were
packed into a new innovation, the Cluster Projectile.

An original wartime press photograph of a Bomber Command attack on the railyards of Trier, Germany in late 1944. Author's collection.

The Small Bomb Container was slowly being replaced by the Cluster Projectile, which was an improvement in that it carried its load of flares or incendiaries in a casing that was dropped from the bomb bay and fell to a pre-set height, at which point it broke open and spewed its contents. The problem with the SBC was that its contents tended to bump into each other and scatter as they fell from the bomb bay—the Cluster Projectile improved accuracy by avoiding this issue.

The German defenders lit smoke screens and set off decoy Target Indicators, a tactic that had often worked effectively in the past, but no longer, thanks to Bomber Command's tactics, equipment, and battle experience. The attack was successful, destroying a large swath of the city, including dockyards, railway marshalling yards, and factories.

The post-raid reports mention that night fighter opposition was "astonishing light."

There are likely multiple reasons for the lack of Luftwaffe presence this night, including the work of 100 Group, who had staged a fake raid in the area two hours earlier. Bomber Command's destruction of aircraft factories and oil plants was also putting tremendous pressure on the German's ability to resupply, replenish, and fuel their Nachtjager force. By 1945, the Luftwaffe's potentially game-changing new jet fighters often had to be towed by horses or oxen to their runways for take-off due to the critical shortage of fuel. However,

I think much credit must go to the American Mustang, Lightning, and Thunderbolt pilots who had been savaging the Luftwaffe for months while escorting the USAAF's B-17 armadas into Germany. The losses they were inflicting on the Luftwaffe were crippling and unsustainable.

The Luftwaffe leadership also has to take a good portion of the blame for the Nachtjager's waning power as well—the policies they put in place for their aircrew were shortsighted and self-defeating.

Night fighter aircrews had no tours of operations like their adversaries in Bomber Command: they flew until they were killed. Over the course of several years, this led to a severe shortage of combat-experienced mentors for the new recruits in the force. A critical lack of fuel also meant that the fledgling pilots had far less flight training than previous graduates—some were sent to combat squadrons with only a few hours of flying time.

All these factors led to the downward spiral of the Luftwaffe's effectiveness—they were still a force to be reckoned with, but their power was declining by the day.

After returning from Kiel, our crew spent the next two weeks or so focusing on training, honing their skills as Pathfinders. In reading over my Dad's logbook, we can see that very shortly they would be assigned to the challenging role of Blind Sky Markers for two of their upcoming operations. Perhaps this period of training was in preparation for this step up in responsibility, which involved marking the aiming point using only their *H2S* radar.

Whatever the reason, the Coffey crew flew seven training exercises ranging from fighter affiliation and air-to-air firing to cross-country bombing and Standard Beam Approach landings, each of them about two hours long. Ted Rutherglen's logbook records that he got a chance to take over the mid-upper turret for part of the September 26th air-to-air firing exercise—I am sure he thoroughly enjoyed blasting away at the canvas drogue!

The German town of Saarbrücken is right on the French border, south of the Ruhr Valley. It wasn't a major city in WW II, but still an important medium-sized town. It was a centre for coal and steel production, and home to a central railway hub, and infantry and artillery barracks. The residents of Saarbrücken had last endured an RAF bombing raid of any size in September of 1942, but on the night of October 5th, 1944, they were again slated as the "target for tonight."

The 1942 raid had been a typical ineffective early-war operation, involving mostly medium Wellington bombers—the bombing was scattered that night, and the net result was a dozen or so homes destroyed and one man killed. Any Saarbruckener who had experienced the raid that night might be forgiven for not being overly worried when they heard the air raid warnings sounding on the night of October 5th, 1944.

YEAR 1944		AIRCRAFT		PILOT, OR 1ST PILOT	2ND PILOT, PUPIL OR PASSENGER	DUTY (INCLUDING RESULTS AND REMARKS)
MONTH	DATE	Type	No.			
—	—	—	—	—	—	—
						TOTALS BROUGHT FORWARD
SEPT	26	LANC. III	T	SELF	CREW	AIR TO AIR, XCTY.
SEPT	28	LANC. III	M	SELF	CREW	XCTY, BOMBING
		SUMMARY	FOR	405 SQDN.	4 LANCASTER III	SEPT. TOTALS.
		DATE:	Sept. 30/44	TYPES	2.	
		SIGNATURE:	JKCoffey F/o		3.	
					4.	F/L S/DR for O.C. "B" FLT.
OCT.	1	LANC. III	M	SELF	CREW	XCTY, BOMBING
OCT.	4	LANC. III	T	SELF	CREW	AIR TO AIR, F/A.
OCT.	5	LANC. III	M	SELF	F/O BAYNE	OPERATION - SAARBRUCKEN
					F/O DINGWALL	4 X 1000 H.E.
					F/O WILLOUGHBY	10 CANS FLARES
					F/O RUTHERGLEN	1500 GALS, 18000 Ft.
					SGT. HART	
					F/O McWHIRTER	(BLIND ILLUMINATORS)
OCT.	6	LANC. III	K	SELF	F/O BAYNE	OPERATION - DORTMUND
					F/O DINGWALL	11 X 1000 H.E.
					F/O WILLOUGHBY	WANGANUI FLARES
					F/O RUTHERGLEN	1500 GALS, 18000 Ft.
					SGT. HART	
					F/O McWHIRTER	(EMERGENCY SKY MARKERS)

GRAND TOTAL [Cols. (1) to (10)]
786 Hrs. 45 Mins.
TOTALS CARRIED FORWARD

However, the town of Saarbrücken was about to receive a very unwelcome lesson in the exponential advancements that had been made in Bomber Command's destructive power, tactics, and accuracy over the twenty-four months since then.

The October 5th operation was organized at the request of the American Third Army, which was about twenty miles from Saarbrucken, advancing quickly. They wanted Saarbrucken's railways and communication lines smashed.

Dad and crew took off early in the evening, timed to arrive over the target at 10:30. There were two aiming points, one right on the railway yards and one in the city centre. Dad and crew reported that they could see no target indicators on their first run over the city, so they orbited Saarbrücken and came in a second time. On this next run, the target indicators had appeared, and Jimmy Willoughby loosed Maisye's load, first the hooded flares to light up the area and then four 1,000-pound bombs.

Some flares appeared over open countryside about thirty miles away (perhaps decoys), but the Master Bomber kept the incoming Main Force on task and away from this distraction. The 531-strong force devastated Saarbrucken, levelling whole areas of the town, including the rail yards.

Our crew arrived safely home to Gransden Lodge, and after debriefing and the traditional egg breakfast, caught some exhausted sleep before waking on the morning of October 6th to find that they were "on" again that night.

While they had slept, their ground crew, the tireless and unsung "erks" of Bomber Command, had been frantically working on Maisye (and every other Lanc on the station), preparing her for another night's work.

Every inch of the huge aircraft would be gone over—it was a never-ending task, and it was not performed in a warm, dry, well-lit hanger, but outdoors on the dispersal pad, exposed to whatever the weather had to offer, be it driving rain, frigid winds, or even snow.

The ground crew must have found something amiss with Maisye that day, something that required more than an afternoon to fix; when the Coffey crew took off at 5:17 p.m. on October 6th, it was in Lancaster K for King.

They joined a force of over five hundred headed for the long-suffering industrial city of Dortmund, which had the misfortune to be in the running for the title of being the recipient of more Allied bombs than any other single target in the Reich. It was home to synthetic oil plants, steel mills, factories, rail marshalling yards, and coal mines, and was a target the crew had last visited on May 22nd.

Our crew were designated as Emergency Sky Markers and carried *Wanganui* flares along with a heavy load of eleven 1,000-pound bombs. The sky was clear and cloudless, and their flares were not needed— Jimmy dropped their load of high explosives on the green target markers the Pathfinder Mosquitoes had placed on the aiming point, and my Dad turned the Lancaster onto the course Bob Bayne gave him, towards home.

The Coffey crew reported they had seen decoy flares about four miles west of the aiming point, but the fakes attracted little attention. The Germans tried desperately during the bomber campaign to try to duplicate the British target indicators, but an experienced aircrew could tell the difference by the intensity, colour, and duration of the burning pinks, reds, and greens.

Whether they knew it or not (and I doubt they did—how ops were counted and when a crew was to be "screened" was not an exact science), most of the Coffey crew had only six more operations to go before crossing the finish line and completing their second tour. One member of the team had only five more to go, as we shall see.

For a week after returning from Dortmund, the crew did no flying, but the following week we can see two training flights in Dad's logbook cross-country nighttime *H2S* navigation exercises. It seems a relatively quiet schedule, but Bomber Command, in general, was quite low profile during this two week period in October of 1944—I wonder if the members of the force sensed something big was in the offing... I wonder if the Germans sensed it as well?

"Bomber" Harris had indeed planned something big: a massive, coordinated attack on the Ruhr that he dubbed *Operation Hurricane*. The attack would involve thousands of aircrew, not just from Bomber

Command, but also from the American Eighth Air Force. It would be a twenty-four-hour show of strength, designed to make it clear to the Nazi leaders that the Allies unequivocally ruled the skies over Europe and could strike devastating blows at will.

Gone were the days that Harris had to press into service obsolete aircraft and trainee crews from Operational Training Units in order to assemble a force of 1,000, as he had done in 1942.

Operation Hurricane would show that the Allies could mount, not just one, but *three* 1,000 bomber raids in a twenty-four-hour period. Harris told the Allied leaders that the overwhelming display of power would help end the war quickly by showing the Germans the futility of further resistance to the Allied armies fighting their way into the Reich.

Bomber Command chose Duisberg as the focus of their two attacks, one an escorted daylight raid, the next coming that same night; meanwhile, the Americans would hit Cologne in a massive daylight attack.

Gransden Lodge must have been a beehive of activity on October 14th, beginning in the wee hours of the morning, as the crews taking part in the daylight attack took off just after 7 a.m.

I was astonished to see in the squadron records that five of the crews taking off that morning also took part in the operation that very night, taking off for a second time in twelve hours. The thirty-five airmen must have barely had time to be debriefed from the morning raid and grab a few of hours sleep before being awoken to prepare for the next. The tireless ground crews at Gransden Lodge (and at dozens of other airfields like it around England) must have worked like galley slaves to prepare their aircraft for the first op and then turn them around for the second.

Maisye was part of a group of thirteen Lancasters from 405 Squadron who took off at about 11:30 on the night of the 14th, making up a small part of the massive main force of over a thousand heading for Duisburg, timed to arrive in two waves. The Coffey crew were designated as Blind Sky Markers this night, tasked with using their *H2S* radar to find their assigned aiming point and mark it with their *Wanganui* flares—this was a significant increase in responsibility for them and a reflection of their level of experience and training.

The crew were in the first wave of the attack, and Bob Bayne and Malcolm Dingwall likely had little trouble navigating their way to the unfortunate city of Duisburg, as some crews reported they could see the fires still burning from the daylight attack from a hundred miles away. Once over the city, the Coffey crew reported that the aiming point was clearly marked, and Jimmy Willoughby dropped their load of eleven 1,000-pound bombs onto the red target markers, and the crew turned for home. At about the same time they landed back at Gransden Lodge, the second wave of the 1,000 RAF heavies was beginning their attack on the city.

Over 9,000 tons of high explosives fell on Duisburg in one twenty-four hour period, devastating the city. However, *Operation Hurricane* failed in its stated aim of cracking the will of the Nazi regime—the fanatical resistance continued.

The following night (October 15th, which was, in fact, the same day as their return from Duisburg), the crew again climbed into their bombed up Lancaster and went through their pre-trip routines in preparation for a long trip to the German seaport of Wilhelmshaven.

The naval yards and shipbuilding facilities in Wilhelmshaven were extensive, including U-boat factories and repair docks. The city also contained something that, sadly, seems to have been commonplace in wartime German industrial cities, a forced labour camp. Thousands of French labourers were imprisoned at the Alter Banter Weg camp, a satellite of the infamous Neuengamme concentration camp near Hamburg. They toiled in the shipyards and were used to clear bomb damage, something Wilhelmshaven had no shortage of, it being a favourite target for the heavy bombers of the American Eighth Air Force.

The Coffey crew were designated as Blind Illuminators this night. They carried a load of flares and four 1,000-pound bombs. Their task was to illuminate the area, finding the aiming point using their *H2S* ground mapping radar, which gave an especially clear return in places where bodies of water met the shore. There was lots of cloud over Wilhelmshaven this night (in their post-raid report, our crew reported the conditions were "very hazy with poor visibility"), but they and many of the other Pathfinders reported getting very clear pictures on their *H2S* sets. The aiming points were accurately marked for the main force who arrived right on time and subjected Wilhelmshaven to a pounding attack, reportedly the heaviest the city experienced during the war.

Most of the Coffey crew got a three-day break after this twenty-four-hour marathon, the exceptions being Jimmy Willoughby, who was pressed into service as flight engineer on Wing Commander Lawson's crew for a training flight on October 17th, and Malcolm Dingwall, who flew as 2nd navigator with Flying Officer Cormic's crew on a training exercise on the 18th.

On the 19th, the crew flew an air-to-air firing and fighter affiliation exercise during the day; then they learned they were "on" for that night, and began briefings for another raid deep into Germany.

Their target this night was the major industrial city of Stuttgart, a destination most of the crew had seen before, way back in March when they had flown in a Halifax out of Tholthorpe. It was Jimmy Willoughby's first trip to Stuttgart, though, as Sgt. Porter had been the crew's flight engineer the last time.

The route chosen by the planners must have been more direct this time, as they carried three hundred gallons less fuel and spent ninety minutes less time airborne than they had the previous trip.

The attack involved almost six hundred Lancasters and Mosquitoes, arriving in two waves some four hours apart. Dad and crew must have been in the second wave, as they reported seeing the "glow of fires… on clouds over target when thirty miles away." Our crew arrived over their assigned aiming point just before midnight, dropped their illumination flares, and then added their four 1,000-pound bombs to the destruction below.

Stuttgart was covered with 10/10ths cloud this night, but with *H2S* it mattered little—the Pathfinders got an excellent visual on their radar displays, and the target indicators, flares, and high explosives rained down on the already burning city for the second time that night.

YEAR 1944		AIRCRAFT		PILOT, OR 1ST PILOT	2ND PILOT, PUPIL OR PASSENGER	DUTY (INCLUDING RESULTS AND REMARKS)
MONTH	DATE	Type	No.			
—	—	—	—	—	—	— TOTALS BROUGHT FORWARD
OCT.	12	LANC. III	M	SELF	CREW	X.CTY, No.14
OCT.	13	LANC. III	M	SELF	CREW	XCTY, No.14
OCT.	14	LANC. III	M	SELF	P/O BAYNE	OPERATION - DUISBERG
					P/O WILLOUGHBY	11 X 1000 H.E.
					P/O DINGWALL	WANGANUI FLARES
					P/O RUTHERGLEN	1400 GALS, 18000 Ft.
					SGT. HART	
					P/O McWHIRTER	(EMERGENCY SKY MARKERS)
OCT.	15	LANC. III	E	SELF	P/O BAYNE	OPERATION - WILHELMSHAVEN
					P/O WILLOUGHBY	4 X 1000 H.E.
					P/O DINGWALL	10 CANS FLARES
					P/O RUTHERGLEN	1500 GALS, 18000 Ft.
					SGT. HART	
					P/O McWHIRTER	(ILLUMINATORS)
OCT.	19	LANC. III	W	SELF	CREW	AIR TO AIR, F/A.
OCT.	19	LANC. III	M	SELF	P/O BAYNE DFC	OPERATION - STUTTGART
					P/O WILLOUGHBY	4 X 1000 H.E.
					P/O DINGWALL	10 CANS FLARES
					P/O RUTHERGLEN	1700 GALS, 18000 Ft.
					SGT. HART	
					P/O McWHIRTER	(ILLUMINATORS)
OCT.	24	PROCTOR	HH 431	F/LT HOLLAND	SELF	WYTON - HIGH WYCOMBE (B.C.H.Q)
				GRAND TOTAL [Cols. (1) to (10)]		
						TOTALS CARRIED FORWARD

Squeezed onto the final line of this page of Dad's logbook is a brief entry that has caused me more frustration and research time than any other single line item. I call it the "Mystery Flight," and it is comical how much effort I have put in to try (unsuccessfully) to unpack its secrets.

The line itself seems innocuous—simply a notation that Dad had flown as a passenger with Flt. Lt. Holland from Wyton to High Wycombe in a Percival Proctor on October 24th. Big deal, right?

For some reason, the entry got under my skin, and I couldn't let go of the nagging questions it raised. To start with, what was my Dad doing at RAF Wyton, home of the Pathfinder Force's 128 Squadron and their de Havilland Mosquitoes? The base was about twenty-five miles north of Gransden Lodge, more than a bike ride away, to be sure. Then there was the mystery of Flt. Lt. Holland: who was he, and how did Dad know him? The name Holland is not on the roster of pilots at either Wyton or Gransden Lodge, so where was he from? And what was the purpose of the flight in the first place? They made a half-hour hop down to High Wycombe, home of not only Bomber Command Headquarters, but of Sir Arthur Harris himself.

And the trip seems to have been one-way—how did Dad get back to Gransden Lodge? Despite my efforts, I have managed to find out next to nothing about the Mystery Flight beyond what Dad wrote in his logbook.

I did learn that the Percival Proctor was an ugly little single engine monoplane that the RAF used as a communications aircraft—ferrying messages and messengers, transporting VIPs, and so on. This particular Proctor (coded HM431) was assigned at the time of the "Mystery Flight" to the 8 Group (Pathfinders) Communications Flight, so that adds up. I also learned that Proctor HM431 went on to a long and colourful career, leaving England after the war and finally ending its flying days in 1965 when it made a crash landing in the Australian outback, with its final destination in the scrap yard.

The homely and diminutive Percival Proctor.
Original wartime postcard in author's collection.

One scenario has come up in my mind: Dad had recently been awarded a Distinguished Flying Cross (the DFC award was mentioned in 405 Squadron's Operations Record Book on October 16th), so is it possible Dad was flying down to High Wycombe with Holland, as they were both going to attend some kind of award presentation? But I can find no Holland with a DFC whose particulars fit the bill, so this scenario is pure conjecture.

Then there is the final page of Dad's logbook, where he lists all the aircraft he has flown: the very last one, a Percival Proctor! So was Flt. Lt. Holland teaching him to fly the plane during their trip? A second pilot was certainly not needed in the diminutive Proctor, so Dad was either a student or a passenger. Questions and more questions, which lead to more questions!

Although I have gained *some* proficiency during the past six years, my research skills remain decidedly amateurish, and it is not for the first time during my inquiries into my Dad's time in the RCAF that I have had to remain content to leave some things (for now) a mystery. Someday I hope to pay a visit in person to the National Archives in Kew, England, where all of the U.K.'s paper and photographic archives are housed. Many have been scanned and are available online for download, but many more must be viewed in person. There, tucked away in a file folder or cardboard box, there may be a document that clears up all my questions about the "Mystery Flight."

The Coffey crew's final three operations all took them into the heart of Germany.

They must have all known they were very close to being deemed "tour expired", or "screened," approaching the magic number of sixty operations, signifying the completion of a second and final tour.

I can't help pondering what their state of mind must have been like by this point, knowing that they had been living on borrowed time, month after month. Did the mental strain increase as they entered the home stretch, or were they resigned to whatever fate had in store for them, burned out and numb to the danger? Or were they confident and positive, eager to complete their last few ops, their eyes on the finishing tape that was so close they could almost touch it?

Bob Bayne and Bob McWhirter, exact date unknown. Photographer likely Teddy Rutherglen. Photo courtesy of the Rutherglen family.

Ken Hart, Jesse Coffey and Teddy Rutherglen, Gransden Lodge, summer 1944.
Photographer unknown, photo courtesy of the Rutherglen family.

On the night of October 31ˢᵗ, our crew took off from Gransden Lodge along with eight other Lancasters and joined the bomber stream, five hundred strong, as it began its journey to the long-suffering German city of Cologne, which was to be the recipient of a heavy attack for the second night in a row.

Cologne was an important transportation hub and major industrial city, and had been on the receiving end of Bomber Command and USAAF attacks on many occasions. By the end of the war, the historic city was virtually a wasteland, and photos taken of the ruins after Germany's surrender have become iconic, showing the magnificent Cologne cathedral standing virtually alone in a sea of broken brick and rubble.

The tactics used during the October 31ˢᵗ attack were typical of the sophistication that Bomber Command had developed by this stage of the war. The main force approached Cologne behind a screen of *Mandrel* radar jammers from 100 Group, and another group of spoofers used *Window* foil strips to fake a major attack on Frankfurt.

Then, fifteen minutes before the main force arrived over Cologne, a group of fifteen Pathfinder Mosquitoes staged a small attack. Once they left, the defenders of the city no doubt thought that would be the end of their night's work… and then came the ominous thunder of some 2,000 Merlin and Hercules engines as the Main Force approached.

YEAR 1944		AIRCRAFT		PILOT, OR 1ST PILOT	2ND PILOT, PUPIL OR PASSENGER	DUTY (INCLUDING RESULTS AND REMARKS)
MONTH	DATE	Type	No.			
—	—	—	—	—	—	— TOTALS BROUGHT FORWARD
		SUMMARY FR OCTOBER, 405 SQDN.				OCTOBER TOTALS :
		DATE: October 31/44			TYPES: 1. LANCASTER III	
		SIGNATURE. JR. Coffey F/Lt.			2 PERCIVAL PROCTOR	
						W.J. Marion S/Ldr
						O.C. "B" FLIGHT
OCT.	31	LANC. III	M	SELF	F/Lt BAYNE DFC	OPERATION - COLOGNE
					P/O WILLOUGHBY	1 X 4000, 6 X 1000, 4 X 500 H.E
					P/O DINGWALL	WANGANUI FLARES.
					P/O RUTHERGLEN	1275 GALS., 17,600 Ft.
					SGT HART	
					P/O McWHIRTER	(BLIND SKY MARKERS)
NOV.	2	LANC. III	M	SELF	F/L BAYNE, DFC	OPERATION - DUSSELDORF
					P/O WILLOUGHBY	1 X 4000, 5 X 1000, 5 X 500 H.E
					P/O DINGWALL	WANGANUI FLARES
					P/O RUTHERGLEN	1400 GALS., 18000 Ft.
					SGT HART	
					P/O McWHIRTER	(BLIND SKY MARKERS)

GRAND TOTAL [Cols. (1) to (10)]

914 Hrs. 30 Mins. TOTALS CARRIED FORWARD

Dad and crew were assigned as Blind Sky Markers and added their *Wanganui* sky marking flares to the continuous stream that the Pathfinders were dropping on the aiming point. Cologne was covered in a thick layer of cloud, topping out at 5,000 to 10,000 feet, but the *H2S*-placed sky markers made bomb aiming straightforward for the crews in the Main Force.

Maisye's contribution to Cologne's misery was a load of six 1,000-pound and four 500-pound bombs, and one 4,000-pound cookie, all of which Jimmy sent plummeting through the cloud just after 9 p.m. when they had finished their sky marking duties—they were back home before midnight.

Two nights later, Maisye roared off the runway once again, heading for Dusseldorf in the Ruhr Valley. The November 2nd operation against Dusseldorf was to be the last time Bomber Command would mount a major raid on the city, as by the time the almost 1,000 strong force left the unfortunate city, there was literally nothing left to bomb—Dusseldorf was left a moonscape of rubble.

There were two other ways this night's raid would involve "last times:" it would be the crew's last time flying at night, and it would the last time all seven of the Coffey crew would fly together, as one of them was destined to be "screened" upon their return from the Ruhr.

The crew arrived over Dusseldorf around 7 p.m. and added their green *Wanganui* flares to the already well-skymarked aiming point. The weather was perfect, with no cloud and just the usual industrial ground haze to contend with.

In the early years of the war the smog belching from the smokestacks of countless factories, filling the Ruhr from end to end, had bedevilled Bomber Command's attempts at accurate bombing. *H2S* had solved the problem, allowing the Pathfinders to see through the smaze and mark aiming points with bright target indicators and flares.

The flak this night over Dusseldorf was reported as heavy, but Maisye avoided any trouble, it seems, and after the crew unloaded their 10,000 pounds of high explosives, they headed back for England.

Another 405 Squadron Lancaster was not so lucky. K for King, skippered by Flying Officer Hannah, was hit by flak over the city. Although the aircraft remained airworthy, Hannah was badly wounded in the chest and knocked unconscious, going limp over the control column. Bomb aimer George Martin struggled for minutes before finally being able to pull Hannah's dead weight from the pilot's seat, whereupon he took over piloting the Lancaster, having never flown anything but a Link trainer before! With the help of the crew's navigator, he managed to get them back to England and make a wheels-up crash landing in a field.

Their mid-upper gunner remained in Germany as a P.O.W., having misinterpreted the panicked intercom chatter when they were hit as an order to bail out. Sadly, Flying Officer H. A. Hannah succumbed to his wounds two months later, having never left the hospital.

Ken Hart likely didn't know for sure that the Dusseldorf trip would be his final operation, but he must have known he was close. After the war, he wrote in his scrapbook that he reckoned the ops he completed to Cologne and Dusseldorf with the Coffey crew were the start of his "third tour"! He must have been anticipating those magic words "you're screened" at any time, and he finally heard them after debriefing from his trip to Dusseldorf.

I can only imagine his feelings.

There must have been elation and relief, of course, but I wonder if there was some hesitation as well? Although the rest of the Coffey crew were not far behind him, they had not finished their tours yet, and would carry on without him. Did Ken even have a twinge of an urge, I wonder, to carry on with them, so they could all finish together?

It's not likely, and I don't fault him one little bit—more than one bomber crew fell victim to flak or Nachtjager cannon fire on what was supposed to be their successful final operation, and Ken would have been foolhardy to risk it.

At any rate, Ken wasted no time in sharing the good news, and that same day fired off a laconic telegram to his mother back in London, Ontario, which read:

FINISHED OPERATIONS LOVE

The sight of a telegram boy coming up the driveway was a terrifying experience for any parent with a son in Bomber Command, so I hope Mrs. Hart got the good news quickly, before she had a chance to panic and assume the worst. She and the rest of the Hart family had already had a nasty scare the previous year when the local paper had mistakenly printed a photo of Ken under the bold heading *MISSING* (the notice was actually for Sgt. David Brown, an air gunner with 408 Squadron who had been shot down over Germany).

It took some time for the RAF bureaucracy to decide what to do with Ken next, although a troopship heading back to Canada was likely in the offing. In the meantime, he cooled his heels at Gransden Lodge. I am willing to bet he was on the tarmac on November 9th to wave his friends off and then greet them on their return from Wanne-Eickel, their final operation. But sometime during the ensuing few weeks before Ken was sent home, he had one task he wanted to complete. He wanted to keep the promise that had been made to his new crewmates at No. 1664 Heavy Conversion Unit many months before and tell them why he had been grounded for twelve months.

It is a story about a tragedy, but also very much about courage and resilience.

At about the time Ken arrived at the Personnel Receiving Centre in Bournemouth in May of 1942, my Dad was still on tarmac duty, guarding the perimeter of the Air Observer School back in Edmonton. Three of the other future members of the Coffey crew hadn't even joined up yet—this gives us an idea of how much farther ahead Ken was.

From Bournemouth, Ken was assigned to the No. 7 Air Gunners School at RAF Stormy Down in Wales, where he spent about two weeks honing the basic skills he had already learned back at the No. 4 Bombing and Gunnery School in Fingal, Ontario.

As part of the curriculum at Stormy Down, students were taken to the nearby sand dunes, where they would climb into a powered gun turret on the back of a trailer and blast away (sometimes at night with tracer ammunition) at a target moving on a small rail track. It seems, however, that most of the training was classroom-based, involving the usual drill of stripping and reassembling the .303 Browning, aircraft recognition, types of ammunition, and so on.

From Stormy Down, Ken was sent to the No. 22 Operational Training Unit, where he was put to work as an air gunner with numerous crews. It's unclear why Ken didn't follow the standard route of joining up with one crew during the usual "crewing up" process. In mid-September, Ken left the OTU and travelled north to RAF Topcliffe in Yorkshire, where he joined the RCAF's 405 Squadron, who were equipped with the Halifax Mark II.

Ken's logbook shows he flew training operations with several different pilots and crews for the next three weeks, until he and the rest of the squadron got some momentous news from Bomber Command H.Q.

The squadron was ordered to move lock, stock, and barrel some three hundred miles to an RAF base on the south coast of England—until further notice, they would be dropping depth charges instead of bombs.

405 Squadron had been part of Bomber Command since 1941 and was flying regular operations against targets in Germany, but suddenly they were told that their brief was to change immediately. They had been

temporarily (and much to the consternation of "Bomber" Harris, who fought the decision in vain) placed on loan to Coastal Command to assist in the fight against the German U-boats. The submarines were decimating Allied shipping in the Atlantic and threatening the supply ships that were supporting the imminent Allied invasion of North Africa, *Operation Torch*.

On October 31st, 1942, Ken flew to RAF Beaulieu in Hampshire, manning the mid-upper turret of a Halifax flown by Wing Commander Fraser, the squadron's Commanding Officer.

Moving an entire Bomber Command squadron was no mean feat—the official records give only a scant outline of all the work involved. The squadron's Halifaxes and their crews flew to Hampshire in groups, with the ground crew (and their tons of equipment and tools) following over successive days in truck convoys. Three Handley-Page Harrows (obsolete pre-war bombers pressed into service as transport aircraft) carried priority ground crew and equipment on the first day, and more "erks" followed the next day via bus. Twenty Women's Auxiliary Air Force (WAAFs as they were known) personnel came along as well, and the squadron records state that they were "warmly welcomed by the boys" at RAF Beaulieu.

One of the crews arriving in Hampshire to their new home was piloted by Flight Sergeant Clifford Stovel, and he immediately set about finding a replacement for his mid-upper gunner, who for some reason had transferred to another squadron before they left Topcliffe. Ken Hart was a natural choice, and very quickly after their arrival Ken became a part of the Stovel crew.

After less than a week of settling in and organizing, the Halifaxes of 405 Squadron began their new duties, flying long lonely patrols over the Bay of Biscay. Every member of the crew would be on the lookout, scanning the waves for the outline of a submarine, which travelled on the surface for the most part, submerging only to approach and attack their prey. The two air gunners on the crew would be on double-duty: they had to keep eyes peeled for German fighters as well.

A Halifax B II coded LQ-R, meaning that this aircraft flew with
405 Squadron in 1942, and that Ken Hart may have flown in this very aircraft.
Original wartime postcard, author's collection.

The Halifax B II flown by 405 Squadron at that time would have a load of 250-pound Torpex depth charges to use if they were lucky enough to spot a U-boat—but they had to act fast, as the sub would immediately dive if their lookouts spotted an aircraft. Any submarine in the Bay of Biscay was either returning to its base in France after a weeks-long hunting expedition or heading out into the North Atlantic with a bellyful of torpedoes meant for Allied merchants and troopships.

Ken Hart and the rest of the Stovel crew took off from Beaulieu to begin their first patrol early on the morning of November 6th, 1942.

It ended prematurely and badly.

Some seventy years later, I was becoming more and more immersed in my Dad's Bomber Command experience and was in the early stages of attempting to connect with all the families of his crewmates.

I had tracked down the family of Teddy Rutherglen and Jimmy Willoughby, both of whom were keen to help with my research, and these early successes had boosted my confidence.

Locating the families of Ken Hart and Bob McWhirter took a bit longer and were more involved, but the searches in both cases turned out to be well worth the effort.

As I have mentioned, cold calling strangers out of the blue is not something that comes naturally to me, so before I dialed the number of a possible contact, I had to take a deep breath and remind myself of my goal: to find the families of my Dad's crewmates. Many of those early calls were met with confused pauses, others with suspicion, but then there were those golden moments when, after identifying myself, the response was something along the lines of a delighted, "Oh my goodness, are you Jesse's son?!"

My first call with Susanne, Ken Hart's daughter, was one of the latter. She was so pleased to connect, and it became plain during our conversation that she revered her Dad, and that although she already knew quite a lot about his RCAF experience, she was keen to learn more.

Susanne sent me copies of her Dad's scrapbook and his logbook, both of which made for thought-provoking reading. I was puzzled by Ken's time with the Stovel crew in particular—why did it end after only a few operations, and why then a twelve-month blank period in his logbook…? Susanne could not offer any insight; it was a mystery to her and her family as well.

And then there was the odd entry in his logbook for November 6th, 1942 (his first operation with the Stovel crew). He had written a brief comment of some kind as part of the entry but then, at some point, thoroughly redacted it with a black marker. I asked Susanne if she could hold the original page up to the light to see if she could make out what was written, but the entry is permanently lost. What could have been written there that needed to be so meticulously expunged?

Soon after receiving the package of memorabilia from Susanne, I had the privilege of meeting the last surviving member of the Coffey crew, Bob McWhirter, at his home in Kelowna. At one point in the conversation, I decided to ask him if he could clear up what I thought was just a small nagging mystery of little significance.

My time with Bob that day had flown by, and most of the conversation was very lighthearted, as he recounted stories like that of my Dad terrorizing the Land Army girls or of him "beating up" the airfield at Tholthorpe. Bob laughed as he talked about some of the lousy food they were fed and the nickname of "Button" (or sometimes even "Verbutton"!) that Teddy Rutherglen had bestowed upon him. He recounted how he would tease the other members of the crew about how being in the rear turret made him the "senior" member: since the tail was the first part of the aircraft to leave the ground on take-off, and the last part to touch down upon landing, he had more "airtime" than any of them! I felt like the tiny, faded black and white photo of the Coffey crew that the Rutherglen family had sent me was coming to life and that I was getting to know these seven young men.

But solemnity descended in the room when I casually asked Bob about meeting Ken Hart at the No. 1664 Heavy Conversion Unit in the spring of 1944, and whether the crew had asked Ken where he had been for the past year.

Bob's smile faded, and he hesitated. I put the hesitation down to him searching his memory, but looking back, I don't think it was his memory that caused him to hesitate—it was his undiminished loyalty to his crewmate and friend, and to the confidence that had been entrusted to him. After a long, pregnant pause, Bob spoke.

"He was clearing his guns on the ground," Bob told me, "...and accidentally fired into his rear turret, killing his own rear gunner. He didn't want to tell us about it then; he said he would tell us when our tour was over. True to his word, he told us then."

Shocked by the implications of the revelation, it was my turn to hesitate—what, if anything, was I going tell Susanne and the rest of the Hart family?

When I got home I decided I would do some research into Bob's story and try to dig up some corroborating evidence before I told the Hart family anything. I meant no disrespect towards Bob's powers of recollection, but it *had* been seventy years, after all, and before I dropped a bombshell on Susanne and her family, I wanted to know I had my facts right.

The 405 Squadron records that I could access online gave me part of the story, and a very kind researcher in Ontario forwarded copies of original wartime documents that filled in more detail. After several weeks of going over these documents, I felt I had as complete an account of what happened as I was likely to get.

In the end, Bob's memory was spot on but for one detail—the tragedy that Ken had told the Coffey crew about happened at 5,000 feet over the Bay of Biscay, not on the ground.

When I telephoned Ken's daughter again, I told her that I had some information that cleared up the mystery of her Dad's missing logbook year, but that it was an unhappy story and that I would leave it up to her as to whether she wanted to know the details or not. I knew that there were members of her family who had made it clear they thought it best to let sleeping dogs lie, but without hesitation, she told me she wanted to hear everything. I remember thinking that her decision took grit and courage, and that she was obviously her father's daughter.

The Stovel crew left Beaulieu at 7:30 on the morning of November 6, 1942 in a Handley-Page Halifax coded LQ-G. It was a typical late fall morning on the south coast of England, cloudy and wet, with poor visibility.

Flt. Sgt. Stovel steered a course into the Bay of Biscay, and they began their assigned patrol route and the often monotonous task of scanning the endless ocean, looking for the telltale conning tower of a submarine.

Less than two hours later, at 9:38, Sgt. Ken Hart requested permission from his skipper to test his guns. This check was a standard routine for every air gunner in Bomber and Coastal Command, and something that happened hundreds, perhaps thousands of times a day across the skies of England as armadas of Lancasters, Halifaxes, Stirlings, and Wellingtons made their way towards Germany.

But on this occasion, when Ken tried to fire a quick burst from his twin .303 Brownings, nothing happened—they were jammed. This malfunction had to be addressed quickly as the Halifax might come under attack from a German fighter at any time.

How things managed to go so tragically sideways at this point is unclear, but in the process of trying to unjam his guns, one of them suddenly went off—Ken testified later that "the firing controls were not touched" and that the gun "went off by itself."

A single .303 bullet from the errant burst sliced through the fuselage of the Halifax and through the doors of the rear turret before tearing into the back of Sgt. Hugh Gillespie, the crew's tail gunner. The bullet hit Gillespie's spine and ricocheted off into his belly, leaving his intestines terribly torn up.

Chaos must have ensued at that point, but they were a well-trained, professional crew, and they did what needed to be done. Flight Sergeant Stovel turned the Halifax around and set course for the nearest friendly airfield, in this case the RAF base at St. Eval in Cornwall. The crew's wireless operator radioed ahead to warn St. Eval of their arrival and requested a medical team meet them.

Sgt. Gillespie was gingerly pulled from the rear turret and made as comfortable as possible on the Halifax's rest bed—he likely got a shot of morphine from the emergency first aid kit and then had compression applied to his wound by one of his crewmates.

One can only imagine what state Ken was in—he must have been beside himself with guilt, remorse, and concern for his crewmate. But there was no time for emotion in the moment, as they were still over an hour away from land… with the mid-upper guns jammed and out of commission and the rear gunner wounded, the Halifax was entirely undefended. My jaw dropped in amazement as I reread Ken's logbook entry for the trip and realized what happened next: Ken Hart steeled himself and climbed into the blood-stained rear turret to take Gillespie's place and resume his job of scanning the skies for enemy fighters.

Not for the first or last time, I sat blown away by the pure courage and dedication of the young men of Bomber Command.

Flt. Sgt. Stovel landed the Halifax safely at St. Eval, where they were met by medics who loaded Sgt. Gillespie into an ambulance and sped away to the Royal Cornwall Infirmary in Truro. Gillespie arrived at the hospital in a "dangerous condition," according to the official records.

In reality, Sgt. Gillespie stood little chance of survival—the stray bullet had torn up his intestines and rectum badly, resulting in spreading infection, which would have been difficult to control even in a modern-day hospital.

Gillespie was conscious but in obvious pain when he arrived at the hospital, and was operated on by Dr. J. H. Hood, who removed the .303 bullet and repaired the damage as best he could. Over the next few days, Gillespie was given morphine to make him comfortable, and antibiotics, which fought a losing battle with a raging infection. He died in the evening of November 13th, 1942.

Hugh Gordon Gillespie was older than most Bomber Command aircrew, thirty-three at the time of the accident. He hailed from Port Coquitlam, British Columbia, which is only a few kilometres from where I live, but I have been unable to find any of his descendants. He was unmarried, and his parents had died years before his death. A very kind letter was sent to Gillespie's closest relative (his brother) from Wing Commander Fraser, the squadron's Commanding Officer. The family was told that their brother had been "fatally injured due to an air accident" and that "he was liked, and admired, and respected by all those with whom he came in contact."

Sgt. Gillespie was buried with full military honours on November 17th in Major Cemetery in St. Columb, Cornwall. The Stovel crew, including Ken, flew an anti-submarine patrol the day after his funeral, so I think it was unlikely they attended, as their base was some two hundred miles to the east of where the service took place.

Ken continued to fly with the Stovel crew while the accident was investigated and the powers-that-be decided what, if any, action to take against him. The fact that Ken carried on flying clearly shows that the Stovel crew had confidence in their mid-upper gunner. One word from Sgt. Stovel to his Commanding Officer and Ken likely would have been grounded, and to me, it once again demonstrates the tight bond formed among Bomber Command aircrew.

Ken flew about six more patrols with the Stovel crew before he got what must have been devastating news: he was to face a court-martial for his role in the deadly accident. On his final operation with his crew, they sighted and attacked a U-boat in the Bay of Biscay, dropping six depth charges into the swirling water that the sub had left behind as it made an emergency dive. They were unable to stick around to see if any wreckage or oil came to the surface to indicate a kill, as they were at the far edge of their range and had to beat it home before their fuel ran out. As it turned out, they barely made it back to the English coast, landing once again at RAF St. Eval to refuel and flying back to RAF Beaulieu the following day. The bad news was waiting for them when they landed—their mid-upper gunner was being removed from the crew and grounded pending the outcome of the court-martial.

Ken Hart faced his court-martial in February of 1943. I have been unable to find the original court-martial documents (they are likely in a file box somewhere in the National Archives in Kew), but really, the details of the proceedings matter little to our story. Ken was found guilty of negligence, ordered detained for two months, and reduced in rank back to Leading Aircraftman.

It should not have been possible for Ken to fire into his own aircraft; there were mechanical systems in place in the turret that were supposed to prevent a gunner from accidentally firing into his own plane during the heat of combat. It is pure conjecture on my part, but perhaps Ken went against his training by having his turret facing towards the rear of his Halifax instead of off to the side, towards the sea, as he attempted to clear his jammed Browning .303 machine gun.

Ken spent about two months in detention and was then reinstated as a Sergeant and assigned to the RCAF's Air Command Headquarters on General Duties. It is a vague description, and he may have been assigned as anything from a transport driver to a mail clerk to an Officers aide. At any rate, after six months of this, Ken must have become frustrated and decided to ask for a change. With his prior training and interests (remember that jalopy he fixed up back in Ontario?), he could have been an excellent candidate to become an engine mechanic or armourer, but Ken Hart volunteered once again for aircrew duties.

The choice, I think, highlights this young man's courage and character—after what he had been through, it would be perfectly understandable if he had decided to contribute to the war effort while keeping his feet firmly planted on the ground.

His request was granted, and in November of 1943, he was back at No. 22 Operational Training Unit in Wellesbourne, manning the rear turret of a Vickers Wellington for various crews over the course of a month. In January of 1944, he was transferred to the No. 1664 Heavy Conversion Unit, where he flew as mid-upper gunner with the Baldwin crew, the Peterson crew, the Bissett crew, and then the Coffey crew, with whom he found a permanent home.

Ken Hart's story is one of remarkable determination and resolve; many men in his shoes would never have even considered returning to flying after what he had been through. I think the Ju88 night fighter attack over Wizernes that the Coffey crew survived shows that Ken's decision, although likely not an easy one, turned out to be the right one—he proved himself to be a valuable, reliable, and skilful member of his new crew.

He was no doubt haunted by the memory of that tragic accident over the Bay of Biscay. In his post-war scrapbook, he posted several pictures of the Stovel crew. The caption he wrote above the grainy black and white snapshots suddenly acquired new, saddening significance when I reread it after learning the full story of Ken's accident.

Clifford Stovel and his crew were shot down over Hamburg in July of 1943, and five of them, including Flt. Lt. Stovel, were killed. Ken wrote above their photos, "…due to sickness I did not go with them. Some break."

The wording of the caption, coupled with that redacted logbook entry, makes it obvious Ken was not at peace with the part he played in the tragic accident. He never spoke to his family of the incident, although his daughter thinks he may perhaps have confided in his older brother Bev, who was a paratrooper and had visited Ken at Gransden Lodge in the summer of 1944.

This theme of hidden burdens, of young men carrying their fears and troubling memories buried deep inside, is one that kept recurring for me throughout my research.

One particular light-hearted story that Bob McWhirter told me when I interviewed him took on new and troubling significance when I recalled it after learning the details of Ken Hart's accident.

Sometime that summer of 1944, "Button" McWhirter gleefully approached the rest of his crewmates with a .303 bullet in the palm of his hand and an amazing story to tell.

The night before, in the dark skies over Germany, some nervous tail gunner in another Lancaster or Halifax had mistaken Maisye for a German night fighter (it wasn't an uncommon occurrence, apparently) and fired a burst from his four .303 machine guns at them. My Dad, swearing colourfully into his oxygen mask, had thrown their Lancaster into an evasive turn and escaped the "attacker," and they were soon back on track toward their target. No one gave any further thought to the incident—it was par for the course, I suppose.

The following day, as their "erks" were going over the Lancaster from stem to stern, one of the armourers spotted an indentation in Bob McWhirter's rear turret seat. Perhaps using a screwdriver or pocket knife, he soon found the source of the dent: a single .303 bullet was embedded in the back of the seat. It had penetrated the fuselage, the doors of the rear turret and finally the first few millimetres of Bob's seat before its force was spent. Bob recalled that he must have been leaning forward when it hit, or he likely would have felt the impact or even been wounded or worse. The ground crew dug out the slug and gave it to Bob the next time he saw him.

"I almost bought it last night, boys!" Bob laughed as he showed the rest of the Coffey crew the spent bullet. I am sure they all laughed and kidded him about his close call… but perhaps not all of them? I can't help but imagine what Ken Hart's reaction was when he heard the story and saw the bullet. Did his friends wonder why he looked so serious, why his face suddenly drained of colour?

The Coffey crew took off at about 8:30 on the morning of November 9th, 1944, on what was to be the final operation for most of them. Only Jimmy Willoughby would carry on after the 9th, as he still owed the RAF a few more operations, having started a bit later than the rest of the crew.

Although Ken was not with them, they were certainly in good hands as far as manning their mid-upper turret went. Joining them for this one trip was Flt. Lt. Melvin Hamblin, a seasoned veteran and a regular member of 405 Squadron's Marcou crew. Hamblin had been born in the U.S.A., but with Canadian roots, as his father was a Canadian entrepreneur who ran a furniture business in Detroit.

After lifting off the tarmac at Gransden Lodge they, along with nine other Lancs from 405, joined a force of about three hundred (not including their cover escort of almost two hundred Spitfires and P-51 Mustangs) heading for the Ruhr Valley city of Wanne-Eickel, home to a major synthetic oil plant, the coal mine that supplied it, and the GAVEG chemical plant.

YEAR 1944		AIRCRAFT		PILOT, OR 1ST PILOT	2ND PILOT, PUPIL OR PASSENGER	DUTY (INCLUDING RESULTS AND REMARKS)
MONTH	DATE	Type	No.			
—	—	—	—	—	—	— TOTALS BROUGHT FORWARD
Nov.	9	Lanc III	M	SELF	F/L Bayne	OPERATION - WANNI EICKEL RUHR
					P/O Willoughby	1 x 4000, 6 x 1000, 6 x 500H
					P/O Dingwall	1225 Gals. 10.0.0 P/L
					P/O Rutherglen	
					F/L Hamblin	
					P/O McWhirter	
		SUMMARY FOR NOVEMBER, 1944				NOVEMBER TOTALS.
		UNIT - 405 SQDN.	TYPES - LANC III			
		SIGNATURE - J.R. Coffey F/Lt.				
						SECOND TOUR COMPLETED NOV. 9/44.
		NUMBER OF SORTIES - 59				OPERATIONAL HOURS:
						NIGHT - 227:25 DAY - 36:05
						TOTAL: 263:30
						GRAND TOTAL:
						D. J. McQuiad S/LDR. O.C. "B" FLIGHT.

GRAND TOTAL [Cols. (1) to (10)]
818 Hrs. 05 Mins.

TOTALS CARRIED FORWARD

Germany had been building up its capacity to produce synthetic oil (derived from processing coal) for years, ever since Hitler had foreseen the need for alternatives to traditional sources of oil and had ordered the industry to scale up. He knew Germany did not have the oil reserves needed to fuel the war he planned—one of his Panzer divisions could easily devour a thousand gallons of gas for every mile it advanced. Numerous plants were built in the late '30s, usually adjacent to large coal mines. Names like Gelsenkirchen, Wanne-Eickel and Castrop-Rauxel became very familiar to Allied bomber crews as their leaders sent them to try and destroy the plants and thus choke off Germany's supply of fuel.

It would be gratifying for me to report that the Coffey crew's last operation was a glorious success, a fitting swan song to their service in Bomber Command, but the attack was a dud.

It appears that the synthetic oil plant at Wanne-Eickel led a bit of charmed life—Bomber Command's records show the plant was attacked repeatedly, right up to the end of the war, but was never even seriously damaged.

On November 9th, the approaching bomber force was met with solid cloud up to 22,000 feet and crews reported severe icing and temperatures down to -26 degrees Fahrenheit. The Mosquitoes of the Pathfinder Force gamely dropped their skymarker flares, but they disappeared into the dense cloud immediately, and the frustrated Master Bomber soon gave the order over the radio for crews to bomb as best they could, using whatever method they could.

Dad and crew made a timed run from the city centre of Wesel, which Bob Bayne and Malcolm Dingwall could see clearly on their *H2S* set, and, with confirmation from their *GEE* navigation system, dropped their 13,000-pound load of high explosive on a point they estimated was over the plant. Everyone else was in the same boat, and the bombing was scattered and ineffective.

Reading about the attack on Wanne-Eickel was another one of those times when a story my Dad told me as a teenager suddenly came into sharper focus and took on added significance. Dad had told me that, after dropping their bomb load on their final flight, he told the crew to hang on, as he was going to head for home at treetop level.

What possessed my Dad to take such an unorthodox (and unauthorized) break from the plan? The weather over Wanne-Eickel perhaps gives a clue: the thick, relentless cloud substantially increased the risk of a mid-air collision, especially during that day's chaotic attack, which likely meant some crews were coming back across the target area in an attempt to find the aiming point. Maybe my Dad felt it was safer to leave the bomber stream and descend below the cloud cover so they could see what they were doing and avoid the crowds at 20,000 feet? It's a plausible explanation, but something tells me that at least part of Dad's decision was more personal and emotional than logical. I think he knew it was their final trip, and I wonder if their idiosyncratic last flight home wasn't partly a gesture, a big, joyful middle finger to the deck of cards and the statistics that had been so cruelly stacked against their survival for so long.

"Screw you, Fate; we made it!"

Whatever the reason, my Dad peeled off from the assigned route over the Ruhr and put Maisye into a fast descent while Bob and Malcolm quickly charted a new course back to Gransden Lodge. Jimmy Willoughby cranked up the power on the four Merlin engines, and they roared back west, across the nearby front lines, across France and then the English Channel, finally touching down back at Gransden Lodge at 12:18 pm. Dad taxied Maisye to her dispersal pad, Jimmy shut down the engines, and they all climbed out of the Lancaster, all but one of them for the very final time.

Their job was done.

CHAPTER SIX:
DISPERSAL

NOVEMBER 1944 AND AFTER

I'm betting there was a party!

A crew safely finishing a second tour of operations was not something that happened very often, although in the latter half of 1944, it was thankfully becoming more common than in previous years.

A party was certainly a well-justified way to mark the occasion, and it's likely they held it at the local pub rather than at the officer's mess at RAF Gransden Lodge. The Coffey crew would have wanted their ground crew to be there, and the officer's mess would have been off-limits to the Aircraftmen, Corporals, and Flight Sergeants who had worked so hard to keep them flying. And not just them: all our crew were officers now—Dad and Bob Bayne were Flight Lieutenants, the rest Pilot Officers, except for Ken Hart, who remained a Sergeant, his lack of a much-overdue promotion a consequence of his court-martial. He, too, would have been barred from the officer's mess. Within two weeks, the seven comrades would part ways, never to meet as a complete group again. It is sad in a way, but I am sure a familiar story—comrades-in-arms who return home and move on to new lives when their jobs were done.

Dad posing self-consciously for a portrait in a very English-looking back garden.
Photographer unknown. Author's collection.

Before he left Gransden Lodge, my Dad totalled up his logbook: his summary lists sixty completed "ops" (he credited himself with one more than the official tally, perhaps mistakenly including one of the sea searches conducted at No. 1664 Heavy Conversion Unit) during which he and his crew had dropped almost 600,000 pounds of high explosives and incendiaries on enemy targets, burning 83,006 gallons of gas in the process. He had spent 263 hours and 30 minutes flying in combat, the vast majority at night, and glad he must have been to get it over with, gleefully writing "**last trip YIPEE!**" at the end of the List of Operations.

YEAR		AIRCRAFT		PILOT, OR 1ST PILOT	2ND PILOT, PUPIL or PASSENGER	DUTY (INCLUDING RESULTS AND REMARKS)	
MONTH	DATE	Type	No.				
						TOTALS BROUGHT FORWARD	
				LIST OF OPERATIONS AND TIMES.			T.O.T.
MONTH	DAY	TARGET		BOMB LOAD	GAS LOAD	HEIGHT / TIME NIGHT / DAY	
Aug.	7	BEACHHEAD CAEN (FR)		14,000 lbs.	1400 GALS	14000	2:30	2342
Aug.	8	LA HEST DE LUMONT (FR)		14,000 lbs.	1450 "	15000	2:55	2346
Aug.	12	RUSSELSHEIM (GR.)		10,040 "	1500 "	17000	4:30	0009
Aug.	16	KIEL (GR.)		10,100 "	1500 "	17000	5:00	0010
Aug.	18	BREHEN (GER.)		11,200	1500	15000	4:50	0012
Aug.	25	RUSSELSHEIM (GER.)		8,200	1970	14000	7:15	0108
Aug.	26	KIEL (GER)		9,600	1500	17000	5:25	2314
Aug.	29	STETTIN (GER)		7,400	2100	17500	8:35	0153
Sept.	15	KIEL (GER.)		7,400	1650	17000	5:10	0108
Oct.	5	SAARBRUCKEN (GER)		10,600	1500	18000	4:50	2023
Oct.	6	DORTMUND (GER)		11,400	1500	18000	4:50	2033
Oct.	14	DUISBURG (GER)		11,400	1400	18000	3:55	0137
Oct.	15	WILHELMSHAVEN (GER)		10,600	1500	18000	4:05	1938
Oct.	19	STUTTGART. (GER)		10,600	1700	18000	5:25	0100
Oct.	31	COLOGNE (GER.)		12,800	1275	17600	4:10	2100
Nov	2	DUSSELDORF (GER)		11,800	1400	18000	4:10	1915
Nov.	9	WANNI EIKEL (GER.)		13,000	1275	17600	3:35	last trip
TOTALS		60 OPS		589,320 lbs.	83,006 GAS.		227:25 36:05	YIPEE!!!
							263:30

GRAND TOTAL [Cols. (1) to (10)] Hrs. Mins.	TOTALS CARRIED FORWARD

Final page of Dad's List of Operations and Times, with a last gleeful note at the bottom.

Ken Hart was the first to go, leaving Gransden Lodge on November 27th and travelling to the RCAF "R" Depot, a clearinghouse near Liverpool where airmen were processed for "Repatriation" back to Canada.

Ted Rutherglen left next, on November 30th, but he was ordered to RAF Exning, in Suffolk, which was HQ for Bomber Command's 3 Group, where he would act as a Canadian liaison staff officer for the next five months. The delay in going home to Canada was not something he was upset by, and was at his request, as we shall see.

My Dad, Bob McWhirter, Bob Bayne, Malcolm Dingwall, and Teddy Rutherglen all left together on December 4th, and made their way as a group to "R" Depot, where most of them were soon assigned to troopships re-crossing the Atlantic. Bob Bayne somehow managed to score himself a faster trip home, flying across the Atlantic in a Canada-bound Lancaster on December 18th.

This tally leaves only Jimmy Willoughby unaccounted for, and since I want to tell a bit about our crew's lives after they came home from the war, it seems logical to start with him.

For two weeks or so after his final operation with the Coffey crew, Jimmy Willoughby flew various training flights with several other crews, and then returned to ops on November 27th with the McIntyre crew on a trip to Neuss, a medium-sized industrial town in the Ruhr. Over the course of the next few weeks, Jimmy flew operations to Duisburg, Essen, Nuremburg, Hanover, and finally Munich on January 7th, 1945. Upon return from his 56th operation, he was told he was screened. His job was done now, too (well, almost).

It seems 405 Squadron kept Jimmy busy in an administration capacity of some kind over the next four or five months as the noose tightened around what remained of Nazi Germany, and bombing operations started to wind down.

The squadron's final bombing operation was at the end of April, and in May, Germany finally surrendered. The Lancasters of Bomber Command (including those of 405 Squadron) were then put to work in an incredible month-long operation to ferry tens of thousands of Allied P.O.W.s back to England. Some of these poor young men had been in captivity since the fall of France in 1940, and many, I am sure, had never been in an aircraft before. Still, skinny and in threadbare uniforms, they were loaded into fuselages of Lancasters, about twenty-six at a time, and flown back to receiving centres in England.

In June, the squadron was officially disbanded, and their Lancasters prepared to fly back to Canada. As a member of the RAF, Jimmy would, of course, not be going with them. At the end of May, he was transferred to the RAF's 128 Squadron at Wyton, where he took to the air for the final few times as a flight engineer with three different pilots as they flew "Cook's Tours."

"Cook's Tours" was the humorous name (a reference to the famous travel company) given to daytime flights made to Germany to show support personnel like ground crew and staff officers the destruction wrought by Bomber Command on Germany. They could fly (without fear, now that German forces had surrendered) at a low level over the Ruhr or Berlin and see for themselves the devastating damage that the Bomber Campaign had inflicted. It must have been a sobering experience for those who had previously only heard stories or seen photographs.

Jimmy must have had some leave that spring of 1945, as at some point he attended a dance in London and met a young English girl named Winnifred Palmer. One dance led to another, and the next thing you know, the couple was getting married, exchanging vows on June 20th. Winnifred's new husband was officially discharged from the RAF in November of 1946 with the rank of Flying Officer and awarded the Distinguished Flying Cross for his service.

Mr. and Mrs. Willoughby leaving England, bound for a new life in Jamaica.
Photo courtesy of the Willoughby family.

Jimmy and Winnifred Willoughby sailed from England in July of 1946, and the Willoughby family sent me a photo of the couple on board the ship as it left port, headed for Jamaica. Winnifred looks very excited and happy—leaving war-torn Britain, a land of rationing and austerity, for a new life in the tropics must have been a wondrous adventure for her!

The couple stayed in Jamaica for a few months, then decided to emigrate permanently to Australia, a country that Jimmy's brother had sold them on—he had visited and fallen in love with it during his time in the Merchant Marine during the war. Australia was actively promoting immigration in the years after WW II, and there was little in the way of red tape for any British citizen who wished to relocate "down under." There were so many takers that there was even a slang term among Aussies for the wave of new arrivals: "Ten Pound Poms" they were dubbed, referring to the one fee they paid to immigrate.

The Willoughbys returned to England for six months and then, accompanied by many of the members of Winnifred's family, boarded a ship for Sydney, arriving there in early December of 1947.

In January of 1949, the Distinguished Flying Cross that Jimmy had been awarded in 1945 finally caught up to him, and he was presented with the decoration by the Governor-General at Admiralty House in Sydney. The couple's eldest son, Keith, was a year old by then, and they went on to have two more sons, John in 1957 and Craig in 1965. The family lived in the Sydney suburb of St. Mary's, where they owned a modest home on a quiet street.

Jimmy had a head for engineering and mechanics and a logical mind and soon found work in this field as a Design Engineer, first with Kellogg's Australia and then with a firm called W. E. Cuckson. At the latter firm, he worked on projects as diverse as packaging machinery for zippers to a new suspended ceiling design. His sons tell me their Dad was a very hard worker, probably too hard for his own good. After his first heart attack in early 1965, he insisted on having his drawing board brought from his office to home to continue working from his sickbed. Two months later, Jimmy was back in the office, and on November 11th, 1965, had a second heart attack, this one fatal.

Digby "Jimmy" Willoughby was only 44 when he died, and his early death seems especially tragic and unfair considering the very recent birth of his youngest son, Craig.

Jimmy and the rest of the Coffey crew lost contact with each other after the war, and Bob McWhirter expressed shock and sadness in 2015 when I told him the year in which Jimmy had passed away.

Bob Bayne was the only member of the crew who decided to make a career in the Air Force, and he joined the regular RCAF in 1945. It is indicative, I think, of the respect his superiors had for him that he was allowed to keep his wartime temporary rank of Flight Lieutenant, as it was often the case that a man was required to sink a rank or two in order to stay in the regular peace-time military. The two Distinguished Flying Crosses that Bob had won probably helped his cause!

Bob went on to have a long, distinguished career with the RCAF, rising to Squadron Leader and eventually to the rank of Wing Commander. He was deployed all over the world, and at one point, assisted NATO with the debriefing of East Bloc pilots who had defected. He went on to teach Ethics and Tactics at the Royal Military College in Kingston.

In 1948, Bob was one of "18 expert air navigators" who took part in an expedition of seven RAF Lancasters who made an epic 5,300-mile flight from England to Gibraltar, and then north to the Arctic Circle, and finally back to the U.K. The RAF said the trip proved that "flights to polar regions now are routine and present no abnormal hazard."

Bob had gotten engaged before he left to serve overseas in 1943, and married June when he returned in 1945. They had three children over the years. Bob's grandson told me he recalls his grandfather fondly, remembering him as a "consummate gentleman," highly intelligent and passionate about geography and world events. He was an avid reader (with a large, well-stocked bookcase in his home) and had a wonderful sense of humour—he especially loved to tell long, funny stories and jokes, never bothering with "one-liners."

In 1988, Bob and Malcolm Dingwall exchanged letters and photos—the snapshot of Bob shows him on the balcony of his apartment, looking fit and steely-eyed, with an impressive head of thick grey hair. The baggy grey V-neck sweater he wears was apparently a bone of contention, however—he told "Ding" that he wished his wife would buy him sweaters that fit!

Bob Bayne in 1988. Photo courtesy of the Dingwall family.

Bob and Malcolm continued to correspond into the 1990s, and in one letter Bob expressed sadness that Ken Hart, my Dad, and Ted Rutherglen were all dead, noting, "it is hard to realize that over fifty years have elapsed since we 'crewed up' at OTU… a crew that was lucky enough to survive."

After retiring from the RCAF in the late 1960s, Bob and June wintered regularly in Florida, where Bob indulged his passion for golf. Bob Bayne enjoyed robust good health until the insidious disease of Alzheimer's took hold of him late in life. His grandson was the first to notice a problem, alerting the rest of the family that there was something odd about his grandfather's speech and that he seemed a bit confused and having trouble with his memory. After some tests and a diagnosis, the horrible disease advanced quickly.

Bob Bayne passed away peacefully on August 23, 2006, at the age of eighty-eight.

Pilot Officer Malcolm Dingwall DFC, arrived back in Canada on December 18th, 1944, and was soon reunited with Edith and his daughter Diana, who had been a newborn babe when he left for England eighteen months earlier. The young family set to work getting to know each other again, remaining settled in

Shellbrook, Saskatchewan. Malcolm started a business with a partner, a general store named *Dingwall and Kopping*, and a bakery/cafe. Over the next ten years, the family grew, with the addition of daughter Sandra and son Lorie. In 1952, the Dingwalls packed up and moved their lives to British Columbia, prompted by Saskatchewan's poor economy and Malcolm's emphysema. He had picked up the smoking habit while serving with Bomber Command, where the crews often sat around in front of their bombed-up aircraft, nervously chain-smoking while waiting for take-off time. The flour dust from the bakery had exacerbated the condition, irritating his smoke-damaged lungs.

Once settled in Prince George, Malcolm put his business skills to good use, becoming an accountant and eventually the de facto General Manager of several large, successful car dealerships.

Over the decades, Malcolm became a well-loved figure in the local community. He was soft-spoken and reserved, but not at all shy and would sometimes play subtle, good-natured pranks on his friends and co-workers. People were drawn to him—Malcolm was personable and didn't put others off with overbearing opinions or loud talk. And he certainly didn't talk much about the war—his children told me you had to ask a specific question to get their father to speak about that time in his life. Son Lorie recalled that on one occasion, his father looked pained as he quietly recalled looking down on the "burning cities" and seeing the winds created by the incendiaries "sucking furniture and people down the street into the fire."

It was not a line of questioning that Lorie ever brought up again.

After retirement, Malcolm and Edith decided to leave Prince George and move to Courtenay, on Vancouver Island, a popular area for retirees. There they could be close to first-born Diana and their grand-children. Over the years, the couple explored the beautiful Island countryside, and Malcolm delighted in "heading down a road to see where it would take him."

Malcolm Dingwall in the 1990's, proudly showing off part of his grape harvest.
Photo courtesy of the Dingwall family.

Malcolm was diagnosed with an aneurysm in his heart late in his life, but he declined to have the surgery that might fix the problem. His doctor, concerned, warned him that he would get no warning that the issue was getting worse, that it would simply be like "a grenade going off in your chest..." Malcolm accepted the odds, declining the risky and invasive surgery, preferring to carry on with his life.

In 1998, at the age of eighty-three, Malcolm was listening to the humorous monologue of a Master of Ceremonies at a charity gala, and began to chuckle, then guffaw. The grenade finally exploded, and Malcolm's children told me their father, quite literally, died laughing. We should all be so fortunate.

Teddy Rutherglen was undoubtedly anxious to get home to British Columbia and to the mountains, lakes, and forests he loved so much, but (at the risk of sounding mawkish) another love needed to be attended to first. He asked for an assignment in England so that he could arrange to bring his new wife back to Canada. Irene Cox was a London girl who had joined the Women's Auxiliary Air Force and was assigned as a transport driver at RAF Gransden Lodge. Her job was to load up the aircrew before an operation and drive around the dispersal to drop off each crew at their Lancaster. At some point, Bob McWhirter asked her on a date, but there was no spark, and nothing came of it. Teddy decided to try his luck with the young Englishwoman, and they hit it off and quickly became an item.

What could it have been like to drop off the man you were in love with at his bombed-up Lancaster night after night, knowing that there was a very real chance you would never see him again...? It must have been pure hell for Irene to wait each night for Maisye to return safely.

Once all the paperwork was in order, Ted was released from the RCAF with the rank of Flying Officer, and recipient of the Distinguished Flying Cross. He travelled back to Canada to prepare for the arrival of his now pregnant bride (and his new mother-in-law), who arrived a month later, in the summer of 1945.

The couple settled in Nelson, a picturesque small town in B.C.'s Kootenay region. Irene and her mother were Londoners, but they gamely made a new life in the unfamiliar surroundings, although the Rutherglen children told me their mother and grandmother would have moved to a condo in downtown Vancouver in a heartbeat, given a choice! At some point in the 1970s, Ted surprised his wife with a trip back to London (he saved up the money over several years), where she had a joyful reunion with her family, especially her beloved brother.

Ted Rutherglen, quite naturally, found a job with the B.C. Fish and Game Department as a Game Warden, a career he loved and that suited him perfectly.

Ted was a larger-than-life character in Nelson and the surrounding countryside. Although of average height, Ted was a strong, fast, barrel-chested tank of a man who had learned to box while in the RCAF—and one you did not want to mess with. Although a gregarious, easygoing, and kind-hearted fellow, his children remember him as being ready for anything—they would often stay in wilderness cabins with their Dad, and if there was a noise in the night, they would awake to find him standing at the cabin door, fully alert and absolutely fearless. There was never any chip-on-the-shoulder bluster about Ted Rutherglen: he just meant business in whatever he did.

For example, there was the time that Ted, in his capacity of Game Warden, was tasked with serving an arrest warrant on a local logger. The culprit was a head taller and fifty pounds heavier than Ted, but when the man "got aggressive," he was quickly "put on the ground," according to Ted's son.

A post-war photo of Teddy Rutherglen, date uncertain. Courtesy of the Rutherglen family.

Fearlessness was a trait he worked hard to instill in his children, and his son remembers one occasion when his Dad brought him along when he went to put a wounded bear, who had been hit by a car, out of its misery with a shotgun. The call about the bear had come in the middle of the night, but Ted loved animals and could not abide to see one suffer. Their Dad also had a softer side and continued to play the guitar and sing after the war—he serenaded his children every night at bedtime, perhaps with some of the same songs he had sung to his crewmates.

Ted was well known and well-loved by the people in the Nelson area—writing in an online forum in 2012, one local man vividly recalled "Ted the Game Warden" bringing an orphaned fawn into his Grade One class for a sort of impromptu "show and tell."

Ted pioneered the use of tranquilizer darts and traps to deal with problem bears and invented the Culvert Bear Trap that is still in everyday use throughout North America. He much preferred drugging the problematic bears (using a dart attached to a ski pole in the early days—that's how close he got!) and transporting them into the wilderness, as opposed to killing them, but there were times he was given no choice. On one occasion, his job was put on the line when he vehemently protested an order from his boss to kill two young grizzlies who were getting habituated to humans. Ted's superior ordered him to get the dirty job done or quit. Backed into a corner, with a family to support, Ted had little choice but to obey the order to shoot the bears, but it was very hard on him, according to friend Ted Burns.

He also started a firearms safety training program that ultimately evolved into CORE, the safety and education program that all new hunters in B.C. must take to get their license.

I was surprised to see that Ted continued to use his RCAF wireless operator's logbook after the war. His duties as a Game Warden (later Conservation Officer) entailed regular flights to remote lakes to take samples of fish, or to conduct a census of local waterfowl, and the flights are all recorded in his logbook. On one occasion, he assisted the police searching for some missing trappers, flying as an observer and guide in a Grumman Goose flown by an RCMP pilot—they found at least one of the missing men on their second day of searching.

I had to laugh when I saw the first few post-war entries in his logbook—Ted records that the B.C. Forestry aircraft he flew in (as an observer) was the Junkers W34. This ugly single-engine transport plane was manufactured by the same company, perhaps in the same factory, as the Junkers Ju88 Nachtjager that had attacked the Coffey crew that summer night over France. I am betting Ted saw the humour and irony as well and pointed it out to Charlie Wilson, his pilot.

Despite his lifelong good humour and positive attitude, Ted was not unaffected by the stress and terror of what he had been through while serving in Bomber Command. His children have shared with me that their Dad suffered from horrible nightmares, the most memorable was the night, still half asleep, he punched right through a bedroom wall to protect his young son from "the Germans" who were "after him."

After each of these terrible dreams, their mother would soothe the children, tell them to go back to bed and not to worry—"it was just some things from the war," she would reassure them. Ted also carried around tiny fragments of perspex lodged in his face, causing not just physical pain but what must have been a very unwelcome daily reminder of his brush with violent death over France that night in 1944.

Teddy's daughter, Christine, told me that one Christmas she spotted her Dad's Distinguished Flying Cross in a drawer and decided to have it mounted and framed as a surprise. When Teddy opened the gift, he was overwhelmed. Fighting back tears, he left the room to compose himself but not before quietly telling his daughter, "I didn't think anyone cared."

Ted continued with his Game Warden duties for the rest of his life. At the age of fifty-seven, he muscled a group of boulders around in a small creek to create a pool, thus trapping a pair of particularly interesting fish that he wanted to show some local schoolchildren. He complained to his wife that evening that he had "pulled a muscle" in his chest, but it may have been more consequential than that. A week later, while visiting a friend in Calgary, Teddy Rutherglen had what was likely his second heart attack and died on August 25th, 1977.

Ken Hart returned to Canada like almost all returning airmen, via a troopship, and he arrived back in Canada before Christmas in 1944, just a few days before my Dad did. He spent a few weeks at a Bombing and Gunnery School in Quebec as an instructor, sharing his knowledge and experience with the recruits, and was then released from service and returned home to his family in London, Ontario. Around this time, Ken finally got some long-overdue official recognition for his service, and was promoted to Pilot Officer and awarded the Distinguished Flying Medal.

There is no doubt Ken was haunted by troubling memories upon his return to civilian life—Ken's father remembered his son as "being like a lost soul," who would sit at a piano in his parent's home and play with the keys for hours, in another world. But Ken's naturally buoyant spirit and upbeat personality soon reasserted itself. A few months later, he had risen above the gloom and signed up for an education program specially organized for veterans by the Government of Canada. A year later, he received a diploma in Business Administration and had landed himself a job with the large insurance firm of London Life.

His social life had gotten busy as well—Ken began dating Edna Reidhead (literally the girl next door!), and in the fall of 1947, they were married, honeymooning at Niagara Falls. Over the years, they raised four children together, three daughters and a son.

Ken Hart posing for a London Life promotional photo in the early 70's.
Photo courtesy of Susanne (Hart) Thrasher.

Ken continued to work for London Life for the next thirty-six years, rising to Manager of Marketing Services by the time he retired in 1982, and was respected and beloved by his co-workers.

I think Ken must have missed the camaraderie of military life, as it wasn't long after the war that he joined the RCAF reserve, working as a supply officer at a local base in his spare time. When the base was closed in the early 1960s, Ken held the rank of Flight Lieutenant, and he and his friends so missed the good times they had shared they decided to join the Navy. Ken spent almost four years in the naval reserve, retiring with the rank of Lieutenant.

Ken Hart was a man who loved a party and was a natural entertainer. In 1976, he formed an elite fraternity called the "Old Buggers," an exclusive social club with a membership of nine military veterans, with Ken being their "commander-in-chief." They met on November 11th each year for laughs, drinks and remembrances, and each meeting began with Ken's witty, tongue-in-cheek "parade orders."

Ken kept in touch with some of the ex-members of the Coffey crew, including my Dad, who he visited in the mid-70s in our home in Kelowna. He wrote to Bob McWhirter in 1982, and like Bob Bayne, somewhat wistfully recalled their collective past: "In many ways we were probably a strange mix of personalities; however, must have done something right to survive."

In the late 1970s, Ken's health began to deteriorate, which prompted his retirement and a move for him and Edna from a house with a yard to a downtown apartment. Ken's older brother Bev died of lung cancer in 1986, and Ken was diagnosed with the same disease the following year. Ken passed away on December 5th, 1988, at the age of sixty-six, but not before he had made up a detailed, colour coded book with instructions for his family—the last line of the book made his final wish very clear: "Have a hell of a party," he wrote. According to daughter Susanne, "...if there is a party where he is, I know that not only is he part of it, he is the star."

Bob "Button" McWhirter made a rough, eight-day crossing of the Atlantic in December of 1944, disembarking in Boston and then taking the train to Montreal. From there, it was another train east, which arrived in Prince Albert, Saskatchewan, the day after Christmas. He was officially discharged from the RCAF in April of 1945, with the rank of Flying Officer and a Distinguished Flying Cross. Bob's family was unaware of the medal until it was found in a drawer during the packing up for a move in 1955—typical of the modesty of his generation, Bob had never mentioned it.

Bob returned to his parent's farm for (in his words) "a brief stint," but it was clear that he wouldn't stay—he had travelled a bit ("there is a whole world out there!" he told his disappointed parents) and he had no desire to return to farming.

He may not have been a farmer, but Bob certainly stayed an integral part of the Canadian farming community. In the summer of 1945, he was offered a job as a clerk in the Veteran's Land Administration (VLA)—he remained in the business of helping farmers with their credit and insurance needs for the rest of his working life, in increasingly senior positions.

Bob met Florence, a widow with two sons, in Prince Albert soon after joining the VLA, and they were married in early 1946—a year later, they added son Tim to the family. Bob and Florence were married for sixty-five years, until her passing, and by all accounts, they enjoyed a wonderful life together. Bob held a succession of farm credit-related posts over his working life, which took the family from the small rural town of Ogema, Saskatchewan, to Weyburn and finally to the Provincial capital of Regina toward the end of Bob's career. Over the years, Bob kept busy, becoming deeply involved in volunteering with their church (Bob had become a devout Christian after returning from wartime service), school, Legion, and Reserve Army. They spent winter holidays in Phoenix, often travelling with friends from Bob's work.

After retirement, the couple returned to their roots in Prince Albert and enjoyed travelling every winter to someplace sunny and warm, with additional trips on cruise ships to places like Alaska and the Baltic, and tours of Morocco and Portugal.

After Florence passed away, Bob moved to Kelowna, a medium-sized town in the interior of British Columbia, to be close to his son Tim, and it is there that I had the privilege of meeting him.

We had spoken on the phone once or twice, but Bob was a bit hard of hearing, and the conversations had to be facilitated by Tim, so I was anxious to meet the last remaining member of the crew in person. My wife, Tasnim, and I made the three-hour drive to Kelowna in the spring of 2015, staying overnight in a local bed and breakfast.

Bob lived in a spacious and homey assisted-living apartment building, and he was a gracious host and in phenomenal health, mentally and physically, for a man of 93. He was not a big man by any means, which was not uncommon with tail gunners—they had to fit into a very cramped rear turret. It was easy to see at a glance why Ted Rutherglen had given Bob the cheeky nickname of "Button"!

The skipper's son and Button. The author visits Bob McWhirter in 2015.
Photo by Tasnim Coffey.

Bob was kind and open, with a twinkle in his eye and a sharp wit, and best of all, he was keen to share his memories and show me his memorabilia. I interviewed him for two hours or so, and he shared some marvellous stories and cleared up some mysteries for me, as well as dropping that bombshell about Sgt. Ken Hart's accident.

Soon after we arrived, Tim joined us, and Bob insisted on taking us all to lunch in the dining room of his apartment building—on the way down, proudly introducing me to many of his friends.

"This is my skipper's son, come to visit me!"

Needless to say, I was touched and humbled.

Bob and I stayed in touch over the next year, but in 2016, he took a nasty spill on the ice while curling, badly dislocating his shoulder and breaking his arm. While he was in the hospital for an extended convalescence, I sent a get-well card and a package of information to him via Tim. I enclosed some copies of documents I had obtained during my research into the Coffey crew that I thought he might find interesting.

Tim told me his Dad was especially tickled by Dr. T's 1942 assessment of my Dad as "not impressive as aircrew material in any position."

Bob did manage to mend well enough to go home, but it wasn't to last too long—he never really made a full recovery, and was soon back in the hospital. Surrounded by family, "Button" passed away peacefully on July 30, 2017, at the age of 95.

My Dad was processed at the RCAF's "R" Depot at Houghton Green, Warrington (just outside Liverpool), on December 12th, 1944. He was officially labelled as being "supernumerary to training requirements" and sent for "disposal in Canada." This designation seems to me to be a very unnecessarily cold and callous way of saying, "we don't really need you for anything right now, so go back to Canada," like Dad was a broken rifle or obsolete airplane being sent to be scrapped.

It seems Dad had to cool his heels for ten days before a berth on a troopship was available. He was given accommodation at Damhead House, a gorgeous seventeenth-century farmhouse in Mobberley, about fifteen miles outside Warrington. His combat-frayed nerves probably welcomed the quiet country setting, and I hope he enjoyed long walks in the picturesque Cheshire countryside. After a fortnight at Damhead, he boarded a train and headed north to Scotland.

My Dad left England the way he had arrived, on a luxury passenger ship pressed into service for the duration as a troop transport. His ride home to Canada was the Holland Line's *Nieuw Amsterdam*, launched in 1937 for the trans-Atlantic trade. In one of those strange coincidences that pop up now and then in life, the only cruise ship I have ever been on in my life, in 2019, was Holland America's *Nieuw Amsterdam*, the replacement for the original ship, which had been scrapped in 1974.

On December 18th, 1944, the *Nieuw Amsterdam* left Greenock, Scotland and headed into the Atlantic with about 3,600 soldiers and airmen on board, most of them heading home after years of service overseas. Two destroyers protected the ship for the seven-day trip, the Royal Navy's *Zambesi* and the Royal Norwegian Navy's *Stord*. Germany's U-boats were on the ropes by this point in the war, being hunted almost to extinction by Allied patrol aircraft, many of them now based in Iceland. From these mid-Atlantic bases, they were now able to hunt U-boats in what had previously been a 300-mile wide gap in air cover that Allied sailors called "the Black Pit." Patrolling aircraft were now also equipped with advanced radar, searchlights and depth charges, making them even more effective than they had been.

Germany had developed highly advanced new U-boat designs, but production and deployment of them had been hamstrung by the Allied bombers, who had destroyed the roads, railways and viaducts required to transport the parts, raw materials and components needed to build them. An almost-complete U-boat was of no use when all the electric batteries and cables it required were hundreds of miles away, with no way of moving them. After the war, Allied investigators found German steel mills full of finished product— months of production was backed up in the warehouses because there was simply no way of transporting it to the tank factories or shipbuilding yards where it was needed. What the bomber crews hadn't destroyed, they made useless by bottling it up.

As a decorated officer, I think it likely that my Dad's trip home was more comfortable than the one he had made in 1942 as a brand new Sergeant. Perhaps he shared a private cabin with another officer rather than sleeping in a dorm-type setting with the enlisted men, and ate in the dining room.

Dad arrived back in Halifax on Christmas Day 1944, some nineteen months after he had left Canada aboard the *SS Pasteur* that spring day in 1943. A train took him to Lachine, Quebec, where the RCAF maintained a receiving centre for returning airmen. From Lachine, he was flown to Calgary, where, on December 29th, he reported to the RCAF's No. 7 Release Centre.

While Dad had been away, my Mom carried on—like millions of other young wives and mothers world-wide, she managed finances, work, maintaining a home, and caring for her child on her own. After Dad had shipped off to England, Mom had gotten a job at a local hotel and then rented a nearby house, one that was far too large for her and baby Gary but had lots of extra bedrooms she could sub-let to other young women. It was a savvy move that brought in some extra income and provided a handy pool of potential babysitters for young Gary.

As I have mentioned before, I regret not asking my Dad more questions than I did about his wartime service, but I now realize I regret equally (and my regret is tinged with shame) that I never asked my Mom questions about what life was like for her for those two years. She undoubtedly went through some tough times and personal challenges, and I wish I could relate more of her story, but it is now lost, and a sad loss it is.

My Dad only spent a day at the Release Centre in Calgary—the RCAF's seemingly endless bureaucracy needed time to examine and digest his service record before it decided what to do with him. In the mean-time, they granted him "special leave" for a month so he could make the four or five-hour bus trip back to Provost to reunite with his wife and son.

I can only imagine what an emotional scene it must have been as Dad stepped off the bus in Provost—Gary had been a tiny babe in arms when he left and was now a rambunctious toddler approaching his second birthday. It must have been a challenging transition for everyone—in a way, they were all going to have to get to know each other again, almost from scratch.

The village of Czar organized a welcome home for Dad, which was held on January 10th at the Czar Community Hall. The local paper ran an article about the reception: "Czar Welcomes Home Flying Hero." I bet my Dad cut quite a figure at the event as he greeted old friends, neighbours, and family who had not seen him since he had left to join up three years before, and who I have no doubt noticed a change in him. The steely-eyed, confident Flight Lieutenant (dressed in a uniform adorned with ribbons and awards) who now mingled among them was a far cry from the skinny, shy store clerk who had left for Manning Depot three years previously.

After a month, Dad reported back to Calgary for an official meeting regarding his RCAF service and what his government required of him, if anything.

At the end of January 1945, he spent two days with various officials as he was questioned and assessed yet again. The medical officials all wanted to know about any health problems he might have resulting from his service—Dad wrote: "I have no complaints" on the form, and I can't help but wonder if there was a touch of cold sarcasm in the terse comment. After everything he had been through, after all he had given of himself, after everything he had given up to serve, "they" were seemingly trying to ensure he couldn't come back later claiming any sort of service-related disability.

Then came the finances. There was a land grant available to suitable returning veterans, and Dad expressed interest in this program. The assessor wrote:

> A good average education. Very keen and alert. Has a very pleasant manner… Plans
> to become a farmer and wants land under the (Veterans Land Act)… It is recom-
> mended this land be granted him as he appears very capable.

I am not sure why or when Dad decided not to pursue the farm idea—perhaps my Mom expressed an opinion about the prospect of becoming a farmer's wife!

At any rate, even if he didn't get any land, Dad *was* entitled to some money, as per the Statement of War Service Gratuity documents that I got as part of his military records.

Note the word "gratuity"… as if my Dad and millions like him had been waiters while overseas!

Dad was entitled to about $600 in special pay for the time he spent overseas (the eligible period is carefully noted as stopping on Dec 19th, the day he left Greenock on the *Nieuw Amsterdam*). But, incredibly, deducted from this was $70.00 that the bureaucrats claimed they had "overpaid" my Mom in Dependant's Allowance while he had been gone.

With the finances settled up (he didn't actually get the money until May of 1945—all the paperwork had to go to Ottawa for processing) his career with the RCAF was finally over, and he was free to resume civilian life. He received a small enamelled pin which depicted a spray of maple leaves and the words "general service" on it. He could wear it on his civilian clothes to show he had served and prevent verbal abuse (or worse) by those who might wonder why he wasn't doing his bit. Dad was also notified that he had been awarded a Bar to his Distinguished Flying Cross, although I don't know whether he got the award before he left Calgary or whether they mailed it to him.

It was now time to make some decisions about the future of his family. After scrapping the idea of becoming a farmer, Dad decided to go back to work for the Hudson's Bay Company, which would provide a stable income and the possibility of advancement. He was re-hired in short order and found himself assigned to the remote community of Minaki, Ontario, the assistant manager of the HBC outpost there. I can't help but wonder if it was a hard pill to swallow: he had left England only a few short months before an officer and a gentleman, a decorated member of an elite force, the captain of a Lancaster bomber and her crew of six. It must have been the same story for millions of returning veterans, struggling to adjust to a workaday world that was clueless about what they had been through and who just wanted things to get back to normal.

I don't know the reason, but within a year, Dad was transferred, and he, Mom and Gary packed their bags and travelled to their new home on McKenzie Island, another remote community about two hundred kilometres north of Minaki. Dad was again assigned to be the assistant manager, but he would be moving up the ladder within a year. In 1947, he was sent to Montreal to attend Fur Trading School. Five months later, he was assigned as the new Post Manager of the HBC outpost in the tiny Indigenous community of Little Grand Rapids, Manitoba, where he and Mom welcomed a second son, Dwight, into the family.

Dad spent about a year and a half in Little Grand Rapids and then resigned from the HBC—no one in my family recalls why, but a letter Dad sent to the RCAF in late 1948 perhaps gives a clue:

I am writing to you at this time to obtain all the available information you have regarding personnel policies, with the thought in mind of rejoining the RCAF this coming summer. I am particularly interested in the present rates of pay, cost of living allowances, housing facilities and if I could rejoin with my former rank and also what trades are open for me. To assist you in answering my questions, I would give you the following information about myself and former experience: I am 27 years of age, married and with two children. My former rank F/Lt, with two tours of operations with 405 Pathfinder Squadron, total of 850 hours flying one, two and four engined aircraft. Since my discharge in early 1945 I have been Managing a retail store for the Hudson's Bay Company and in constant charge of a number of staff during all this time.

Also I have studied considerably, the subjects of navigation in particular and air-frames and Airmanship to a lesser degree, since my discharge thinking that someday I might want to return to the Air Force.

Dad closed the letter with a hopeful plea for "fullest particulars" at the RCAF's "very earliest convenience."

This letter came as a total surprise when I first came across it in the records the Canadian Government sent me in 2016. Neither my older brothers or I had ever heard my Dad speak about trying to rejoin the Air Force.

While reading through all these old documents from the years immediately following the war, I got the impression that my Dad may have been a bit frustrated. He had a family to support, and the HBC was a stable employer, but perhaps he was chomping at the bit and feeling, as Bob McWhirter expressed to his disappointed parents, that "there is a whole world out there!"

His ambitions, once again, meant little to the RCAF, who sent him a terse, albeit polite, letter stating that "no vacancies exist at present." At that point, it seems, Dad saw the writing on the wall and realized that if being an HBC employee was not for him any longer, that he better take matters into his own hands. He quit the HBC and for the next thirty-five years of his working life, he would be an entrepreneur, owning several small businesses.

The first was an ESSO oil agency in Fort Smith, Northwest Territories, a town where he also served as a Justice of the Peace. Perhaps tiring of life in the far north, the Coffey family (there were four sons now, Gary, Dwight, Stuart, and myself) packed up and moved 2,000 kilometres south, to Kelowna, in British Columbia's Okanagan Valley.

Kelowna is where my memories start, and some of the most vivid are of the business Dad and a partner started there, Okanagan Horseman's Supplies. O.H.S. was a tack shop, as the name implies, and as a kid, I was fascinated by the smells (predominately leather) and textures of all the saddles, boots, clothing, and hardware that Dad and Mr. Mattick, his partner, stocked and sold.

Me and Dad in 1962. Always the trendsetter, I seem to be sporting
one of the first "faux-hawks" ever photographed. Author's collection.

Mr. Mattick was in a wheelchair, having had both his legs horribly mangled by a German 88 that had destroyed the Sherman tank he was driving in 1945. He had lain in a ditch, near death, until German forces found him and took him to a field hospital, where Wehrmacht doctors amputated both legs and saved his life. The War was nearing its end, and Mr. Mattick was soon liberated. I don't know how he and my Dad met, but their business partnership was not to last. After a few years, they closed the business and parted ways—my older brother recalls they had regular friction over the types of items to stock in their limited space, my Dad wanting to cater to the current customer's needs, Mr. M. wishing to go more "upmarket."

After the tack shop closed, Dad tried his hand at being a real estate agent for a few years, and around the same time, he purchased a small fruit orchard and grew the cherries and apples the Okanagan Valley is famous for. Neither enterprise seemed to suit him—the real estate game could be lucrative, but I remember him telling me that he found its "feast or famine" nature too frustrating.

In the end, he went back to small business ownership, purchasing an appliance repair shop that was in serious need of new management.

J.D. Appliance Repair was situated in the corner of a run-down building in a bad part of town. The shop was dirty and cramped, and every available space was stuffed with derelict appliances and other junk. The repairmen drove to see customers in a motley assortment of dented and rusty old vans with faded paint.

The business did, however, have a healthy customer base and was running in the black. Dad saw the potential.

Once Dad had completed the purchase of the business, he set to work building it back up, starting with moving lock, stock, and barrel to a brand new building and buying spiffy new pick-up trucks for the repairmen. Sloppy business practices were put right, and over the next ten years, the business thrived.

When I left home at age eighteen, my parents sold the business, and Dad finally retired. After decades of living in small towns and villages, they both found Kelowna had gotten too large and too busy to suit them, so they sold their home and moved to the small town of William's Lake, in the Cariboo region of B.C.

My memories of Dad are all fond. He was kind and wise, and set an example to me of what it was to be a man—loyal, honest, and dignified—and one with the character to never lower themselves to someone else's level. He taught me how to treat others and to always do the right thing, even if it isn't convenient and even if you get no recognition for it. He taught me that a real man has no need to brag about his accomplishments, that the life he leads and the way he carries himself speaks for itself. Dad was a quiet man—I never heard him raise his voice in anger, but when he spoke, people listened respectfully. It seems to me that his quiet nature came from a place of great strength, a place of calm confidence.

There was an incident when I was about eight years old that leapt vividly back to my mind as I sat writing about my father's calm nature.

Dad and I were in the backyard one spring day, having gathered a pile of garden refuse into a burn pile. Dad lit the pile, but it was not dry enough to do much more than smoulder, so he poured a small amount of gasoline from his nearby lawnmower into an empty plastic margarine container. This plan would no doubt fail a modern safety sniff test, but this was 1970! At any rate, Dad stood back from the smoking pile and carefully tossed the gas onto it, with me standing next to him. It immediately erupted into proper flames, but Dad was a fraction of a second tardy in pulling the container back, and the flames raced back across the tiny stream of gas and ignited the container, still in his hand. My eyes widened in horror and I remember backpedalling away as I saw Dad standing there with a burning container in his hand.

Rumours that I screamed like a little girl are just that: rumours.

I watched, amazed, as Dad calmly and deliberately turned the burning containing upside down in his hand and bent down to firmly place it upside down on the grass, extinguishing the flames.

I am not sure if Dad's imperturbable manner was just his nature or the product of his RCAF experience (perhaps a combination), but I am certain he would have been equally calm had the entire house been on fire.

Dad taught me to appreciate the outdoors, taking me camping regularly, and to value a good book, fiction or non-fiction. He always led by example, and I can't recall ever getting a lecture from him—the most devastating thing he could say was that he was disappointed in me (my grade 11 algebra marks come painfully to mind, even some forty-five years later).

Around 1988, at the age of sixty-seven or so, Dad had his first heart attack. I can still recall how surreal it was to see my Dad, always so vital and upright, lying on a hospital bed hooked up to wires and tubes. Dad left the hospital shortly after with a prescription for nitroglycerin tablets and a doctor's order to quit smoking (which he stubbornly ignored).

On one of my visits to see my parents the following year, Dad told me he had used the nitro pills not long before I arrived. While flipping channels on the TV he had stumbled onto a WW II documentary, just at the moment it depicted a Lancaster bomber lifting off the runway. His heart began racing, and he broke out in a cold sweat. I realize now that what he experienced was likely a panic attack, but at the time we laughed about it. Dad told me he turned the TV off and popped a nitro pill under his tongue—he felt better in short order.

My favourite picture of Dad. I surprised him early one morning in 1983. Photo by author.

How vivid, how visceral, how terrifying must the memories have been for Dad to have that kind of reaction some fifty years later, over a few seconds of grainy, black and white footage on a TV screen? Can any of us really appreciate or understand?

About two years later, in 1990, Dad had a second heart attack, this one instantly fatal, much like Malcolm Dingwall's "grenade."

My Mom found him sprawled on the grass just outside his small backyard workshop and called 911, but there was nothing the first responders could do.

Jesse Coffey's four sons arrived over the course of the next two days to comfort their mother and see to the funeral of their father.

When Gary, Dwight, Stuart, and I went to close up Dad's workshop, Gary found a half-finished bottle of beer (Molson Old Style Pilsner) on his workbench—he had been enjoying a cold one while he puttered.

Two days later, we've come full circle, and return to the scene that started this journey, back to Mom's kitchen, the reading of my Dad's will, and my unexpected inheritance.

I sit here in the summer of 2021, trying to find the words to sum up the last six years of what started as a research project and turned into what I can't help but call a pilgrimage. It has been a profound journey of discovery into a subject I thought I knew a bit about—it turns out I was woefully ignorant.

Three recurring, fundamental lessons or themes stand out in my mind.

The first is that the campaign that Jesse, Bob, Jimmy, Bob, Malcolm, Ken, and Teddy fought in was decisive in winning WW II for the Allies. It didn't win the war on its own, as Bomber Harris had hoped it would, and it wasn't without missteps, missed opportunities, and wasted efforts, but it played an absolutely key role in the Allied victory. If Hitler's Fortress Europe had been left unmolested by bombers from 1941 to 1944, what would invading Allied armies have faced when they hit the beaches of Normandy? Would Operation Overlord, the D Day invasion of Occupied Europe, even have been possible?

The resources that Nazi Germany had to pour into defending itself against the Allied heavy bombers was staggering. If those resources could have been used instead on the Eastern Front, against the Russians, the history of WW II might be very different indeed.

Then there is the actual damage inflicted to consider as well. Factories, steel mills, mines, bridges, dams, railway marshalling yards, ports, oil refineries and, yes, millions of homes belonging to the people who ran all those facilities, were all destroyed. The devastation was appalling—and, for the Third Reich, crippling. It was "total war" (to use Herr Goebbels's term), unlike the world had ever seen before. It doesn't take a wild imagination to picture what the highly efficient Nazi regime, with all the resources of Occupied Europe under its brutal control, could have accomplished had they not been constantly "put on the back foot" by the bomber campaign.

By destroying U-boats before they could be put to sea, destroying V-1 and V-2 rockets before they could be launched, and destroying Panzer formations before they could begin their attack, the bomber boys constantly hampered the Nazi war machine's effectiveness, and made possible its defeat.

In the lead-up to D-Day, the bomber crews laid a cornerstone in the foundation of success by destroying Germany's ability to efficiently transport, maneuver, and reinforce their troops and armour. As President Roosevelt put it, Hitler made Europe into a fortress, but he forgot to put a roof on it.

The second lesson that has struck me is how little recognition the young men of Bomber Command received. When the war ended, the airmen and ground crew were sidelined when it came to tributes or recognition, receiving no campaign ribbon and not so much as a mention in Winston Churchill's victory speech. The Few of the Battle of Britain and the soldiers who won the beachhead on D-Day received universal, lasting, and well-deserved respect and admiration—the bomber crews were mostly forgotten. These brave young men had too much pride and character to complain aloud, but it must have hurt them deeply, in a very personal way, to be passed over so callously.

The campaign they had fought was ugly and best forgotten—that seemed to be the attitude of many. When the bomber boys were remembered in post-war history books, it was all-too-often to disparage their campaign as immoral or controversial. Almost half a million young men served in Allied bomber squadrons in WW II, over the course of five long years, and yet all some pundits seemed to be able to focus their 20/20 hindsight on was one single attack on Dresden in the final days of the war. Tellingly, the "historian" who seems to have set the ball rolling on disparaging the Bomber Campaign in the mid-1960s turned out to be a Nazi sympathizer and Holocaust denier.

The final theme that has sunk in for me is how ill-prepared the tens of thousands of young airmen were for the task that was put in front of them. We threw these young men, most teenagers or barely older, into the cauldron of night bombing and told them to get on with it. Their training was technical in nature, focused on flying, air gunnery, and bombing. Nothing could prepare them for the mental ordeal they faced night after night, operation after operation. Like so many of their generation, they became adept at hiding the lingering psychological toll it took on them.

A young man joining the Army or Navy (or even aspiring Air Force fighter pilots) in 1942 could at least rely on the exploits of predecessors or mentors to give them some inkling of what to expect. There were hundreds of books and movies about being a soldier or sailor, and many young men would have had fathers or uncles who had served in WW I, and who could provide useful advice and encouragement.

The bomber crews would have no such help—their war was unprecedented. Other than perhaps the submarine crews, I can think of no branch of service that subjected their men to the kind of sustained, claustrophobic terror that the bomber crews faced.

In six years of research, I have found no more eloquent a tribute to the men of Bomber Command than that written by H.R.H. The Duke of Kent, in his dedication for the book *So Many:*

> …it was the crews of Bomber Command who carried our message of defiance into the very heartland of the enemy. This they did with extraordinary courage and in the full knowledge that, statistically speaking, their chances of surviving the War unscathed were minimal. For as long as they survived they faced one of the most daunting tasks fighting men have ever been asked to undertake, a task calling for courage sustained for hour after hour during night after long night, in conditions of desperate danger and discomfort. They did not fail us, and 55,573 of them paid the supreme sacrifice. They deserve to be remembered…

With this moving tribute, far more eloquent than I could ever write, my pilgrimage is at an end…except for one last memory.

Sometime in the late Sixties, most of the surviving members of the Coffey crew had a weekend reunion at the home of Teddy and Irene Rutherglen in Nelson, B.C.

My Dad, Malcolm Dingwall and Bob McWhirter were there, but poor Jimmy Willoughby had already died by this time, and it seems Bob Bayne and Ken Hart were unable to make it.

Teddy's son and daughter both remember the weekend as being full of laughter and camaraderie. The bonds that had tied the crew together during that one year as a team were still palpably strong. Ted Rutherglen recalls that his Dad was "so proud" to have his old comrades staying in his home, and Christine Rutherglen remembers her Dad still fondly referring to Bob as "Button." One of the crew took young Tim

McWhirter aside and told how his Dad had "saved their bacon" on several occasions. When Christine Rutherglen overheard her Dad having a conversation with mine, she remembers, "I could hear in Dad's voice and the way he spoke to your Dad, how much he respected him. Personally, I think they all admired him and were grateful he brought them back safely." I suppose it was only natural for them to give their skipper credit for their miraculous survival, but I know my Dad would have scoffed at the idea.

Thanks, once again, to the generosity of the Rutherglen family, I have a photo taken at the reunion. In it, the four ex-warriors sit around a small Formica table in Irene Rutherglen's kitchen. There seems to be a decanter of wine on the table, but that must have been for the ladies, as the crew are all drinking Columbia beer from the iconic "stubby" brown bottles that were phased out in Canada in the early '80s.

Malcolm Dingwall, Bob McWhirter, Jesse Coffey and Ted Rutherglen circa late 1960's.
Photo courtesy of the Rutherglen family.

The crew must have all been their forties by this point, but they are all lean, fit and tanned—they all look like they could quite ably don a uniform and serve again if called upon. As I spent time looking at the colour snapshot that Ted Rutherglen sent me, I remember being struck by the look on my Dad's face. It is remarkably similar to the black and white photo Teddy had taken of him looking out a cockpit window in 1944—the same look of cool, confident assessment.

The Rutherglen kids remember a "lot of laughter" that evening, but at one point, the wives and children sensed that the four men needed some quiet time to talk and left them alone for a time. Ted recalls that it seemed that his Dad and the others needed to "clear the air."

One can only speculate about the subjects they unburdened themselves about.

The evening soon returned to boisterous laughter, and the abiding memory that Ted has from that evening is that Jesse, Teddy, Malcolm, and Bob were "like family, they were like brothers."

SOURCES AND REFERENCES

I would like to especially acknowledge the contribution of three books in particular. I read all three multiple times, and they were fundamental to my understanding of the Coffey crew's time in aircrew training and of the psychological stresses they were put under: Spencer Dunmore's *Wings for Victory*, Mark Wells' *Courage and Air Warfare*, and Allan D. English's *The Cream of the Crop*.

BOOKS

Titles especially recommended for further reading are in **bold print**.

Bashow, David L. *None But The Brave*. 2009. Canadian Defence Academy Press.

Bennet, D. C. T. *Pathfinder*. 1958. Frederick Muller Ltd.

Bowman, M. *Legend of the Lancasters*. 2009. Pen and Sword Books Ltd.

Bowman, M. *Bomber Command: Reflections of War, Volume 4*. 2013. Pen and Sword Books Ltd.

Bowyer, C. *Wellington at War*. 1982. Ian Allen Ltd.

Bowyer, C. *Pathfinders at War*. 1977. Ian Allen Ltd.

Broadfoot, B. *Six War Years 1939-1945*. 1974. Doubleday Canada Ltd.

Cave Brown, Anthony. *Bodyguard of Lies*. 1975. Harper & Row.

Chandler, C. *Tail Gunner*. 1999. Airlife Publishing.

Charlwood, D. E. *No Moon Tonight*. 1956. Angus and Robertson.

Cormack, A. *Men at Arms Series, The Royal Air Force 1939-45*. 1190. Osprey.

Cotter, J. *Living Lancasters*. 2005. Sutton Publishing.

Cotter, J. & P. Blackah. *Avro Lancaster Owners' Workshop Manual*. 2008. Hanes.

Currie, J. *Lancaster Target*. 1981. PaperJacks Ltd.

Darlow, S. *D-Day Bombers: The Veteran's Story*. 2004. Grub Street.

Deighton, L. *Bomber*. 1970. Jonathan Cape.

Dunmore, S. *Wings for Victory*. 1994. McClelland & Stewart Inc.

Dunmore, S. & W. Carter. *Reap the Whirlwind*. 1991. McClelland and Stewart.

English, A. *The Cream of the Crop: Canadian Aircrew 1939-1945*. 1996. McGill-Queen's University Press.

Falconer, J. *RAF Bomber Command Operations Manual*. 2018. Haynes Publishing.

Feast, S. *The Pathfinder Companion*. 2012. Grub Street Publishing.

Freeman, R. *The British Airman*. 1989. Arms and Armour Press.

Garbett, M. and Goulding, B. *Avro Lancaster in Unit Service*. 1970. Osprey Publishing.

Garbett, M. & B. Goulding. *The Lancaster at War*. 1971. Ian Allen Ltd.

Garbett, M. & B. Goulding. *The Lancaster at War 2*. 1979. Ian Allen Ltd.

Garbett, M. & B. Goulding. *The Lancaster at War 3*. 1984. Ian Allen Ltd.

Gibson, G. *Enemy Coast Ahead – Uncensored*. 2003. Crecy Publishing.

Gray, P. *Ghosts of Targets Past*. 1995. Grub Street.

Grehan, J. & M. Mace. *Bomber Harris: Sir Arthur Harris' Despatch on War Operations 1942-1944*. 2014. Pen and Sword Books Ltd.

Griehl, M. *German Night Fighters in World War II*. 1990. Schiffer Publishing.

Hall, M. *Operation Hurricane*. 2013. Fighting High Ltd.

Hampton, J. *Selected for Aircrew*. 1993. Air Research Publications.

Harris, Arthur Sir. *Bomber Offensive*. 1947. Collins.

Harvey, J. Douglas. *Boys, Bombs and Brussels Sprouts*. 1981. McClelland & Stewart Limited.

Hastings, M. *Bomber Command*. 1979. Michael Joseph Ltd.

Jones, E. *L.M.F.: The Use of Psychiatric Stigma in the RAF During the Second World War*. 2006. Journal of Military History.

Jones, R. V. *Most Secret War*. 1978. Hamish Hamilton.

Keegan, J. *Six Armies in Normandy*. 1982. Penguin Books.

King, B. & T. Kutta. *Impact*. 1998. Spellmount Publishers Ltd.

Lake, J. *Halifax Squadrons of World War 2*. 1999. Osprey Publishing.

Lake, J. *Lancaster Squadrons 1944-45*. 2002. Osprey Publishing.

Mackay, R. *Lancaster in Action*. 1982. Squadron/Signal Publications.

Manchester, W. *The Arms of Krupp*. 1969. Michael Joseph Ltd.

Manning, M. & B. Granstrom. *Tail-End Charlie*. 2008. Frances Lincoln Ltd.

Mawdsley, T. *An Erk's Eye View of World War II*. 2003. Woodfield Publishing.

McCaffery, D. *Battlefields in the Air*. 1995. James Lorimer & Co.

McKee, A. *Caen: Anvil of Victory*. 1964. Souvenir Press.

McKinstry, L. *Lancaster*. 2009. John Murray.

Middlebrook, M. & C. Everitt. *The Bomber Command War Diaries*. 1985. Viking Press.

Middlebrook, M. *The Nuremburg Raid*. 2009. Pen and Sword Books.

Moorhouse, R. *Berlin at War*. 2011. Vintage Books.

Moran, Lord. *The Anatomy of Courage*. 1967. Houghton Mifflin Co.

Neillands, R. *The Bomber War*. 2001. John Murray Ltd.

Overy, R. J. *The Bombers and the Bombed: Allied Air War Over Europe, 1940-1945*. 2015. Penguin Group.

Overy, R. J. *Why the Allies Won*. 1995. W. W. Norton and Company.

Page, Bette. *Mynarski's Lanc*. 1989. The Boston Mills Press.

Probert, H. *Bomber Harris: His Life and Times*. 2001. Greenhill Books.

Royal Air Force Benevolent Fund. *So Many*. 1995. W. H. Smith.

Rapier, B. *Halifax at War*. 1987. Ian Allen Ltd.

Revie, A. *The Lost Command*. 1971. David Bruce and Watson Ltd.

Smith, R. *Rear Gunner Pathfinders*. 1987. Crecy Publishing Ltd.

Streetly, M. *Confound & Destroy*. 1978. Jane's Publishing.

Sweetman, B. *Avro Lancaster*. 1982. Wing and Anchor Press.

Terraine, John. *The Right of the Line: The Royal Air Force in the European War, 1939-1945*. Hodder and Stoughton.

Thompson, W. *Lancaster to Berlin*. 1987. Totem Books.

Wells, M. *Courage and Air Warfare*. 1995. Frank Cass & Co. Ltd.

Wilson, K. *Men of Air*. 2007. Weidenfeld and Nicholson.

Yates, H. *Luck and a Lancaster*. 1999. Wrens Park Publishing.

PERSONAL CORRESPONDENCE AND INTERVIEWS

Ted Rutherglen and Christine Rutherglen	"Teddy" Rutherglen's son and daughter
Bob McWhirter	The crew's rear gunner. *RIP Bob.*
Tim McWhirter	Bob McWhirter's son
Lorie and Sandra Dingwall	Malcolm Dingwall's son and daughter
Glenn Dingwall	Malcolm Dingwall's grandson
Keith and Craig Willoughby	Digby "Jimmy" Willoughby's sons
Cathleen Willoughby and Francoise Cote Seguin	"Jimmy" Willoughby's nieces
Chad Bayne	Bob Bayne's grandson
Susanne (Hart) Thrasher	Ken Hart's daughter
Don Hart	Ken Hart's brother
Gary, Dwight, and Stuart Coffey	Jesse Coffey's sons

WEBSITES

In the early days of my research, before the thought of writing a book had even entered my mind, I visited dozens of websites that I neglected to keep track of. The ones listed below were those I visited often and recorded. I apologize for any I have missed.

The following two websites are invaluable resources for viewing original records and documents from World War II. Especially valuable to me were Operational Record Books and Daily Diaries from RAF and RCAF units, which I quote from throughout the book.

www.discovery.nationalarchives.gov.uk

www.heritage.canadiana.ca

Other excellent websites:

www.newspapers.com

www.ancestry.com

www.aviationarchaeology.com

www.backtonormandy.org

www.lancaster-archive.com

www.lancasterdiary.ca

www.aircrewremembered.com

www.rafcommands.com

www.bbc.com (WW2 People's War Archive)

www.rcafassociation.com

www.V2rocket.com

www.masterbombercraig.wordpress.com

www.atlantikwall.co.uk

www.bunkerarcheodieppe.com

www.tracesofevil.com

www.vintagewings.ca

www.convoyweb.org.uk

www.tedburns.net

CPSIA information can be obtained
at www.ICGtesting.com
Printed in the USA
LVHW071417060423
743676LV00009B/99